*For all the cyclists and racers who want to improve.* — HHA

*For Debbie, my tandem partner on and off the bike.* — SSC

# Contents

# Cutting-Edge Cycling

HUNTER ALLEN

STEPHEN S. CHEUNG, PhD

**Human Kinetics**

**Library of Congress Cataloging-in-Publication Data**

Allen, Hunter.
  Cutting-edge cycling / Hunter Allen, Stephen S. Cheung, PhD.
    p. cm.
  Includes bibliographical references and index.
  ISBN 978-0-7360-9109-1 (soft cover) -- ISBN 0-7360-9109-2 (soft cover)
  1.  Cycling--Training.  I. Cheung, Stephen S., 1968- II. Title.
  GV1048.A53 2012
  796.6--dc23

                                     2011049602

ISBN-10: 0-7360-9109-2 (print)
ISBN-13: 978-0-7360-9109-1 (print)

The web addresses cited in this text were current as of January 2012, unless otherwise noted.

**Acquisitions Editor:** Tom Heine; **Developmental Editor:** Carla Zych; **Assistant Editor:** Claire Marty; **Copyeditor:** Bob Replinger; **Indexer:** Nan N. Badgett; **Permissions Manager:** Martha Gullo; **Graphic Designer:** Bob Reuther; **Cover Designer:** Keith Blomberg; **Photographer (cover):** Peter Blakeman/Action Plus/Icon SMI; **Photo Asset Manager:** Laura Fitch; **Visual Production Assistant:** Joyce Brumfield; **Photo Production Manager:** Jason Allen; **Art Manager:** Kelly Hendren; **Associate Art Manager:** Alan L. Wilborn; **Illustrations:** ©Human Kinetics, unless otherwise noted; **Printer:** McNaughton & Gunn

Human Kinetics books are available at special discounts for bulk purchase. Special editions or book excerpts can also be created to specification. For details, contact the Special Sales Manager at Human Kinetics.

Printed in the United States of America    10 9 8 7 6 5 4 3 2

The paper in this book is certified under a sustainable forestry program.

**Human Kinetics**
Website: www.HumanKinetics.com

*United States:* Human Kinetics
P.O. Box 5076
Champaign, IL 61825-5076
800-747-4457
e-mail: humank@hkusa.com

*Canada:* Human Kinetics
475 Devonshire Road Unit 100
Windsor, ON N8Y 2L5
800-465-7301 (in Canada only)
e-mail: info@hkcanada.com

*Europe:* Human Kinetics
107 Bradford Road
Stanningley
Leeds LS28 6AT, United Kingdom
+44 (0) 113 255 5665
e-mail: hk@hkeurope.com

*Australia:* Human Kinetics
57A Price Avenue
Lower Mitcham, South Australia 5062
08 8372 0999
e-mail: info@hkaustralia.com

*New Zealand:* Human Kinetics
P.O. Box 80
Torrens Park, South Australia 5062
0800 222 062
e-mail: info@hknewzealand.com

E5089

# Preface

Look through the archives of your favorite cycling photographer or magazine. The feel and ambience of hard athletes performing a hard sport remains the same, but the overall look of the sport today is far different from years past. Except for the basic diamond shape of the frame, bicycles are almost completely unrecognizable from 20 or even 10 years ago—from clipless pedals, brake lever and electronic shifting, aerodynamic road bikes and time trial–specific bikes, oversized and integrated headsets and bottom brackets, eleven-cog cassettes, compact cranksets and bike geometries, ceramic bearings, and wind tunnels to pretty much carbon everything. The dizzying pace of technological improvements has been such that cycling has often been likened to Formula 1 racing on two wheels, and this focus on technology is one of the underlying fascinations of the sport for many people.

Although the techno-geek angle within cycling continues to advance by leaps and bounds, the basic awareness and application of the science of training and fitness is unfortunately lagging behind for many amateurs and even professional cyclists. True, many cyclists would never head out for a ride without their bike computers, heart rate monitors, or power monitors. But numbers are just random digits without any meaning unless cyclists have the knowledge and understanding of what the values mean and how to use that knowledge to their advantage. Many athletes are still stuck in variations of the "just ride more and harder" mentality of training. Meanwhile, despite the scientific advances in equipment, which result in the ascendance of designs that prove better, training itself continues to be rife with old-school ideas that seem to gain added cachet simply because they're old. These ideas include such chestnuts as riding long steady distances and avoiding intensity in the off-season, riding a fixed gear to improve pedaling technique on the road, and using the knee over the pedal spindle as the optimal seat setback position. Such ideas and beliefs may or may not have merit, but rather than examine the evidence, many coaches and athletes blindly accept them simply because they've been handed down through the generations.

This concept of an evidence-based approach to cycling science and training is the philosophy underlying this book. Our goal is to bring a science-first perspective to cycling by digging into the scientific basis behind concepts such as lactate threshold, periodization, bike positioning, pedaling technique and cadence, nutrition, and recovery. From there, we develop proven and practical strategies to enhance your performance on the bike. Our hope is that this book will be equally useful to athletes and coaches by creating a common knowledge set and improving communication between the two parties and ultimately the performance of both. Just as a public that is better educated about health can cause doctors to become better educated themselves and more accountable, informed athletes and coaches spur one another to greater heights. We hope to increase the awareness of and appreciation for cycling sport science among athletes of all levels. Throughout the book, we not only examine the science but also present it in ways that are accessible and practical regardless of your level or experience. Case studies of individual cyclists illustrate how various concepts come into play when the rubber hits the road.

Chapter 1 focuses on the fundamentals of cycling science. With scientific advances comes marketing geared toward exploiting science as a magic ingredient. Therefore, chapter 1 begins with a simple primer on what science can and cannot tell us and how we can separate the wheat from the chaff when hearing about the latest "scientifically proven" advice. From there, we explain in chapters 2 and 3 how the body responds during cycling and how to quantify training and performance. What does lactate threshold actually mean, is it important, and how can cyclists plan their training around it?

The next few chapters give you the basic scientific knowledge and tools needed to translate physiology so that you can optimize your fitness while avoiding pushing yourself to the point of overtraining. Interviews with professional cyclists in the popular press are rife with references to building form and peaking for goals, but rare is the examination of what "form" actually entails. Therefore, we examine the dual nature of training stress and recovery, and we explain how to optimize both components to maximize your physical capacities. Chapter 4 outlines the scientific foundations of periodizing training to build your fitness throughout a season and over the years. Chapter 5 gives you practical insight into tools and techniques for optimizing recovery from hard training, and it takes you over the edge of fitness into overtraining so that you can avoid taking the actual plunge yourself. Chapter 6 is unique in examining the critical art and science of pacing your effort throughout a race. How you pace yourself in expending your finite energy over various events, from criteriums to flat and hilly time trials, can make the difference between stepping up on the podium and falling far off the back.

The next few chapters examine the important details that go into perfecting the man–machine interface. No matter how fit you become and how much energy you have in the tank, it all goes for naught if you squander it by being uneconomical and spending that energy when you don't have to. Chapter 7 takes you through the current scientific knowledge about proper positioning on the bike and outlines how to blend the science and art of proper bike fit. Chapter 8 looks at optimizing the fundamental act of pedaling properly, from biomechanics through the ongoing debate about optimal cadence.

The final chapters of the book cover the cutting edge in hydration, ergogenic supplements, and adaptation to extreme environments. Because innovations are becoming increasingly accessible to both professional and recreational athletes, understanding the science and applicability of these emerging technologies is important. The classic saying in computer science is "Garbage in, garbage out." Similarly, taking in the wrong nutrients at the wrong time can wreak havoc on your performance capacity; thus, chapter 9 focuses on some of the latest findings in hydration and sports supplements both on and off the bike. Finally, chapter 10 examines the latest knowledge on maintaining performance in extreme environments from enhancing performance through hypoxic and respiratory training to optimizing exercise capacity in inclement conditions.

One argument sometimes heard against the encroachment of scientific training is that using objective data turns us into robots enslaved by our gadgets. Another claim is that greater emphasis on science takes away from the mystique and beauty of cycling. Who cares about science when we all know that we should just ride more and harder? True, a basic attraction of cycling is the meshing of man and machine that may occur when you are completely "in the zone" while carving switchbacks down a mountain pass or riding in a great rhythm while climbing. But in cycling, as in other fields, art and science can not only coexist but also magnify and enhance the enjoyment of the whole. A great artist cannot be great without an inherent understanding of the physics of light and perspective, and a scientist aware of the complex biology of plants cannot help but become even more fascinated by the beauty of a flower. Our respective careers as scientist and coach have sprung from this precise philosophy—that the more we know about how the body works, the more enjoyable the already amazing experience of cycling becomes. Besides, at the end of the day, cycling is about speed, and it is just plain more fun to ride faster!

# Acknowledgments

Cycling has been a central theme in my life since my early years of BMX racing. The support of so many friends, family, teammates, and coaching clients have kept me focused on my quest for more knowledge, lighter bicycles, faster computers, and the latest in cycling training. I owe each of them a big thank you and pat on the back for their continued support and help. From my own racing and training experiences, I have learned so much, but coaching others has taught me more than I thought possible. Each of my clients deserves a thank you for the opportunity they afforded me to work with them. The advent of power meters brought about a brand new dimension to this amazing sport, and I owe a debt of gratitude for all those power meter manufacturers out there that brought about these amazing tools for our continued improvement. All of my partners at Peaksware have my lifelong appreciation and gratitude as well, and I continue to be amazed by their incredible abilities to make my ideas, thoughts, and dreams come to reality. Thanks to my coaches at the Peaks Coaching Group as well, as their questions keep me on my toes, force me to create new presentations and ways of teaching that inspire them and their clients.

My co-author, Stephen, has been incredible with his dedication, motivation and outstanding writing ability. I only wish I had half his writing brilliance. Thank you for making this book outstanding.

Tim Cusick has made a huge difference in many parts of this book, and his incredible organizational ability and clear thinking helps me every day. There are so many others that have helped this book come to fruition: Joe Friel, Kevin Williams, Dr. Allen Lim, Tom Coleman, Paul Swift, Paraic McGlynn, Gear Fisher, Todd Carver, Cliff Simms, Katrina Vogel, Kate Allen, Ben Pryhoda, Dirk Friel, Juliann McCarthy, Brandi Jones and Dr. Stephen McGregor. Thanks to all.

Dr. Andrew R. Coggan has been a great wealth of knowledge and motivation over the years as well, and his mentorship and friendship is something that I appreciate daily. Thanks to my Dad and Mom for their support and encouragement over the years, as their positive attitude and belief in my abilities have molded me into the person that I have become. Thanks so much to my kids, Thomas, Jack, and Susannah, as their excitement for cycling, racing, and learning has helped to reinvigorate my own passion for the sport as I get to explain the intricacies of training stress score, power meters, and threshold heart rates to each of them. Finally, a deep debt of gratitude goes out to my loving wife, Kate, as she has put up with all the challenges throughout every project that I undertake and makes sure I keep a proper balance in my life.

**—Hunter Allen**

Where would my life have wound up without two wheels under me? I did my first degree in oceanography, but my passion for cycling was what led to my switch to kinesiology, with hopes of becoming a cycling scientist and learning more about how my body works. So cycling has brought me some of the greatest moments and joys of my life—especially because it was through cycling that I met my wonderful wife Debbie. It has also been through cycling and science that I have met the most diverse and entertaining group of friends, including not only the numerous folks that I have shared the miles with, but also many of the fellow scientists that are interviewed in this book. Truly our sport is like no other in its freedom to take you on the journey of a lifetime.

My thanks go to Richard Pestes and the crew of PezCycling News. Being with Pez has given me the perfect outlet for combining my love for cycling along with my scientific background, fulfilling the dream I first started out with when I entered graduate school.

Finally, thanks to Graham Jones for hovering over my shoulder all these years!

**—Stephen S. Cheung**

## CHAPTER 1

# Evaluating Cycling Science

**A**lthough the human body itself doesn't evolve on a yearly basis, scientific information about exercise physiology is increasing exponentially. This growth can be seen in the number of papers published each year and in the ever-increasing number of scientific journals devoted primarily to sport and exercise. The way that the body works is not fundamentally changing; rather, the body of knowledge about how it works is expanding.

A number of factors are fueling the growth of the field of sport science. First, health professionals and governments are recognizing that physical activity is a preventive medicine for many illnesses. Research funding is therefore becoming more readily available. Indirectly, the Olympics have played a role by highlighting and stimulating research into particular exercise topics. Examples include altitude training from Mexico City (1968), heat stress and cooling measures from Athens (2004), and pollution effects on exercise from Beijing (2008).

Second, new tools and techniques for quantifying activity, such as portable power and portable metabolic analyzers along with metabolic machines for obtaining real-time data on riders during training and races, have broadened the avenues of study in the field. In the lab, new techniques and advances in molecular and genetic analysis permit scientists to investigate questions that simply could not be asked a decade or two previously.

Changes in the professionalism of sport itself are also driving the development of sport science as a field of research and work. With the dominance of sport in popular culture comes an increasing call by sponsors, athletes, and the public for performance. In turn, this demand motivates teams to seek advantage in every available avenue (only legal ones, we hope!) for improving performance. One by-product is that athlete care and training support has been largely taken out of the hands of traditional team staff members, who are often former amateurs or professionals who have minimal scientific training. Instead, teams are now open to hiring sports medicine specialists and sport science professionals who have been trained in the field. University graduates can make a career out of working with teams and athletes, and they come into the field with an appreciation for new ideas and approaches. Probably the most publicized example is the work of Allen Lim, PhD, with Jonathan Vaughter's Slipstream program. Although not the first to introduce technology like ice vests and compression garments to pro cyclists, Lim and Slipstream popularized their use, and the team's success has spurred others to explore the same advantage.

# Technological Breakthroughs

Probably the seminal event in the scientific evolution of cycling was the systematic approach used by Francesco Moser in his shattering of the world hour record in 1984. Along with pioneering the use of an aerodynamic time trial frame and disc wheels, Moser used the newly developed Conconi test to determine anaerobic threshold and trained with specific heart-rate-based methods based on such testing (Conconi et al. 1996). This approach was supplemented by the development and use of portable heart rate monitors to enable real-time monitoring of effort. Since that time, heart rate monitors have become ubiquitous for cyclists and multisport athletes of all levels. Unfortunately, without the knowledge to analyze and interpret the data, heart rate just becomes another meaningless number on a screen. Over the past decade, power monitors have become the new standard in training tools, and coaches such as Hunter and scientist Andy Coggan, PhD, have been pioneers in the systematic and detailed use of this tool to quantify training and maximize fitness. However, power is a random number unless the user knows how to interpret it.

But how much science and how much high-tech gadgetry do most people need to enjoy cycling? How do sport science improvements filter down to the everyday cyclist? Our view is that even the recreational age-group cyclist who simply likes to ride the occasional century or Gran Fondo event can enjoy keeping up with new ideas as they emerge, because doing so advances the sport and the cyclist's enjoyment of it. Yes, getting a new set of high-end carbon tubular wheels and getting faster that way is neat, but adopting a new and proven training idea is the physiological equivalent to those wheels, and it will get the cyclist faster in the end.

The influence of training and technological advances were nicely summarized in a study by Dr. Asker Jeukendrup (Jeukendrup and Martin 2001), who in addition to his cycling research has worked with the Rabobank professional cycling team. How much faith should we place in technology to enhance our performance, and where should we place our priorities and spend our money? Using a baseline cyclist of 70 kilograms racing a 40K time trial at either untrained (48 milliliters $\dot{V}O_2$max, 72:56 time), trained (66 milliliters, 58:35), or elite (80 milliliters, 52:02) fitness while riding on the handlebar hoods, Jeukendrup and Martin (2001) modeled and ranked in relative importance the effects of various interventions, both fitness and technological. A summary of some of the possible improvements is presented in table 1.1.

For a novice athlete, big improvements in a simulated 40K time trial (TT) can come from improvements in both training and aerodynamics. So although equipment changes and buying stuff will indeed get the cyclist "free speed," similarly large benefits come from enhancing physiological performance and bike fit, and that is where training and coaching based on sound evidence come into play.

As seen in table 1.2, scientific evidence can also guide us in our equipment choices. In the tradeoffs between aerodynamic versus lightweight equipment, the former is often seen to be a priority in flat races, whereas the quest for light equipment dominates when climbing. The modeling from Jeukendrup and Martin (2001) provides strong support for this view, but with an important caveat. Namely, at moderate grades, aerodynamics remains important, especially with higher fitness because of the higher speeds.

**TABLE 1.1  Relative Benefits of Various Strategies for Improving Performance in a 40K Time Trial**

|  | Training | Decreasing body weight by 3 kg | Hoods— drops | Hoods— aerodynamics | Hoods— optimized aerodynamics |
|---|---|---|---|---|---|
| Novice | −5:27 | −0:25 | −3:46 | −6:49 | −9:21 |
| Trained | −1:45 | −0:21 | −3:06 | −5:36 | −7:42 |
| Elite | −1:02 | −0:19 | −2:47 | −4:59 | −6:54 |

**TABLE 1.2  Relative Importance of Bike Weight and Equipment Modifications During a 20K Climbing Time Trial**

|  | DROPPING BIKE WEIGHT FROM 10 TO 7 KG | | | SWITCHING FROM AERODYNAMIC TO LIGHT WHEELS | | |
|---|---|---|---|---|---|---|
| Grade of climb | 3% | 6% | 12% | 3% | 6% | 12% |
| Novice | −1:34 | −3:38 | −7:25 | +0:10 | −0:25 | −1:12 |
| Trained | −0:42 | −1:52 | −4:02 | +0:20 | −0:03 | −0:35 |
| Elite | −0:29 | −1:15 | −2:48 | +0:21 | +0:06 | −0:22 |

# Evidence Versus Dogma

Despite such advances in understanding how the body works and how to maximize its physical potential, changing the ideas held by individual riders remains difficult. Too often, new riders rely on advice that they hear from their riding partners or club members, who heard the same advice when they started. Such knowledge becomes ingrained in the culture of the sport, and persuading successful athletes to try something that is out of their normal routine can be challenging. After all, why fix it if it isn't broken? For every rider like Greg LeMond, who was always open to new training ideas and equipment and who popularized everything from sunglasses and aerobars to power-based training and peaking for particular events such as the Tour de France and Paris–Roubaix, there are countless riders who will stick with what they know and therefore trust. Old advice is not always bad, of course, but a better approach is to assess information rather than blindly accept it without analysis. It is time to take a hard look at what does and doesn't work in the world of training and fitness. But if we are going to dig into the underlying science to develop training ideas, first we need to have a clear understanding of both the strengths and the limitations of the scientific literature.

Here are some examples of ways in which scientific advances have improved cycling performance and the lessons that we can draw from them about the benefits of the scientific process. We examine these topics in detail in subsequent chapters:

- **Precooling.** Cooling garments were initially developed by NASA for use by astronauts during spacewalks, and the Australian rowing teams first popularized their use for precooling before races in the mid-1990s (Flouris and Cheung 2006). Did Team Slipstream win the 2008 Giro d'Italia team time trial (TTT) because they used cooling vests? Or did they win because of particular equipment choices, the specific training that they did as a group in the weeks prior, better fitness, or simple luck? Certainly, Slipstream's success that day has probably caused other teams to consider the use of cooling vests, but how can we tell for sure whether such interventions work? Rather than a blind "monkey see, monkey do" process of emulating what others did, the most notable characteristic of most scientific investigations is the use of a control group versus an experimental group. This aspect is the heart of the scientific method. A control group refers to a group that receives the same testing but without the experimental intervention. Such a design permits the isolation of that particular intervention and the removal of confounding factors. For example, a study on precooling should have a trial in which a subject is precooled before testing and another trial in which the subject rests for a similar length of time but receives no precooling (Cheung and Robinson 2004). Without this control trial, determining whether precooling is effective is simply impossible. In chapter 10 we look closely at whether the evidence suggests that precooling results in improved performance across all types of exercise.

- **Altitude tents.** Altitude training was first stimulated by the Mexico 1968 Olympics. The development of artificial altitude facilities in the late 1990s and early 2000s helped to reduce the need for high-altitude training camps. The emergence of such commercial technologies demonstrates the symbiosis between sport and science in that greater demand by athletes drives scientific inquiry because scientists need to keep up by developing scientifically validated and safe protocols for their use.

- **Fluid replacement and sports drinks.** Although athlete feedback is important, some information can only be gained through using laboratory techniques in a controlled setting. One example is the direct measuring of emptying rates from the stomach and intestines of various fluids during exercise. New advances in cellular analysis have also provided information on how the body's metabolic demands change with different exercise durations and different environments like heat and cold. Such laboratory-specific techniques have enabled the development of sports drinks calibrated for optimal nutrition during exercise. Some of the latest advice on hydration strategies is surveyed in chapter 9. The use of scientific data quickly accelerates the development of new products, because it provides concrete information that can then be complemented by athlete testing.

## Q&A     With Ben Sporer: From the Lab to the Road and Back Again

| Current position | Physiologist with Canadian Sport Centre Pacific. |
|---|---|
| **Professional relationship and background with cycling** | Physiologist and sport scientist with Canadian National Cycling and Triathlon Teams. |
| **Personal background with cycling** | Road and mountain bike—some recreational racing. |
| **Favorite ride (either one you've done or always wanted to do)** | Spruce Lake in British Columbia's Chilcotin region—beautiful alpine passes, epic downhills, and flowing single track. |
| **Favorite cycling-related experience** | Coffee rides and annual riding trip. |

*(continued)*

**Ben, you're a PhD who's worked a lot with top cyclists and triathletes in and out of the lab. Do ideas come from the athletes out on the road and trails, or do they come from the lab?**

It's funny that you ask this because I was recently having a discussion on this exact matter with sport psychologist Dr. David Cox. Our outcome was that science drives practice while practice leads science. It really is a bit of both. Cyclists and coaches live and breathe the pursuit of performance every day and because of this are constantly on the lookout for strategies, techniques, and modifications to training that enhance performance. Some of these ideas may have originated in science, but many also come from personal experiences of the coach and athlete. As a scientist who works with athletes, you need to be a student of the sport. At the same time, athletes and coaches need to embrace the fact that science can provide innovative ideas and real solutions to the challenges of cycling. I believe it is a mutual respect for both that advances our understanding of the sport.

 **Then what's the biggest single thing that you've learned about how the body works from working with athletes?**

The single biggest thing? There are many but I guess I'd have to say that the body truly works like a machine but that each machine is unique. Often in science, we take a reductionist approach and break down the parts of a complex system like the human body to determine how its various components function. Obviously, this has great benefits and has driven our understanding of how the human body operates immensely. But when working in elite sport, you need to take a holistic approach to understanding individual responses to different stressors in different situations. It's critical to have a good understanding of each individual's strengths, weaknesses, and responses in an integrated context that takes into account the many factors affecting performance—nutrition, psychology, environment, training history, level of competition, and so on.

 **With so much information out there in books, on the Internet, and from coaches, how do you advise athletes in terms of sorting out the wheat from the chaff? How do you help them to figure out the science?**

This is a big challenge because there is an information overload, and it's a difficult task to make sense of it all. The most important thing is to help athletes understand whether or not there is a physiological basis for an idea or strategy. That said, there's not always scientific evidence for some of the things that athletes and coaches do, yet their actions are very effective in real-world situations. I try to get them to think critically to see whether there's a physiological basis for it and to think about where they're getting the information from.

**If you come across something in the lab that just doesn't jibe with current practice, how do you tell athletes that what they're doing has no scientific basis? Is that advice different if it's something that's benign versus something that's both wrong and potentially harmful or a real waste of their time and effort?**

This ties in closely with the previous question. Part of the art of being an applied sport scientist is in the ability to differentiate when and when not to talk about scientific evidence. Science is not perfect, and it has its limitations—especially when you're looking at individual responses. As scientists we look for statistical significance to qualify as scientific evidence, but this is based on mean group data. In high-performance sport we're looking at individual athletes. Part of my job is to read, study, and look at trends in data and determine whether they apply to a given situation. I try to lay out the pros and cons to any practice so that athletes can understand what it is they are doing.

Even when there is no scientific basis, it's really important to keep an open mind because athletes and coaches may be ahead of the evidence. As I said before, they often provide ideas and the inspiration to look deeper and evaluate practices scientifically. There's also a lot to be said about the placebo effect. If there is no detriment to the athlete and the athlete believes in a particular practice, this can be very powerful. Certainly, when there are potentially negative or harmful consequences, or when the practice is unethical, every effort is made to deter the cyclist from doing it.

 **How can everyday cyclists and coaches go about accessing and understanding the physiology better?**

A general exercise physiology book is always a good starting point. The greater your understanding of how the body works, the more critically you can think about the information you come across. Cycling-specific books like this one are excellent resources.

It's also important to have an open mind and surround yourself with good resources. There are a lot of good physiologists who have a passion for cycling, so seek out quality experts who can advise and mentor you. This holds true for all aspects of the sport. Those with more time and money to devote to the quest should look for conferences on cycling or endurance sport physiology—it's always good to learn from what other sports are doing.

# Limits of Scientific Studies

Despite the powers of the scientific method, it is by no means a perfect system. Unfortunately, the public has been cajoled into accepting scientific findings as gospel chiseled in granite. Advertisers have exploited this perception by touting their products with claims such as "clinically proven," "demonstrated in university studies," and "scientifically formulated." These statements can give products the veneer of authenticity, but a true understanding of the strengths and limits of science is required to assess such claims. At the same time, understanding these limits does not mean that we should cynically dismiss all scientific claims. In applying scientific studies to practical training and accepting sport science advice, athletes and coaches need to understand a number of serious limitations.

## Statistical Versus Practical Significance

Possibly the biggest hurdle in the field of exercise science is appreciating when a scientific finding is truly significant. For example, a one-second improvement in a 4,000-meter track pursuit race may be statistically insignificant in that it is mathematically impossible to ascertain that such an improvement, even if it is consistent among all subjects, is a true difference or simply a random error given the small number of subjects and the inherent variability in running the test day to day. But a difference of 1 percent or even less may be more than enough to separate the athlete on the top step of the podium from those who are not on it at all. At the elite end of the sport, the margin for success is razor thin, not only in shorter events like a track pursuit but also in three-week stage races that now often seem to be decided by less than a minute over 90 hours of racing. Such tiny differences in top-level performances make even a potentially miniscule advantage critical to explore and exploit. Therefore, even when scientific studies cannot determine a clear benefit from a training method or ergogenic aid, an open mind must be maintained to the possibility that a new way has sufficient merit.

## Humpty Dumpty Effect

The goal of scientific control is to isolate individual factors and test their effects on performance. The experimenter who is investigating the effects of caffeine on time trial performance exerts as much control as possible on everything from diet, hydration, and sleep, to external training the day before and the day of a testing session. This approach prevents those extraneous factors from confounding the results, so that, ideally, any observed changes can be attributed solely to the effects of the caffeine. But in the process of focusing solely on the variable being tested, the ability to understand the big picture is often lost, especially in

Whether they strive to be victorious at elite levels or to achieve faster personal bests, cyclists turn to science for new ways to improve performance by even the smallest margin.

©John Giles/PA Wire/Press Association Images

the interaction of various factors with each other. For example, how does caffeine interact with water or vitamin intake, and how might caffeine affect the ingestion of carbohydrate during exercise? Another example is how a change in crank length may interact with changes in saddle height or saddle fore and aft. An equally difficult task is fitting together all the microscopic pieces of scientific studies into the whole human response to exercise, much like the challenge faced by all the king's men and horses as they attempted to put Humpty Dumpty back together after his fall. This jigsaw puzzle is made more difficult when we throw in the question of practical versus statistical significance. Namely, how many "nonsignificant" results, added together, are sufficient to produce a real and definite improvement in performance? If caffeine improves performance by a nonsignificant 0.5 percent, do 10 such little manipulations together mean a significant 5 percent improvement?

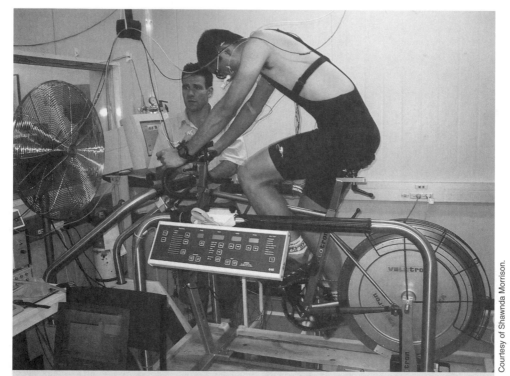

Courtesy of Shawnda Morrison.

**Scientific studies can inform your training, but study results must be thoughtfully interpreted and carefully applied.**

## The Laws of Averages

Individual variability lies at the heart of the reason why scientific studies employ multiple subjects rather than simply report values from individuals. But one of the key things to keep in mind is that statistics demands that individual responses be collapsed into group values to perform comparisons. Therefore, the results are generally average values rather than individual responses. This approach can lead to the classic case of "one size fits none" in which the results are generalized, because group averages may have no bearing on individual responses. For example, in a study on the effects of fatigue from prolonged exercise in response to cold stress, the group response led to the conclusion that fatigue did not affect the ability to maintain shivering and body temperature in the cold (Tikuisis et al. 1999). But that study also published individual values, and the graph clearly showed a huge range in tolerance times in the cold. In addition, some subjects cooled much faster when fatigued than when they were rested. In this case, such variability makes it difficult to predict how a particular individual may respond to cold stress. Occupational guidelines often err on the conservative side to maximize safety, thus underestimating the true capacity of a large part of the population.

For athletes, individual performance cannot be simply extrapolated from the average results reported in a study. Instead, performance may fall within a fairly wide range of possibilities. This conclusion pertains to many of the studies that we mention in this book. As you read the book and draw your own conclusions, realize that what one study might have concluded could be completely the opposite of how you might respond.

Extending beyond individual variability in response to an intervention, certain athletes will simply not respond to an intervention, even if scientific studies demonstrate clear efficacy. Such nonresponders commonly appear in the laboratory, but they are often hidden among a large group of subjects in a study or sometimes not included at all. An excellent example is altitude training and the live high, train low (LHTL) protocol of living at an elevated altitude while training at a lower elevation to maximize both hypoxic and training stimuli. Although this type of training seems to show consistent promise in eliciting an increase in aerobic capacity, the research group that first proposed and systematically investigated LHTL (Levine and Stray-Gundersen 1997) also found that nearly 40 percent of tested subjects did not respond at all to LHTL, regardless of the various protocols implemented (Chapman et al. 1998). Ultimately, even if scientific evidence clearly states a benefit, there is no guarantee that it will be beneficial for all people. Nothing can replace an understanding of how your own body works and responds, supplemented by a review of detailed training diaries of both objective and subjective data.

## Skewed Participant Pool

Little research is done on top professional athletes. Their training and racing lives are simply too busy for them to be brought into the lab on a regular basis. In addition, these athletes and their coaches and team managers are often leery of the restrictions that the testing might place on their regular training routines. Performing a study involving multiple testing sessions over the course of several weeks on elite athletes would be extremely difficult because their training status would have to be fairly even throughout the entire experiment to ensure that changes did not occur simply because of natural variations in their training load. Therefore, most studies of professional or elite athletes are accomplished during a small window of base training in their off-season, between their period of complete rest and their transition to higher-intensity training.

As a substitute, the "elite" athletes used in cycling research are typically second-tier or developing riders. The vast majority of exercise studies are done using "recreational" or "active" subjects, who are typically university-aged males who may or may not be trained in cycling. The use of this population is often simply a matter of practicality and availability because most research laboratories do not have access to a large pool of willing competitive athletes as subjects.

Therefore, the relevance of data on these elite or recreational athletes for either professional athletes or age-group competitors must be evaluated in light of differences in everything from age to training history and level of fitness, as seen in tables 1.1 and 1.2 on page 3. For example, does an improvement in threshold power output from 350 to 380 watts in "elite" subjects automatically translate to a similar 30-watt improvement in age-group or masters athletes who might have thresholds of 250 watts? How would it translate to professionals who have thresholds of 400 watts? Similarly, how can findings be used when recreational athletes with thresholds of 150 watts are employed? Can such findings be directly translated to other competitive groups, or will improvements be greater or smaller in athletes with higher fitness?

## Logistical Constraints

We have previously described why it can be difficult to get elite athletes into a lab for a study. Even when using non-elite athletes as subjects, researchers find it difficult to recruit and retain subjects willing to donate the time and effort required to participate in training studies that involve multiple visits over weeks or months. Even when subjects are willing, running a training study is a major undertaking. Think how tough it might be to schedule 20 subjects, each with time constraints of school or jobs, to come in and train for two hours each day for two weeks! Such logistical issues can make even simple training studies of one to two weeks a daunting proposition. Therefore, we know little about the extent and timeline of adaptation.

The problems associated with short-term courses of scientific study play out all the time in the sport of cycling. Because of the repetitive nature of pedaling, the body becomes incredibly well adapted to that specific motion, even when using a nonoptimal position or pedaling stroke. A classic real-life example of this type of accommodation is the great Sean Kelly, who was so scrunched up when he cycled that he looked like he was riding a bike two sizes too small. Although Kelly was incredibly successful, biomechanists and bike-fitting specialists would probably have recommended a more stretched-out position. But considering that Kelly had adapted to this position through countless hours of riding over decades, would he really have been even more powerful and efficient if he had changed his position? How long would it have taken him to adapt to a new position? Would he ever have been able to adapt?

The difficulty with short-term studies is further illustrated by the quest to determine the effects of varying cadence. Simply investigating the effects of various cadences on time trial performance in a one-off test is not sufficient; it's almost guaranteed that the results of a single experiment would show that the optimal cadence is the one that the subjects normally ride at because their bodies have adapted through months or years of riding at that cadence. So the only way to conduct a fair test of whether a higher or lower cadence is better is to have riders train at a different cadence for months or more to become adapted to that cadence before testing their performance.

# Applying the Science

If science is powerful yet has all these inherent limitations, how should we approach our reading of it or the data that it provides? We believe that one key is to get as broad a picture as possible rather than rely on a single study. For almost any question or opinion under the sun, we can find a scientific study that argues for it and another that argues against it. Keep in mind that no one study will definitively address and resolve every aspect of a question. One of the characteristics of science is that it requires an accumulation of evidence. The weight of many studies that address a similar idea can be used to develop a holistic and comprehensive consensus. We agree with Dr. Ben Sporer that we must keep an open mind about new techniques and strategies. At times athletes and coaches are ahead of the science and lead the science, whereas at other times they are behind the times and base their training on techniques from 50 years ago. You must therefore listen to your body, study the latest training methods, and make your own judgment about the effectiveness of a particular training method, philosophy, interval, product, or supplement. The advantage of science is that you can base your training decisions on solid evidence rather than opinion. Trial and error on an individual level will always be critical, but you can greatly accelerate that process by using the benefits of scientific evidence as the foundation on which to build your training.

# 2

# Producing and Measuring Energy

The body is an incredibly complex engine, which explains why scientists are still busily exploring its inner workings after centuries of study. Indeed, although we know in broad terms the anatomy and physiology of the major systems within the body, we are still nowhere close to understanding a question as simple and yet as fundamental as why we slow down and fatigue during exercise. One reason for this lack of clarity is that the body is so complex that multiple factors are likely involved, each of which may separately or synergistically combine to elicit a state of fatigue (Coyle 2007, Joyner and Coyle 2008). Also, the human body is incredibly versatile in its range of capable activities, so the primary mechanisms that limit exercise capacity may be different for different types of exercise. For example, the physical demands of a single 200-meter sprint on the track are quite different from those of a road sprint in the finale of the Milan–San Remo after nearly 300 kilometers of riding. Similarly, the hard efforts of a 60-minute cyclo-cross race, with its repeated accelerations from low speeds, can be quite different from the short, hard accelerations from high speed involved in a 60-minute road criterium, which in turn are drastically different from the steady power output required in a 40K time trial.

Compared with other animals, humans do not excel at any particular activity. But their trump card is being proficient at a wide variety of exercise demands. For example, cheetahs can outrun humans over short distances, but humans can easily outrun cheetahs and many predator animals over moderate distances or longer. Indeed, some anthropologists believe that the distinguishing characteristic that drove much of human evolution is not necessarily our upright posture or even walking, but rather the evolutionary pressure presented by endurance running to support a hunter–gatherer existence or the prolonged tracking of game (Bramble and Lieberman 2004). Furthermore, in the process of such migrations to follow food sources, humans have become uniquely adapted, through both physiological and behavioral responses, across a diverse range of environments on the planet, from deserts and the tropics, to the Arctic and high altitudes (Cheung 2010).

As scientific research illuminates the complexity of the body and its response to exercise and training, more questions are raised, and ideas are developed about how to extend the limits of human potential (Hargreaves 2008). Therefore, even a non-elite athlete interested in greater understanding and improved training can no longer stick with simple definitions and generalizations when it comes to exercise physiology and the underlying mechanisms of training. Further complicating the search for meaningful information is the confusing jargon and morass of terminology, often used inaccurately by both scientists and coaches. Therefore, we will distill some of the basic principles in exercise science, define the major systems and terminology, and discuss the latest concepts about what limits exercise capacity.

# Energy Production

The end goal of energy metabolism within the body is to produce adenosine triphosphate (ATP), which is the common currency of energy used throughout the entire body for all functions. The basic adenosine molecule can have one (adenosine monophosphate or AMP), two (adenosine diphosphate or ADP), or three (ATP) phosphates attached to it. Each of the three phosphates is attached in series to adenosine and is a store of energy. Most commonly, only the third phosphate bond is broken, and the stored energy within that bond is released to provide energy to the cell, resulting in ADP and a phosphate. But it is also possible for two phosphate bonds to be broken and AMP to be produced.

To enable varied exercise from all-out sprints to riding a century, the human body uses three different but interrelated energy metabolic systems to generate ATP: the alactic or phosphocreatine (ATP-PC) system, anaerobic glycolysis, and aerobic metabolism (figure 2.1).

## ATP-PC System

Although it is the endpoint currency of energy, ATP is not stored in large quantities within a cell, possibly because of its relatively large size compared with glycogen and fat. Therefore, the body needs a system of replenishing ATP as quickly as possible for high-intensity efforts, like the final sprint for a mountaintop or the finish line. The ATP-PC system consists of energy stored within the

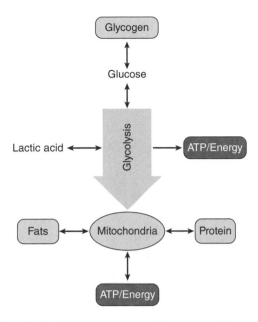

**FIGURE 2.1**    **Interrelationships between energy systems.**

phosphocreatine (PC) molecule, analogous to the high-energy bonds within the ATP. Phosphocreatine acts as an initial reservoir of accessible energy. As ATP becomes depleted to ADP (adenosine diphosphate), PC is broken down, and that released energy is then used to bind phosphate to ADP, turning it back to ATP again. The advantage of PC is that immediate release of energy occurs with a minimum of biochemical steps. Thus, ATP levels within the muscles are fairly well preserved even during intense exercise in the time before ATP becomes readily available from glycolysis (explained in the next section). Training this system can help you extend your top-end sprint speed from a short 50- to 100-meter burst to a distance up to 300 meters, greatly expanding your options in the finale of a race. This ability is the forte of sprinters like Alessandro Petacchi and Mario Cipollini, who can simply outdrag their competitors to the line by keeping their speed as others fade.

The role of phosphocreatine in maintaining ATP levels during brief, intense exercise has resulted in a heavy emphasis and research on the role of creatine supplementation for resistance training and power sports such as weightlifting, football, and many field events in athletics. Although power-based cyclists such as track sprinters may gain some advantage, the benefits of creatine supplementation for endurance cyclists is unproved, except possibly during periods of heavy resistance training (Bemben and Lamont 2005).

## Anaerobic Glycolysis

Glycogen is the primary storage form of carbohydrate in the body. About 500 grams or 2,000 kilocalories are stored in your muscles and liver. This fuel is broken down for energy by both anaerobic and aerobic metabolism. Note that there is no difference in how the body treats carbohydrate when it is first broken down in a muscle. The common initial pathway is anaerobic glycolysis. In this glycolytic ("glucose breakdown") pathway to energy production, glucose or glycogen is initially broken down in the muscles without the use of oxygen (anaerobic means "without oxygen"). If sufficient oxygen is available to the muscle, carbohydrate can then proceed onward to aerobic (or "with oxygen") metabolism. Glycolysis of one molecule of glucose results in only two molecules of ATP. The advantage of this system, however, is that a great deal of glucose can be processed rapidly and, most important, without oxygen. This advantage is important for cyclists, because many of the efforts in cycling are short and intense. When you are doing a hill effort of 30 seconds to 2 minutes, you are taxing the anaerobic system, and some people have better anaerobic systems than others. The riders with the strongest anaerobic systems will excel in races like a criterium with a hill and six turns in it, a hard-paced breakaway in which the pulls at the front are short, and in events like cyclocross.

As related to exercise physiology, keep in mind several important points concerning glycolysis:

- **As the name implies, only carbohydrate is metabolized through glycolysis.** In contrast, fat and protein can only be converted to ATP aerobically with oxygen present. Thus, when exercising at high intensity when oxygen supply to the muscles is limited, you rely heavily on the limited stores of carbohydrate for energy. For that reason, among others, you want to protect your limited glycogen stores during a long ride or race, both by not going hard until you need to and by making sure that you consume carbohydrate early on in the ride.

- **Glycolysis takes place in both Type I (slow-twitch) and Type II (fast-twitch) muscle fibers, although Type II fibers have higher glycolytic capacity.** The main difference between fast- and slow-twitch fibers is the degree of specialization rather than one muscle type being incapable of a particular metabolic step. For example, a top-flight sprinter is still able to climb and an elite climber is capable of an occasional sprint. Neither may be happy about it, but they can still do it!

- **The main by-product of glycolysis is lactic acid (also called lactate).** Lactate is not a dead end, or "waste" product (for more information, see Role of Lactate in Fatigue on page 32). When sufficient oxygen again becomes available, the lactate is converted back to pyruvate and can then continue to aerobic metabolism.

Improving the anaerobic system is a key part of your training in cycling because you will be challenged anaerobically many times in your group rides, races, and events. We examine this topic further in chapter 3 when we discuss training zones and ways in which you can improve your ability to go hard and recover quickly.

## Aerobic Metabolism

With aerobic metabolism, the conversion of fuel for energy becomes much more efficient because carbohydrate can be taken beyond the initial glycolysis and be fully broken down to release more energy. In addition, the large supply of fat and the smaller supply of protein can also be converted to energy aerobically. Compared with glycolysis, aerobic metabolism is much more efficient in terms of energy return; 34 additional ATP molecules are created compared with the 2 created with glycolysis alone. A molecule of fat can produce even greater amounts

Courtesy of Scott Moninger.

**The key to improving cycling performance is to maximize your body's aerobic metabolic capacity.**

of ATP than a carbohydrate molecule can. Aerobic metabolism and the burning of fat remain an important source of energy regardless of cycling speed or effort, so aerobic metabolism does not turn off and the body does not completely switch over to anaerobic metabolism. What does change, at high intensity, is how much extra anaerobic energy production is needed to meet the energy demand that aerobic metabolism alone cannot produce.

As we know from reading food labels, one gram of carbohydrate yields approximately 4 kilocalories of energy, whereas each gram of fat yields approximately 9 kilocalories, because of the higher number of carbon bonds within fat. This higher energy density explains why fat is a preferred fuel storage form within the body. In a lean male athlete of 70 kilograms and 5 percent body fat, 3.5 kilograms of fat, or theoretically 31,500 kilocalories of energy, may be used for aerobic metabolism. Although obviously the cyclist cannot use all of this and survive, this energy reservoir is much larger than the small supply of carbohydrate stored as glycogen. Another consideration to keep in mind with fuel use in the body is that the brain can use only carbohydrate for energy, not fat or protein. If you deplete your glycogen stores, you will not only "hit the wall" and run low on energy but also experience impairment of your mental functioning and mood as your carbohydrate supply becomes too low. Thus, keeping carbohydrate reserves as high as possible is critically important to cyclists. You can achieve this by taking in carbohydrate before exercise, by ingesting carbohydrate early in a ride to minimize the amount of glycogen use, and by starting the refueling and recovery process as soon as possible after finishing a ride to prepare for next day's ride.

Your aerobic metabolism is the bedrock of your cycling fitness, whether you are a century rider or a track sprinter. When we talk about riders with big engines, what we are really saying is that they have extremely well-developed aerobic metabolic systems. Think of it this way: The stronger your aerobic energy system is, especially your fat metabolism, the less reliant you are on carbohydrate use while riding at a set workload (e.g., 200 watts) early in a race. You can therefore ride longer at that workload before running out of glycogen, and you will have more carbohydrate available for the hard attacks that require you to exceed that workload at the end of a race. In day-to-day training, a stronger aerobic metabolism becomes the critical foundation for improving your anaerobic capacity because it permits you to do more or harder intervals. Therefore, if you can do just one thing to improve in cycling, you should train to improve your body's aerobic system and its efficiency at using fat, carbohydrate, and protein as fuel. Because aerobic metabolism relies on oxygen availability, an athlete's aerobic capacity can be quantified relatively simply by measuring the rate of maximal oxygen consumption $\dot{V}O_2$max in the body.

## Interplay Among Energy Systems

Some exercise physiology textbooks present a graph outlining the relative dominance of different metabolic pathways for events ranging from a 200-meter track sprint to a century ride. Often, these figures unintentionally give the mistaken notion that only one metabolic pathway is used at a time, implying that ATP-PC stops after 15 seconds, glycolysis begins at 15 seconds and ends at 3 minutes, and aerobic metabolism kicks in after that. This notion is false. The critical concept to take from our discussion about the various metabolic pathways is that none of them works in isolation. Rather, energy for movement is simultaneously being derived from all three sources, and the relative dominance of each system depends on exercise intensity (figure 2.2). Therefore, different training workouts emphasize

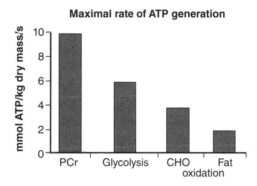

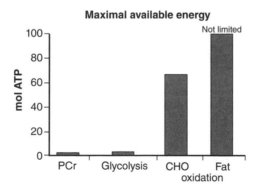

**FIGURE 2.2** **Energy production rates (top) and overall energy availability in the body (bottom).**

Reprinted, by permission, from J.H. Wilmore, D.L. Costill, and W.L. Kenney, 2008. *Physiology of sport and exercise*, 4th ed. (Champaign, IL: Human Kinetics), 58.

different metabolic systems, but all systems are trained to some extent. When you do a $\dot{V}O_2$max interval for 5 minutes, you are primarily taxing the aerobic system, but you used the ATP-PC system in your initial sprint to start the effort. Then when you dug deep to push over that hill, you maxed out the anaerobic glycolysis system. On the whole, however, the aerobic system got the most stress and should respond by improving, and because cycling is primarily an endurance sport, the primary emphasis is to maximize aerobic capacity. Therefore, the bulk of a well-designed training program features large doses of long rides and relatively long intervals to stress the aerobic system, supplemented with smaller doses of hard group rides and races.

# Energy Definitions

Cycling is a sport that relies on equipment, and its technocentric nature is complemented by the jargon used to describe human physiology. People commonly toss around terms like watts, calories, and $\dot{V}O_2$max. Unfortunately, many terms are used without an intrinsic understanding of what they mean, so a great deal of confusion can arise. Moreover, some terms are used interchangeably, further hindering proper communication. This section aims to clarify the meanings of some commonly used terminology and provide some generally accepted definitions.

## Units of Energy

With the development and popularization of portable power monitors such as PowerTap, Quarq, and SRM, the measurement of wattage is steadily becoming the dominant metric of performance and training, taking over from heart rate, distance, speed, or volume measures. But what does wattage actually mean in terms of energy? In sports nutrition especially, the unit *kilocalorie* remains dominant. The following are some of the critical definitions of variables used in quantifying energy (chapter 3 focuses on using these definitions in training):

- **Joule.** The metric standard unit of energy is a joule (J), which is often also quantified in kilojoules (kJ), or 1,000 joules. This unit, kilojoule, is the value that you also see on your power monitor, quantifying how much absolute mechanical work you performed. Because mechanical work is the actual physical load that is being imposed on the body, it can be a more accurate method of quantifying training compared with relatively crude methods such as distance or time.

- **Watt.** Wattage is a rate of energy production, and 1 watt (W) equals 1 joule per second. Therefore, when you are cycling at 200 watts, you are generating

200 joules of mechanical energy each second (1 kilojoule every 5 seconds, or 720 kilojoules every hour). Although the mechanical energy is accurately quantified using such systems, power monitors do not quantify the overall energy expenditure by the body because the body is not 100 percent efficient in metabolically converting the energy stored in carbohydrate, lipids, and protein into mechanical energy (see chapter 8 for a detailed definition and examination of gross efficiency). Rather, like the combustion engine in a car, the vast majority is converted to heat energy, such that the human body is only 20 to 25 percent efficient. Therefore, assuming 25 percent efficiency, to generate the 720 kilojoules of mechanical energy mentioned earlier, the body has to convert approximately three times that much, or 2,160 kilojoules of additional heat energy, for a total metabolic requirement of 2,880 kilojoules for that hour of exercise.

- **Calorie.** A calorie (cal) is an alternative unit of energy to the joule and is defined as the energy required to increase the temperature of 1 gram of water by 1 °C. As with joules, it can be quantified in units of 1,000 (1 kilocalorie), and kilojoules or kilocalories are the typical units of energy that we see when we read food labels. Many exercise machines and heart rate monitor systems indirectly calculate energy expenditure in kilocalories using an algorithm that incorporates heart rate, body mass, and exercise duration. Note that although the algorithms being used are sophisticated and are constantly improving, they remain indirect estimates that are prone to error.

Frustration can arise from the fact that energy units from power monitors are often not the same as those used in nutrition, making it difficult to match energy expenditure during workouts with adequate intake of food calories to achieve nutritional goals. But the conversion between the two units can be roughly assumed to work out to a 1:1 ratio because the relationship between the two is a constant ratio in which 1 kilocalorie equals 4.17 kilojoules. But if we assume that the body is 25 percent efficient in converting energy stored in nutrients to mechanical power, then we first need to multiply our mechanical energy production from the power monitor by 4 before dividing by 4.17 to obtain the number of kilocalories. Let's calculate an example:

200 W effort for 1 h = 200 J/s × 3,600 s = 720,000 J = 720 kJ

720 kJ × 4 = 2,880 kJ total energy expenditure

2,880 kJ / 4.17 kJ/kcal = 690.6 kcal

The conversion between kilojoules and kilocalories is important to know if you use a power meter that measures energy production in kilojoules or a heart rate monitor that calculates energy expenditure in kilocalories. You can see how much energy you have burned and use that as a guide to how much you should eat after a ride. Many cyclists even use the kilojoule data from their power meters or the kilocalorie data from their heart rate monitors to build nutrition protocols for their events based on the energy burned along the way. The data can serve as a reminder to eat regularly during your next event or long ride to prevent running low on fuel and bonking. Of course, if you live in a region where food labels are provided in kilojoules, then you do not need to convert to kilocalories; you can simply multiply your total mechanical power for a workout by four to obtain a good estimate of how much food energy you have consumed. Remember, though, that this factor of four is a general assumption and may differ across individuals and with training. The only way to get an accurate conversion factor is to do a specialized lab-based test (see chapter 8 for more detail on gross efficiency).

## Maximal Oxygen Consumption Terminology

Many athletes and coaches consider the measure of maximal aerobic capacity—or $\dot{V}O_2$max—as the gold standard test for endurance athletes. The primary purpose of quantifying this measure is to provide a good expression of your ability to generate ATP through aerobic metabolic pathways. One important consideration is that $\dot{V}O_2$max values, as with all physiological measures of fitness, are sport specific and will differ for running, swimming, or Nordic skiing. $\dot{V}O_2$max values are typically higher for running and Nordic skiing because of the weight-bearing nature of those activities and the larger muscle mass involved. In contrast, the buoyant nature of water typically results in lower $\dot{V}O_2$max values despite the large muscle mass used. Therefore, multisport athletes need to have sport-specific fitness tests and training zones.

Maximal oxygen consumption can be quantified in a variety of ways:

- **Non-normalized $\dot{V}O_2$max or $\dot{V}O_2$peak.** This value is the highest absolute amount of oxygen that your body can process and is generally expressed in liters per minute (L/min). This is the simplest and most basic way of presenting oxygen uptake capacity because it doesn't take into account any fluctuations in your weight between tests.

- **Normalized to body mass.** This value is your highest oxygen uptake during the exercise test normalized to body weight in kilograms, or liters per minute per kilogram. Thus, this number provides a better basis for comparison between two riders of different sizes and is the value that we most commonly talk about when referring to $\dot{V}O_2$max. Note that this simple division doesn't differentiate between muscle (high metabolism) and fat (minimal metabolism), and fat can be thought of as essentially dead weight. Therefore, higher $\dot{V}O_2$max values can be achieved either by increasing aerobic capacity or by decreasing body mass and fat. For example, a 70-kilogram rider with a $\dot{V}O_2$max of 4.2 liters per minute has a normalized value of 60 milliliters per kilogram per minute. If he drops 2 kg to 68 kg yet maintains an oxygen uptake of 4.2 liters per minute, his normalized $\dot{V}O_2$max increases to 61.8 milliliters per kilogram per minute. For that reason many pro cyclists are obsessed with dropping weight before Grand Tours, assuming that their power output is not affected by the weight loss.

- **Normalized to lean body mass.** To remove the dead weight factor resulting from body fat, $\dot{V}O_2$max is sometimes normalized to lean body mass to provide a better indicator of the actual aerobic capacity of the muscles.

## Maximal Oxygen Uptake as a Performance Predictor

Is $\dot{V}O_2$max the single best predictor of endurance sport performance? Can any method predict who will be a top cyclist based on lab or field test scores? From our interviews with sport scientists, the consensus is that test scores are a broad indicator or starting point at best. Certainly, a higher $\dot{V}O_2$max is rarely a bad thing to have, and it can give you some indication of form and potential. For example, without a minimum value in at least the mid- to high 60s for $\dot{V}O_2$max in milliliters per kilogram per minute, you should probably not be seriously considering a professional cycling career. Hunter and Andy Coggan (Allen and Coggan, 2010), from their vast database of power files, have also compiled a general range of power outputs in watts per kilogram for efforts of various durations typical of riders in categories ranging from untrained through to international professionals (see chapter 3).

Testing is an important way to monitor your progress, but comparing yourself with others is not simple and often not appropriate. Every cyclist brings a unique background and a distinctive set of physical and mental strengths and weaknesses. Therefore, regardless of your category of racing, $\dot{V}O_2$max and other lab-based test measures such as lactate threshold testing are more of an indirect suggestion of ability or a threshold indicator than an actual predictor of success. Think of them as the equivalent of a minimum test score needed to be admitted to a university. That is, although you need to have a particular test score even to apply to a top-level university, having the highest test score doesn't mean that you will become valedictorian of the graduating class after you arrive on campus. Also, although $\dot{V}O_2$max stays fairly stable for a cyclist over the course of a season of training, the functional threshold power, or the highest average power that the cyclist can sustain over an hour, can change dramatically with the phases and peaks of training (see figure 2.3 on page 26). Young cyclists who aspire to be pros should probably get a $\dot{V}O_2$max test to determine whether professional cycling could become a reality for them or whether golf might be a better sport. Fortunately for cyclists, the real measure of performance comes out on the open road or trail, and the strongest, smartest, and luckiest generally win.

*(continued)*

## Maximal Oxygen Uptake
## as a Performance Predictor *(continued)*

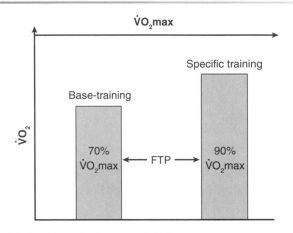

**FIGURE 2.3** Relative changes in $\dot{V}O_2$max and functional threshold power (FTP) with training.

## Q&A   With Chris Abbiss: Why Do We Fatigue

| | |
|---|---|
| **Current position** | Lecturer and research fellow, Edith Cowan University, Australia. |
| **Professional relationship and background with cycling** | In 2008 I completed my PhD in cycling physiology and performance. I have since been employed as a research fellow in high-performance cycling. As part of this position I am employed within the School of Exercise, Biomedical and Health Sciences at Edith Cowan University, the Department of Physiology at the Australian Institute of Sport–Australian Sports Commission, and the Division of Materials Science and Engineering at the Commonwealth Scientific and Industrial Research Organization. |
| **Personal background with cycling** | I have cycled since I was young, but it has only been in the past seven or eight years that I have been cycling competitively. I began cycling road bikes to recover from a broken leg I received playing football. I loved the competitive nature of the sport, so rather than play football I continued to cycle competitively. I am also the vice president and cofounder of the ECU Cycling Club and ECU Race Team. The cycling team is currently competing in numerous local and state cycling competitions. |
| **Favorite ride (either one you've done or always wanted to do)** | I have always wanted to climb up Alpe d'Huez. I am not much of a climber, so I'm not sure why this ride is so appealing to me. I think it is one that you just have to do as a cyclist. |
| **Favorite cycling related experience** | I think the most enjoyable experience has to be the coffee shop at the end of any ride. The actual riding is usually unbearably painful, tiring, and at times nauseating. I'm not too sure what it is that keeps me in this sport. |

**Chris, you wrote an influential review paper in 2005 that focused on the concept of what causes fatigue during exercise. So why do we get tired and slow down? Can you boil it down to one thing, or is it dependent on the situation?**

I really wish that I could simplify things and say that we get tired because of one specific physiological change that occurs within the body. Unfortunately, however, the human body is extremely complex, and phenomena such as fatigue are multifaceted. For instance, exercise in the heat has been shown to cause hyperthermia, increase our dependency on carbohydrate, and possibly reduce our motivation to continue exercising. I am sure that most cyclists have at some stage felt tired before they even got on the bike, which likely had an effect on their performance. When we begin exercising things become even more complicated. This occurs because the fatigue we experience will be heavily influenced by the situation or the specific exercise we perform. For instance, the fatigue you experience in a 4-kilometer individual pursuit performed in a velodrome will be very different from the fatigue you feel at the end of a 100-kilometer road race performed in extreme heat. Understanding the specific factors that may be responsible for fatigue during various cycling events therefore requires a sound understanding of the exercise task (i.e., duration, intensity, and so on) and the situation in which the exercise is being performed (i.e., environmental conditions, dietary intake, sleep patterns, and so on). By being aware of factors influencing fatigue, interventions may be put in place to minimize fatigue and possibly improve performance.

 **How much of fatigue is in the body, and how much is in the head?**

Some recent research is now taking a holistic, or whole-body, approach in an attempt to gain better understanding of fatigue development during exercise. Recently, a model to explain fatigue during exercise has gained significant momentum. This model, the "complex systems" or "central governor" model, suggests that the rate of fatigue, and thus exercise performance, is regulated within the brain to prevent catastrophic failure of any one physiological system. Within this model, the brain continuously receives and integrates feedback regarding the status of various physiological systems in the body. From this, the brain can then set exercise intensity to ensure that the exercise task can be completed without the risk of injury. Consequently, fatigue may originate from various parts of the body, such as the legs, but this information is integrated within the brain. Therefore, the body and the brain work together and both are likely to be responsible for the fatigue that we experience during exercise.

In light of this theory, athletes may ask, if fatigue is controlled by the brain, why can't we just choose to exercise faster and harder? Well, we can do this to a point, but the brain regulates intensity on both a conscious and subconscious level. For instance, when riding in a group or peloton that is slightly faster than we are accustomed to, we may be required to consciously override the desire to stop or slow down just to hold onto the group. This conscious

*(continued)*

control of exercise intensity is a balance between perceived exertion, effort, and motivation to continue exercising. If we have no desire or can't be bothered to ride fast, we will simply slow down and ride back to the coffee shop alone. But if this occurs during the final kilometers of a race that we have a good chance of winning, we would be more motivated to stay in the group. Therefore, in some situations we may be able to will ourselves to continue exercising even when our level of fatigue is high. In certain circumstances, however, even if we want to ride faster, the brain may subconsciously restrict or reduce exercise intensity to preserve homeostasis and protect the body from harm.

**One of the big things that is always talked about in endurance sports is lactic acid and how it causes fatigue. Is that still a valid concept?**

The possible role of lactate in fatigue development and exercise performance is quite complicated. Lactate is continuously being produced in the body. During high-intensity exercise, when energy demands are high, the formation of lactate sometimes exceeds the rate of removal and the concentration begins to rise. This increase in lactate concentration does not directly result in an increase in fatigue or muscle acidosis. Although increases in fatigue sensations and the accumulation of lactate may occur at similar exercise intensities, the two are not causally related. The sensations of pain or discomfort that we experience during intense exercise are likely to be caused by variety of other factors including a decrease in pH or an increase in inorganic phosphate concentrations.

It has been suggested that excessive lactate accumulation during high-intensity exercise may slow the rate of glycolysis and therefore have an effect on the rate of energy production. Lactate accumulation may therefore be indirectly related to reductions in exercise performance, but it is not as simple as stating that someone who has high lactate will be more fatigued than someone who has low lactate. Instead, lactate formation can be thought of as a temporary short-term solution to allow energy production and exercise at high intensities to continue longer than would be possible if lactate were not produced.

**Can you briefly summarize what happens when we train and improve our fitness? What's happening in the body and brain that permits us to ride faster or longer?**

When we train a number of adaptations occur within both the brain and the rest of the body. The specific adaptations that occur because of training will be very much dependent on the particular exercise tasks that we are performing. For instance, performing prolonged low-intensity base training at the beginning of a cycling season will result in very different adaptations from those gained by repeated sprint or high-intensity interval training performed later in the year. Irrespective of training modality, some of the more important changes that occur in response to endurance exercise are to metabolic, neuromuscular, and cardiovascular systems. Essentially, the adaptations that we experience because of training will be dictated by the stress that is placed on each of these physiological systems. Therefore, to improve overall exercise performance, athletes need to stress physiological systems that are important to the specific event that they are competing in.

# Explaining Fatigue

The concept of fatigue is one of the terms on which it is difficult to obtain a consensus definition. Fatigue is a complex phenomenon (Enoka and Duchateau 2008) , and it can be defined at various levels ranging from the cell to the entire organism. For the purposes of this book, perhaps the simplest definition of fatigue during cycling is the inability to maintain the desired or appropriate power output. Using this broad definition maintains the most relevance to what is commonly experienced across various cycling disciplines without being tied to specific mechanisms of fatigue.

At Edith Cowan University in Australia, Chris Abbiss and Paul Laursen (2005) wrote an excellent summary of the multiple models proposed for fatigue during prolonged cycling. None of these models is necessarily completely separate or dominant, because they interrelate with each other (see figure 2.4). Although other

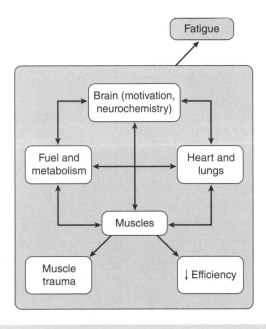

**FIGURE 2.4**  **Schematic of various fatigue models.**

models certainly exist and the specific details of each remain open to debate, this article provides a useful start to seeing the multiple issues that sport scientists, coaches, and athletes alike need to consider in their understanding of fatigue. Each model presents various ideas to consider in terms of avenues for training and maximizing fitness.

## Cardiovascular Model

The cardiovascular model is one of the traditional models of fatigue and the source from which many of the other models derive. With this model, the heart and the circulatory system are central to exercise capacity. When the heart can no longer circulate a sufficient amount of blood to deliver oxygen and nutrients to the muscles to keep up with demand and to remove waste products, a cascade of problems occurs within the muscles, which elicits fatigue. For example, insufficient oxygen availability at the muscles limits aerobic energy production and increases reliance on anaerobic metabolism, depleting the limited stores of glycogen and increasing lactate levels because the body relies more on anaerobic metabolism. As a natural extrapolation of this model, increasing cardiac output, raising the pumping capacity of the heart, and increasing the ability of the blood vessels to deliver blood to the muscles is central to maximizing exercise tolerance. With increased training on the bicycle, focused specifically on relatively high-intensity aerobic efforts, your body will make those adaptations and you'll be able to produce higher wattages and greater average speeds.

Improving the body's ability to use the oxygen and nutrients delivered by the blood is another path to improved fitness through this model. Mechanisms to improve through training can include increasing the release of fat to the muscles for energy. Complementing this, the muscles can be trained to be better able to use fat for energy rather than carbohydrate. The capacity of the body to generate ATP through aerobic metabolism can also be increased through structural changes in the muscle fibers themselves so that they become better able to use the available oxygen and nutrients being delivered by the heart and blood vessels. Together, being able to use more fat and enhance aerobic capacity means sparing the limited glycogen and carbohydrate stored within the body. This point is especially important to road cyclists.

Ever wonder how the pros can ride for five hours and then start attacking each other after mile 130 (km 210)? They have trained their bodies to use more fat at a higher intensity. Imagine that you could do a 100-mile (160 km) race and ride at a relatively high pace, say 25 miles per hour (40 km/h), for the first 80 miles (130 km) and still be burning fat as energy, leaving you with a huge storehouse of liver and muscle glycogen to use in those intense last 20 miles (30 km). Less

**Sparing glycogen and carbohydrate early on conserves fuel for race-winning attacks later in the contest.**

©Philippe Millereau/DPPI/Icon SMI

trained cyclists might be able to burn fat at only up to 22 miles per hour (35 km/h) in the race. Thus the 25-mile-per-hour pace would force them to burn far more glycogen before the serious attacks start later in the race, so they are running out of energy (bonking) with 10 miles (16 km) to go.

Other acute manipulations can involve carbohydrate loading to increase the store of glycogen in the body before a particular event.

# Role of Lactate in Fatigue

Traditionally, lactate has been viewed as the grim reaper in terms of limiting exercise capacity. In turn, aerobic capacity and cardiovascular limitations have been thought of as being dominant in determining exercise limits. On the surface, the general idea of how lactate does this is logical. The following series of events is claimed to occur:

1. We exercise at an intensity so high that our aerobic metabolism cannot produce all the necessary ATP.

2. To maintain ATP production, the body burns carbohydrate, not fat or protein, through the initial steps of glycolysis, and lactic acid serves as a temporary endpoint for metabolism.

3. The continued buildup of lactic acid increases the acidity of the muscle cells, causing what is commonly thought to be the burn that we feel when we're exercising hard.

4. Eventually, the acidity level becomes so high that it impairs the ability of our muscles to contract, forcing us to slow down or stop exercising altogether.

Such a chain of events is implicit in many of our concepts of exercise capacity and testing, such as the idea of an anaerobic threshold. It is also implicit in the more modern concept of lactate threshold, whereby we determine the power output at which the body's blood lactate levels begin to rise significantly and its companion point of onset of blood lactate accumulation (OBLA), the power output at which blood lactate is at a level of 4 millimoles (see figure 2.5). The setting of 4 millimoles as this OBLA point is arbitrary, corresponding to the highest

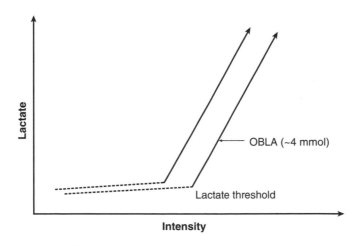

**FIGURE 2.5** The lactate threshold and onset of blood lactate accumulation (OBLA) changes with training.

general lactate level that many athletes seem to be able to tolerate for a sustained period in the initial studies that modeled lactate dynamics. Another common test of threshold power that is based on the idea of lactate being the determinant for exercise performance is the Maximal Lactate Steady State test, which measures the highest power output at which the blood lactate does not continue to rise over a 30-minute steady-state effort.

Using research conducted over the past decade, scientists are coming to realize that a more complex model of fatigue is needed. The central tenet that lactate directly causes fatigue or limits exercise has been proved untenable. One of the fundamental arguments for this comes from Robert Robergs of Australia, who has demonstrated that lactate contributes only minimally to the overall amount of the acidity that develops during heavy exercise (Robergs et al. 2004). Even more important, lactate itself and increased acidity may actually facilitate and enhance muscle contractile characteristics, which is completely opposite to the dogma that acidity changes impair muscular function. Therefore, although lactate levels may remain useful as an index of effort and correlate with the onset of fatigue, we need to rethink the idea that lactate is a direct cause of suffering and agony on the bike.

## Neuromuscular Model

In the neuromuscular model, the focus shifts away from the availability of oxygen or nutrients and the metabolic capacity of the muscle to generate ATP. Instead, this model proposes that the dominant cause of fatigue is a decrease in the ability of the muscle fiber itself to contract. Several mechanisms may be at work here:

- **Decreased ability of the brain to activate and recruit muscles.** Repeated exercise may alter the chemistry within the brain. Using improved technology, scientists are beginning to trace neurotransmitters and explore their complex role in both fatigue and overtraining (Meeusen et al. 2007). This line of research may lead to the development of nutritional supplements that directly manipulate brain chemistry.

- **Changes in the ability of the muscles to respond to incoming signals from the central nervous system.** Simply put, the brain may be sending the same signals, but the muscles cannot receive them as well. The cause may be a slight decrease in the ability of the muscle to contract following repeated stimulation. Because of this impairment, as we continue to exercise we become less efficient in our movements, requiring more muscles to work to maintain the same power output. A negative spiral ensues in which greater rates of energy use are required to maintain a given power output. This greater energy requirement depletes energy stores more rapidly, increases the production of waste metabolites, and increases the rate of heat storage, producing a rise in body temperature because of the increased metabolic rate (see the thermoregulatory model in the following section).

- **Trauma from repeated contractions may cause local damage within the muscle itself, resulting in impaired function.** Within the muscle itself, damage from the large stresses imposed on the muscle fiber during exercise can cause microscopic tears within the muscle structure itself. This model is familiar to anyone who has jumped into a hard running or resistance-training workout with no preparation. Sore and aching muscles in the following days are the consequence. Such damage occurs normally with any hard workout or series of workouts, especially when pushing large gears in an unaccustomed position, such as doing a hard time trial effort in the aerodynamic position. Besides the reduction in the functional ability of the muscles to contract normally caused by the physical damage, the increased activation of the pain sensors from the muscles may act as negative feedback to the brain, reducing subsequent recruitment of muscle by the brain to minimize the risk of further damage.

Unfortunately, changes or improvement in muscle function on the bike are relatively difficult to identify for most athletes, because the tests require either specialized equipment or invasive procedures such as taking blood or muscle samples.

## Thermoregulatory Model

As described earlier in the chapter, the body produces about three to four times as much heat as the actual mechanical power going to the pedals. Although some heat generation is critical to maintaining normal body temperature, especially during cold exposure, the excess heat must be dissipated from the body to prevent body temperature from rising to dangerous levels of hyperthermia. Failure to do so can result in heat-induced cramps or illnesses such as heat exhaustion and heatstroke. We have long known that exercise capacity declines in hot or humid conditions, and most of us have experienced how much more difficult it can be to ride on a blazing hot summer day than on a cooler day. Traditionally, the main dangers from heat stress from an exercise capacity perspective were presumed to come from increased demands on the cardiovascular system. To dissipate the excess heat, blood flow to the skin increases, decreasing the amount going to the active muscles. In addition, sweating for evaporative heat loss decreases our plasma volume, increasing the stress on the cardiovascular system through increased viscosity of the blood. This increased pressure in the blood vessels needs to be compensated for by greater pumping pressure from the heart. The decreased plasma volume also reduces blood flow returning to the heart, forcing an increased heart rate to maintain cardiac output and blood flow to the body. The effect of this chain of events can be commonly seen in the "cardiac drift" during sustained exercise, in which the heart rate gradually increases over time even with no change in power output. From a training and monitoring perspective, this drift needs to be taken into consideration when setting training based on heart rate alone and when analyzing training data.

Popular cycling coach Joe Friel uses the term *decoupling* to describe the point at which the ratio between heart rate and power output no longer displays its normal association. Friel uses this point to determine when an athlete is ready for the next level of higher-intensity training. When less than 5 percent decoupling occurs in a ride of more than 2 1/2 hours that contains at least 60 minutes of fast tempo-paced riding, then the athlete is ready to begin training at her or his threshold power and above. This decision to train at or above threshold must be carefully reviewed and made only when factors such as heat, overall fatigue, and hydration can be ruled out as the cause of the cardiac drift.

High body temperatures can cause a cascade of problems in the body, and a great deal of scientific research in the past decade has focused on the direct effects of elevated body temperature on physiological responses. What scientists have observed is that there is indeed a direct effect and that it is pervasive across multiple physiological systems. For example, work in Stephen's lab has demonstrated that an elevated core temperature progressively decreases the ability of the brain to activate and recruit muscles (Thomas et al. 2006). Other researchers have demonstrated reduced brain arousal in the heat, reduced blood flow to the brain, and altered brain chemistry, each of which may decrease the ability to activate muscles or elicit a mental state of fatigue according to the psychological models presented in the following section (Nybo 2008). Furthermore, heat stress impairs the ability to maintain blood flow to the digestive tract. One resultant problem is that the ability to take in fluid and nutrients during exercise becomes impaired. Beyond that, recent work has also demonstrated that heat stress may cause increased leakage of the bacteria normally sealed within the gut into the bloodstream, resulting in an inflammatory response that may shut down the ability to exercise and accelerate the risk for heat illnesses (Lambert 2004). From a straight performance standpoint, some excellent studies have demonstrated that the body may have the equivalent of a thermal safety fuse, whereby a high body temperature consistently leads to fatigue regardless of starting body temperature or rate of temperature rise (Gonzalez-Alonso et al. 1999).

Consequent to this thermoregulatory model, it is clear that maintaining a cool body temperature, or at the least decreasing or delaying the rate of temperature rise, can dramatically delay the onset of fatigue and improve exercise performance (Marino 2002). The natural method of adapting to hot environments is to spend time training in the heat before a warm-weather competition such as the Hawaii Ironman. This exposure to heat stress results in an increase in both total blood volume and sweating rate to improve cooling. Another possibility is to use cooling strategies to keep body temperature as close to baseline as possible before exercise. The use of such systems began in the 1996 Olympics with the Australian rowing team, and numerous professional cycling teams and federations have adopted them. These ideas range from wearing ice vests or liquid cooling garments during warm-ups to ingesting cold drinks or ice slurries to keep body temperature down. Overall, it is clear that body temperature maintenance, or even precooling by a small (0.5 °C) amount, can produce significant performance benefits with endurance exercise, although the benefit during a short, high-intensity exercise such as sprinting remains unclear. Further information on the science and practicality of cooling strategies is provided in chapter 10.

## Psychological and Motivational Model

We have all had days when all was right with the world and we just flew on the bike as a result. Conversely, we have all had days when we felt dreadful and just could not find the motivation to train or race, regardless of our physical ability. An athlete's response to the environment and exercise encompasses not just physiological changes but also psychological components that may be dominant in many circumstances. These issues can range from the simple emotional reaction to the prospect of riding on a sunny and warm day versus facing the same ride in cold rain and wind. We all know riders who are mentally beaten even before the race begins—perhaps a sprinter facing a day in the high mountains or a physically strong rider who dreads the tight pack riding and bumping in criteriums. On a broader level, this mind–body connection is clearly dominant in the concept of overtraining (see chapter 5), which is primarily a psychological and mental response to high physical and emotional stress, most likely mediated by changes in brain chemistry (Meeusen et al. 2007). Actual physiological damage or physical impairment to the muscles and cardiovascular system likely plays only a relatively minor role (Anish 2005).

Another variation of psychological limits on exercise is self-regulation within the brain to protect athletes from damaging themselves by exercising too hard (Tucker and Noakes 2009). Within this model, the aim of a "central governor" within the brain is to exercise efficiently yet safely. For example, in riding a 16-kilometer time trial, the rider wants to reach the point of exhaustion at the finish line rather than at the 10-kilometer mark. Exactly how the body determines the particular power output for this 16-kilometer TT could be based on previous experience, motivation, environmental conditions, and continuous monitoring of feedback from multiple physiological systems throughout the body. In essence, the brain, or governor, learns what the body is capable of for any particular exercise, constantly monitors itself, and anticipates physiological problems by controlling the power output to prevent damage.

What this model highlights for cyclists appears to be the importance of experience in regulating performance. Simply put, unless you have had experience in a particular effort, whether it's a 16-kilometer time trial or a hard hill on a race circuit, you will have difficulty regulating and modulating your effort for maximal efficiency and performance (Mauger et al. 2009). Therefore, you need to simulate the key efforts required for your event during training, not only to prepare yourself physiologically but also to imprint that response pattern into your brain so that it can be added to your database of experiences (e.g., "Just how hard can I ride this hill without blowing up?" or "What does it feel like to ride at 350 watts for five minutes to establish the break?").

Although no amount of sport psychology can replace proper physical preparation, it is critical to be both physically and mentally prepared for training and racing. Therefore, you should view proper psychological preparation not as a separate and optional part of training but as an integral component of maximizing fitness, training, and ultimately performance.

# Applying the Science

A sound understanding of basic exercise physiology as it relates to metabolism, energy dynamics, and fatigue can go a long way toward advancing a cyclist's appreciation of the various body systems at work during cycling. Such information is important if a cyclist is to be able to interpret the numerous claims and counterclaims out there among scientists, coaches, and companies about what works and what does not work when it comes to training and sport science. The important advice here is not to be afraid of the technical jargon of scientific literature but rather to use the basic principles in this chapter to dig deeper and examine the underlying scientific rationale and evidence for and against different training ideas. Therefore, this chapter sets the stage for subsequent chapters that examine various aspects of cycling science.

## CHAPTER 3

# Tracking Effort and Performance

**W**e are using numbers more than ever before, in all areas of life and increasingly in the world of fitness. With the advent of heart rate monitors, power meters, GPS units, and other devices, we have truly moved into a new age of computer-assisted training. This new age has brought many new insights into the human body and the way in which it performs. One of the greatest advantages of this technology is that we have much better ways of tracking changes in fitness. No longer do we have to speculate on whether we have improved after a windy ride; when used and interpreted correctly, the data from our monitors indicate whether the ride was faster than normal because of a tailwind or because of improved fitness. These new technological tools give us access to more data channels such as heart rate, power, and respiration rate, providing information that we can use to make each training session more efficient and help prevent overtraining. These data channels relate to each other in various ways, and understanding what is important and what is not will allow you to optimize your training and minimize your junk distance. This chapter looks at ways to track training using numbers from your downloaded data files and includes sample charts and graphs to help you better understand what this data means.

## Subjective Rating Systems

The past quarter century has seen the rise of scientific training, led by the introduction of heart rate monitors and now power monitors. These tools are fantastic, and it's almost inconceivable for many of us to ride without at least a bike computer and HRM on the bike. Yet you need to remember that one of the fundamental uses of monitoring devices is to help you learn how to feel and gauge

©Human Kinetics

**A well-tuned perception of effort is an important tool in gauging intensity.**

your efforts better. That is, one important goal is to provide objective quantification of your effort and then match or correlate that to your perceptual sensations of effort. Many experienced endurance athletes can gauge their interval intensity and even their breakaway efforts mainly by feel rather than by blindly adhering to a certain number.

The gold standard for perceived effort is Dr. Gunnar Borg's classic ratings of perceived exertion, or RPE, scale, first introduced in the 1970s and formally published in 1982 (Borg 1982). The classic Borg scale rates perceived effort on a scale from 6 to 20, with 6 being "no exertion at all," 13 being "somewhat hard," 17 being "very hard," and 20 being "maximal exertion." The Centers for Disease Control and Prevention reminds users of the scale that

> this feeling should reflect how heavy and strenuous the exercise feels to you, combining all sensations and feelings of physical stress, effort, and fatigue. Do not concern yourself with any one factor such as leg pain or shortness of breath, but try to focus on your total feeling of exertion. (www.cdc.gov/physicalactivity/everyone/measuring/exertion.html)

So the rating relates not to a localized effort or symptom but to your overall sensation of how hard the workload is.

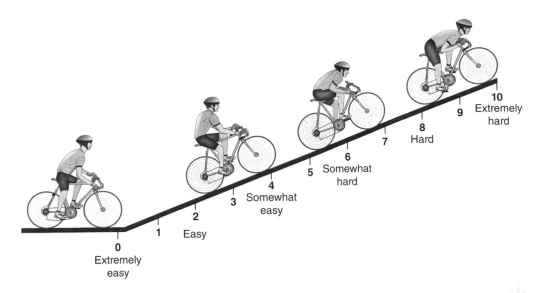

**FIGURE 3.1    OMNI rating of perceived exertion scale.**

From R.J. Robertson, 2004, *Perceived exertion for practitioners: Rating effort with the OMNI picture system* (Champaign, IL: Human Kinetics), 141. Reprinted by permission of the author.

One thing may strike you as strange about this scale: Why does the scale go from 6 to 20? Consider that a prototypical heart rate capacity ranges from a resting rate of 60 beats per minute to a maximum of 200 beats per minute. This correlation between heart rate range and the Borg scale range isn't a coincidence at all, because research has demonstrated that heart rate and perceived effort are closely correlated. Still, for the lay public, a scale from 6 to 20 isn't easy to grasp, so other subjective scales like the Omni RPE generally run from 1 to 10 (figure 3.1), and many coaches prescribe that scale to their athletes for ease of understanding. This RPE scale is based on a lactate threshold effort being perceived as 5 out of 10 by most athletes, and the scale increases exponentially in perceived effort with increasing intensity. Thus, a step of 2 from 5 to 7 is a much harder perceived effort increase than going from 3 to 5.

Another important consideration is that RPE is not meant to be compared across individuals. RPE is not intended to encourage athletes to tough it out and rate a hard effort as easier than their club mates' rating. Garbage in, garbage out! The focus is on comparing your honest responses to workloads over time, just as you would track long-term changes to your training or fitness from your training diary. For example, one complementary gauge of fitness is not only whether you can sustain 200 watts for a particular distance or time but also what your RPE is for that effort (see the interview with Dr. David Martin on page 59 for more information on the importance of monitoring both power and subjective sensations).

# Heart Rate Monitors

With improved fitness, the defining change in your body is that your cardiac output, or the volume of blood pumped by your heart each minute, increases. Cardiac output is simply heart rate multiplied by stroke volume; the latter is the volume of blood pumped with each heart beat. In an untrained individual, the maximal cardiac output can reach approximately 25 liters per minute, but an elite aerobic athlete may have a value of 35 liters or higher. Obviously, as more blood is pumped, more oxygen is delivered to the muscles, increasing your aerobic energy production. Physiologically, what are some of the major adaptations in your cardiovascular system to enable this?

- Your maximal heart rate will not change with fitness. This value is largely determined by genetics and age (see the sidebar on maximal heart rate calculation).

- Overall blood volume will increase slightly, and some correlation is found between higher aerobic fitness and higher blood volume (Sawka et al. 1992). This result occurs mostly because of increased plasma volume rather than more red blood cells, such that hematocrit (the fraction of solid to liquid in blood) usually decreases with fitness.

- The heart, like your leg muscles, becomes stronger and able to pump blood with greater force. This increase in contractility helps to increase the stroke volume, or the amount of blood pumped with each heart beat.

- Stroke volume also increases by improvements in your body's ability to return blood from the body to the heart, resulting in greater filling of the heart each time.

- The capillary network in your muscles increases in density, permitting greater blood flow to the muscles themselves.

As can be seen from the preceding description, the cardiovascular system is a complex interplay of many things going on inside the body. Overall, the body adjusts the heart rate to achieve a cardiac output that will deliver adequate blood, oxygen, and nutrients to the muscles during exercise. Heart rate is also affected by the nervous system, as can be seen at the start line of a bicycle race when your heart rate is at 150 beats per minute before the starting gun even goes off! Or you could be tired and pushing yourself harder than ever, yet your heart rate reaches only 160 beats per minute as compared with your normal 175 beats per minute at threshold. In both cases, your nervous system is sending signals to your heart that override your body's physiological demands for cardiac output.

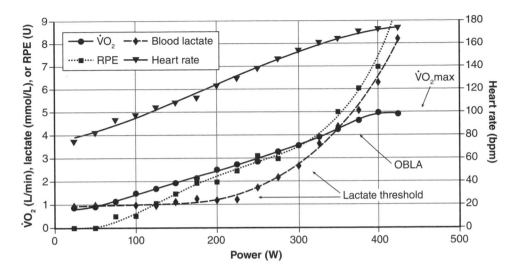

**FIGURE 3.2** Relationship between maximal oxygen uptake, blood lactate, RPE, and heart rate as a means of tracking effort.

Therefore, although heart rate is an indication of effort, it is an indirect one at best. Similar to a tachometer on a car that tells you how fast the pistons are pumping rather than how many horsepower the engine is producing, heart rate does not tell you the speed or power that you are generating on the bike, but only how fast the heart is pumping. Hunter likes to say that "heart rate tells me the 'intensity of an athlete's intention,' and that can help me to better understand the athlete in workouts and races." Also, heart rate can be influenced by many factors related and not related to exercise, such as sleep, caffeine intake, and hydration status. That being said, monitoring your heart rate is beneficial, and you can track fitness changes over time by comparing heart rate with the data channels already discussed (figure 3.2) and other channels discussed later in this chapter.

## Maximal Heart Rate

In gyms and in training manuals, you have likely seen a series of training zones based on your sex and age. You will notice that the heart rate zones decrease with increasing age. The general perception is that your maximum heart rate can be roughly calculated by an equation of 220 minus your age and that your maximum heart rate gradually decreases with age. Note, however, that scientific validation of this age-based formula is limited or absent. For example, Stephen has a nearly 20-year record of laboratory testing throughout his cycling and academic career. In his early 20s his maximum heart rate never exceeded 175 beats per minute,

*(continued)*

## Maximal Heart Rate *(continued)*

compared with a formula-derived 200 beats per minute. Currently in his early 40s, Stephen has a maximum heart rate of approximately 165 beats per minute rather than the 180 predicted by the formula.

The only way to figure out your maximum heart rate is to test yourself. One way is to perform an aerobic capacity ($\dot{V}O_2$max) test in the lab. Barring that, you can perform a series of maximal 1-kilometer efforts and then watch for your highest heart rate, which will occur 10 to 30 seconds after the effort. Finally, if you look through your heart rate data over a month or a season's worth of training and racing, your highest values likely match your true maximum heart rate.

Heart rate training has its own set of training zones, and coaches, scientists, and organizations have proposed many different systems. A commonly used series of heart rate zones has been put forth by Joe Friel in his book *The Cyclist's Training Bible* (Friel 2009); these are presented in table 3.1.

### TABLE 3.1 Heart Rate Zones

| Zone | RPE | Purpose | % of LTHR |
|---|---|---|---|
| 1 | <10 | Recovery | 65–81% |
| 2 | 10–12 | Aerobic | 82–88% |
| 3 | 13–14 | Tempo | 89–93% |
| 4 | 15–16 | Subthreshold | 94–100% |
| 5a | 17 | Superthreshold | 100–102% |
| 5b | 18–19 | Aerobic Capacity | 103–105% |
| 5c | >20 | Anaerobic Capacity | ≥106% |

Reprinted, by permission, from J. Friel, 2009, *The cyclist's training diary,* 4th ed. (Boulder, CO: VeloPress), 48.

The five-zone model is not the only way to look at heart rate training. Scientific debate continues about how to define anaerobic threshold or lactate threshold, so applying the model to athletes is difficult. Countering the idea of a highly compartmentalized set of many heart rate zones, some exercise scientists have been advocating the use of fewer rather than more zones. Specifically, a model of heart rate monitoring used by Dr. Alejandro Lucia from the University of Madrid and other scientists (figure 3.3) uses three broad zones to quantify exercise intensity in top professional cyclists (Earnest et al. 2009; Lucia et al. 1999, 2003; Rodriguez-Marroyo et al. 2009).

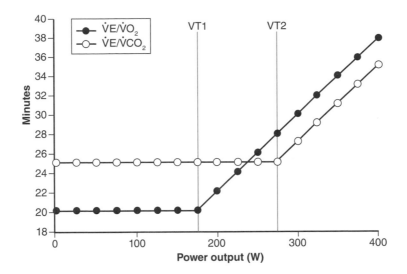

**FIGURE 3.3  A simplified three-zone model for heart-rate intensities.**

VT= ventilatory threshold; V̇E= ventilation rate; V̇O$_2$ = oxygen uptake; V̇CO$_2$ = carbon dioxide production.

   The light-, moderate-, and high-intensity zones used by Lucia and others correspond to the ventilatory thresholds 1 and 2, the two points during an incremental exercise test where the volume of air that you breathe in increases disproportionately compared with oxygen uptake and carbon dioxide production. These intensities can be easily defined in a laboratory test similar to a lactate threshold test in which athletes exercise at increasing wattages every three to four minutes while breathing through a mask so that their breathing pattern and oxygen uptake can be measured. The exact points of these thresholds differ across individuals, but they correspond to roughly 70 percent and 90 percent of maximal heart rate. Compared with the five-zone model, this three-zone model simplifies things for athletes who are exercising in the field. Considering the continuing scientific debate about the validity of lactate as an index of effort and fatigue, along with the discussion about whether an anaerobic threshold truly exists and what it signifies, dividing heart rate zones into three broader zones makes sense. Also, because variations in rate by mechanisms such as cardiac drift (especially at high temperatures or with dehydration) happen over the course of exercise, within the five-zone model HR can easily jump from zone 3 to 4 or from zone 4 to 5 without a concomitant change occurring in metabolic pathways. The three-zone model is more resistant to such errors.

# Features of Heart Rate Monitors

In looking at the features list of heart rate monitors (HRMs), we see that manufacturers appear to be in an arms race to load as many bells and whistles into the watches as possible. Some of the more dubious and unnecessary features include the following:

▶ Body mass index calculator. The equation is weight (in kilograms) divided by height (in meters) squared, but your BMI does not change significantly day to day unless you suddenly lose weight by cutting off an arm. Use an inexpensive calculator instead.

▶ Fitness tests built into the HRM. These tests promise to calculate your aerobic fitness by taking your heart rate, usually at rest, and then comparing it with equations built into the HRM memory. The problem is that these tables are generalized estimates based on other people.

▶ Calorie counters. These counters are typically based on your heart rate along with other inputs such as gender and estimated maximum heart rate, so take these data with a grain of salt. However, a counter in HRMs or cycling computers will give you ballpark values that may be useful as estimates if weight control is a concern.

If you want to use a HRM to improve your performance, you need to understand your situation and needs to assess which monitor might work best for you. Here are some functions to consider:

▶ Preferably, the heart rate data does not stand alone but integrates with other data channels such as speed, cadence, and altitude to give you a holistic picture of your ride.

▶ The greater the sampling frequency and the larger the memory capacity of the monitor, the better the data it will provide. Another good feature allows you to hit a button and record the heart rate at that instant.

▶ A useful feature permits you to record the time spent in various heart rate zones and produce visual or audio alarms. Make sure that the HRM allows you to set the targets manually rather than use set percentages of maximum heart rate. This information is crucial in quantifying the intensity of workouts.

▶ Depending on whether you intend to download HR values into your computer or training diary software for monitoring by yourself or your coach, the ease of downloading or compatibility with your software may be important.

There you have it—a short and simple list of useful features in a HRM! These features are the essential criteria when selecting a HRM, and we would target these features above all others.

# Power Monitors

Although the heart rate monitor began the scientific revolution in cycling, the major advancement in technology for cyclists has been the power meter, which records the mechanical energy that the rider is generating. Bicycles provide an ideal platform for incorporating power measurement because of the relatively steady force generation (in contrast to the large spikes and troughs of power in skating, running, or rowing) and the multiple potential sites for incorporating power on a bicycle. For example, the first commercial power system, SRM from Germany, measured power by placing strain gauges into the spider of the cranks, which deflect and twist slightly during each pedal stroke to provide torque, which is then multiplied by cadence to get an overall value for power in watts. Power-using strain gauges have since been designed by various companies into hubs (PowerTap; figure 3.4), crank spiders (Quarq), bottom brackets (Ergomo), and pedals (Polar). Although each system has strengths and limitations, and indeed will give slightly different values from one another because of the different location of measurement, most of us likely stick with one system, so reliability over multiple rides is generally good if the unit is calibrated correctly.

Courtesy of CycleOps/Saris Cycling Group.

**FIGURE 3.4** The PowerTap G3 hub measures the torsion inside the hub along with cadence and output wattage.

Why do we like power so much as a metric of training, fitness, and performance? First, when you break down the various data channels, power is ultimately the stress that you are imposing on the body. All the other channels are the strain resulting from that stress. For example, 250 watts always means that the body is generating 250 joules of mechanical energy every second (see chapter 2 for basic definitions of power and energy). Therefore, the meaning of watts remains constant and completely independent of terrain, weather, fatigue, hydration status, or anything else. So 250 watts may result in different speeds, heart rates, cadence, or subjective sensations depending on many variables. But the power itself does not change, so it forms an excellent anchor on which to base your analysis of the other data channels.

Another advantage of using power as a fitness index is that you cannot fool yourself when you break things down to power. In simplistic terms, wattage is how hard you are pedaling multiplied by how fast you are pedaling, or torque multiplied by cadence. Ultimately, the only way to produce more wattage is to pedal harder (use a bigger gear), pedal faster, or both! This goal is literally the crux of training and much of racing—to enable yourself to lay out more watts than your competitors can or be able to ride for longer at the same wattage than you could previously. Think of a time trial. Assuming that the weather and your aerodynamic economy do not change, the only way to improve your time is to generate a higher wattage than you did before. Now consider a road race. Take away tactics and strategy, and at some point your success comes down to whether you can generate sufficient power to make the move that you want to make. If you can't, then you've let a gap open, missed the winning breakaway, or lost out in the sprint. You can try to rationalize your failure with various excuses, but at the end of the day it comes down to laying out the watts when needed.

Frankly, the power meter has revolutionized bicycle training, and everyone from top professionals to first-time century riders can use it to improve their cycling. One key benefit is that it is possible to quantify training around a solid and reliable objective using power. For example, the top Tour de France contenders know that they generally need to be able to sustain a power output of approximately 6.5 watts per kilogram for 10 to 20 minutes if they want to be thinking of a podium placing. They plan their training around achieving these wattage goals rather than meeting vague performance goals. Similarly, calculating the power output required to break an hour for a 40K time trial is relatively easy, so training can be based on achieving those unambiguous power thresholds.

# Training With Power

This section introduces power meter training and provides information on how this technology can help you track changes in your fitness. If you are interested in using power to track your training, more detailed information is available in *Training and Racing With a Power Meter* by Hunter and Dr. Andrew R. Coggan (Allen and Coggan 2010).

A power meter not only measures your wattage but also records every second of your ride. It offers a complete diary of your ride from start to finish. It records the hills, the fast flat sections, the rotating pacelines—everything that happens in a race or training ride. With this second-by-second diary of your ride, your power meter captures your best performance for every period. From the best sprint of your life to the best climb of your life, a power meter captures that information for you to review, analyze, and understand. It also captures your mediocre times and your big failures. You can't hide from the power meter!

## Power Training Zones

Training zones, or levels, help us define the intensity at which we need to train to improve a specific physiological energy system. Dr. Andrew R. Coggan created a set of power training levels, outlined in table 3.2, so that riders can create specific and focused training to improve their power in whichever level they desire.

### TABLE 3.2    Coggan's Power-Based Training Levels

| Level | Name or purpose | % threshold power | % threshold HR | RPE (10-point scale) | Typical length of continuous ride | Typical length of interval effort |
|---|---|---|---|---|---|---|
| 1 | Active recovery | <55 | <68 | <2 | 30–90 min | n/a |
| 2 | Endurance | 56–75 | 69–83 | 2–3 | 60–300 min | n/a |
| 3 | Tempo | 76–90 | 84–94 | 3–4 | 60–180 | n/a |
| 4 | Lactate threshold | 90–105 | 95–105 | 4–5 | n/a | 8–30 min |
| 5 | $\dot{V}O_2$max | 106–120 | >106 | 6–7 | n/a | 3–8 min |
| 6 | Anaerobic capacity | 121–150 | n/a | >7 | n/a | .5–3 min |
| 7 | Neuromuscular power | n/a | n/a | maximal | n/a | <.5 min |

Reprinted, by permission, from H. Allen and A. Coggan, 2010, *Training and racing with a power meter,* 2nd ed. (Boulder, CO: VeloPress), 48.

The training levels are anchored in a common concept, which is called functional threshold power, or FTP. This value represents the best average power that you can maintain for one hour, which serves as the anchor point from which all other training zones or levels are developed. This anchor point of a maximal effort over one hour (100 percent FTP) is solidly in the middle of the seven Coggan power levels at level 4, which relates to the lactate threshold energy system. Intensities above 100 percent relate to the $\dot{V}O_2$max(level 5), anaerobic capacity (level 6), and neuromuscular power (level 7) systems. Intensities below level 4 relate to the tempo (level 3), endurance (level 2), and recovery (level 1) levels that are more aerobic in nature.

Take careful note of how each intensity level relates not only to a specific energy system but also to a specific period and intensity in which to train. For example, if you want to improve the $\dot{V}O_2$max system (level 5), you need to do intervals between three and eight minutes long and produce watts from 106 to 120 percent of your FTP. This concept is critical: Improvement of a system requires a stress of both the *correct intensity and sufficient duration* to stimulate that system to improve. In other words, riding five-minute intervals at 100 percent of FTP or training at 110 percent of FTP for one-minute intervals is not going to provide the maximal stimulus for improving this performance zone. Remember also that when you train for maximal improvement in the $\dot{V}O_2$max system, you will see some improvement in other areas as well. For example, a period of heavy training focused at the $\dot{V}O_2$max training intensity will also likely cause an improvement in your endurance performance and your functional threshold power because your body is still being forced to improve its aerobic capacity to cope with the training load.

As you can see, each of the seven training levels also has a heart rate zone that relates to the power level. Note that the heart rate zones are also anchored to the heart rate at FTP wattage (highest average heart rate that you could maintain for one hour). This approach is a departure from most heart rate zones, which are typically anchored in some calculation of maximum heart rate or heart rate reserve.

## Power Charts and Curves

An easy way to see changes in fitness and improvements over time is by tracking your maximal power output for various durations over the course of a ride or a period (some software, such as TrainingPeaks WKO+, automatically calculates mean maximal power for every ride and throughout your training history). Mean maximal power is the best average power that you can maintain for certain periods, ranging from 1 second to beyond 60 minutes. For example, your best-ever wattage that you held for 1 minute would be your mean maximal power for 1 minute. Depending on your training goals, your power will change differently in each different physiological training zone over the course of a season or through the years.

The mean maximal power chart (figure 3.5) shows how a cyclist's power changed over an entire season, including dips, peaks, and periods of stable fitness. Each point on this chart represents the best for that week of training, which makes it easy to track long-term trends at a glance. Peaks that generally decline in height probably indicate a loss of fitness overall. But care must be taken in interpreting sudden changes. For example, a few tall peaks followed by some big drops does not mean that your fitness is so exceptional one day that you could win a race and so low the next week that you would be lucky to finish; the pattern may simply reflect that you did not do the same type of training that week. Overall, the mean maximal power chart can give you a quick view of your progression over a season or a period of training.

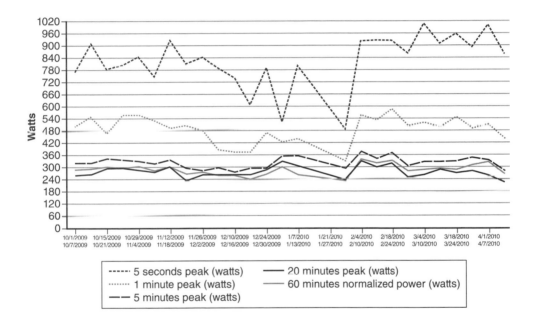

**FIGURE 3.5**   **Mean maximal power chart illustrating changes over the course of a season.**

Another way of looking at the power data is to graph your peak power output over efforts of various duration and compare them to your best performances. The resulting graph would be similar to the mean maximal power chart in that it is a record of best efforts, but the curve represents the best performances over every period, not just a few from a specific energy system. Figure 3.6 on page 52 illustrates changes in this mean maximal power curve. This chart is particularly useful because the shape of the curve from an individual workout, a period, or your best-ever performance gives additional insight into the type of cyclist that you are. For example, in figure 3.6 on page 52 we see two curves. The first solid

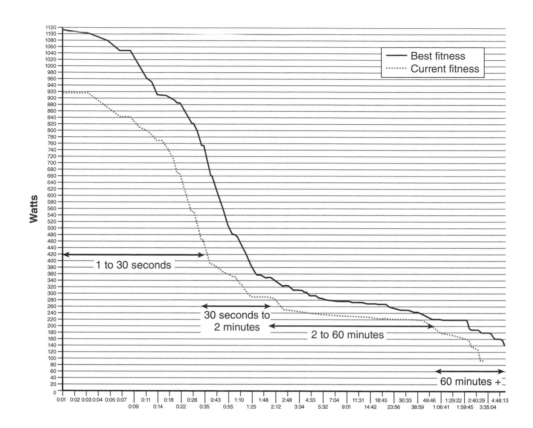

**FIGURE 3.6** Two mean maximal power curves illustrating best performances for a good steady-state time trialist.

line represents the athlete's bests across all times over the past three years of riding, and the dashed line represents the bests from the last month of training. The dashed line located below the solid line for the entire chart tells us that his current fitness does not equal his best-ever fitness. The shape of the curve tells us that this athlete is a good steady-state rider who can maintain steady power after about two minutes without much percentage decrease in wattage. This data would indicate that this athlete is more of a slow twitcher whose muscles are composed predominantly of slow twitch-muscle fibers and who therefore performs better at longer events.

Figure 3.7 shows the mean maximal power curve for a sprinter. The line stays flat at the far left of the chart (zero to 40 seconds) and then abruptly drops off without ever flattening or stabilizing. Also note the sheer number of watts that this athlete produces, which further illustrates strength as a sprinter. The mean maximal power curve highlights the strengths and weaknesses of the athlete, and this curve can be used to define periods that are critical for improvement.

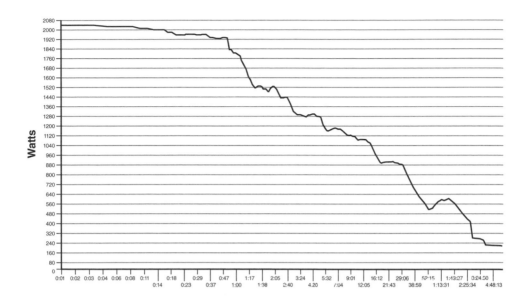

**FIGURE 3.7**  A sample mean maximal power curve for a strong sprinter.

## Power Profile

The previous mean maximal power analyses compare riders' data to themselves. Another way of looking at power and analyzing capabilities is by comparing your data with data from other riders. The power profile chart, outlined in table 3.3 on page 54, allows us to compare an athlete's wattages to others in a similar fitness category and see how the athlete stacks up against the competition. The power profile chart was created from data of more than 300 athletes to define fitness categories for each rider and the corresponding watts per kilogram. To normalize wattages across all riders, the weight of the rider must be taken into account because power-to-weight ratio is paramount in cycling success (see Power-to-Weight Ratio on page 55).

Originally created by Hunter and Dr. Coggan as a way for athletes to compare themselves with others, the power profile chart allows athletes and coaches to visualize the relative strengths and weaknesses of individual riders and their physiological systems.

For the power profile, the index efforts of maximal power outputs over 5 seconds, 1 minute, 5 minutes, and a fourth measure at functional threshold power were chosen because they best reflect neuromuscular power, anaerobic capacity, maximal oxygen uptake ($\dot{V}O_2$max), and lactate threshold (LT), respectively. This does not imply that a 1-minute all-out effort is completely anaerobic

## TABLE 3.3     Power Profile Chart

| | MEN | | | | WOMEN | | | |
|---|---|---|---|---|---|---|---|---|
| | 5 s | 1 min | 5 min | FT | 5 s | 1 min | 5 min | FT |
| | 25.18 | 11.50 | 7.60 | 6.40 | 19.42 | 9.29 | 6.74 | 5.69 |
| | 24.88 | 11.39 | 7.50 | 6.31 | 19.20 | 9.20 | 6.64 | 5.61 |
| | 24.59 | 11.27 | 7.39 | 6.22 | 18.99 | 9.11 | 6.55 | 5.53 |
| World class (e.g., international pro) | 24.29 | 11.16 | 7.29 | 6.13 | 18.77 | 9.02 | 6.45 | 5.44 |
| | 24.00 | 11.04 | 7.19 | 6.04 | 18.56 | 8.93 | 6.36 | 5.36 |
| | 23.70 | 10.93 | 7.08 | 5.96 | 18.34 | 8.84 | 6.26 | 5.28 |
| | 23.40 | 10.81 | 6.98 | 5.87 | 18.13 | 8.75 | 6.17 | 5.20 |
| | 23.11 | 10.70 | 6.88 | 5.78 | 17.91 | 8.66 | 6.07 | 5.12 |
| | 22.81 | 10.58 | 6.77 | 5.69 | 17.70 | 8.56 | 5.98 | 5.03 |
| | 22.51 | 10.47 | 6.67 | 5.60 | 17.48 | 8.47 | 5.88 | 4.95 |
| Exceptional (e.g., domestic pro) | 22.22 | 10.35 | 6.57 | 5.51 | 17.26 | 8.38 | 5.79 | 4.87 |
| | 21.92 | 10.24 | 6.46 | 5.42 | 17.05 | 8.29 | 5.69 | 4.79 |
| | 21.63 | 10.12 | 6.36 | 5.33 | 16.83 | 8.20 | 5.60 | 4.70 |
| | 21.33 | 10.01 | 6.26 | 5.24 | 16.62 | 8.11 | 5.50 | 4.62 |
| | 21.03 | 9.89 | 6.15 | 5.15 | 16.40 | 8.02 | 5.41 | 4.54 |
| | 20.74 | 9.78 | 6.05 | 5.07 | 16.19 | 7.93 | 5.31 | 4.46 |
| Excellent (e.g., cat. 1) | 20.44 | 9.66 | 5.95 | 4.98 | 15.97 | 7.84 | 5.21 | 4.38 |
| | 20.15 | 9.55 | 5.84 | 4.89 | 15.76 | 7.75 | 5.12 | 4.29 |
| | 19.85 | 9.43 | 5.74 | 4.80 | 15.54 | 7.66 | 5.02 | 4.21 |
| | 19.55 | 9.32 | 5.64 | 4.71 | 15.32 | 7.57 | 4.93 | 4.13 |
| | 19.26 | 9.20 | 5.53 | 4.62 | 15.11 | 7.48 | 4.83 | 4.05 |
| | 18.96 | 9.09 | **5.43** | 4.53 | 14.89 | 7.39 | 4.74 | 3.97 |
| Very good (e.g., cat. 2) | 18.66 | 8.97 | 5.33 | **4.44** | 14.68 | 7.30 | 4.64 | 3.88 |
| | **18.37** | 8.86 | 5.22 | 4.35 | 14.46 | 7.21 | 4.55 | 3.80 |
| | 18.07 | 8.74 | 5.12 | 4.27 | 14.25 | **7.11** | 4.45 | 3.72 |
| | 17.78 | 8.63 | 5.01 | 4.18 | 14.03 | 7.02 | 4.36 | 3.64 |
| | 17.48 | **8.51** | 4.91 | 4.09 | 13.82 | 6.93 | **4.26** | 3.55 |
| | 17.18 | 8.40 | 4.81 | 4.00 | **13.60** | 6.84 | 4.17 | 3.47 |
| | 16.89 | 8.28 | 4.70 | 3.91 | 13.39 | 6.75 | 4.07 | **3.39** |
| Good (e.g., cat. 3) | 16.59 | 8.17 | 4.60 | 3.82 | 13.17 | 6.66 | 3.98 | 3.31 |
| | 16.29 | 8.05 | 4.50 | 3.73 | 12.95 | 6.57 | 3.88 | 3.23 |
| | 16.00 | 7.94 | 4.39 | 3.64 | 12.74 | 6.48 | 3.79 | 3.14 |
| | 15.70 | 7.82 | 4.29 | 3.55 | 12.52 | 6.39 | 3.69 | 3.06 |
| | 15.41 | 7.71 | 4.19 | 3.47 | 12.31 | 6.30 | 3.59 | 2.98 |
| | 15.11 | 7.59 | 4.08 | 3.38 | 12.09 | 6.21 | 3.50 | 2.90 |
| Moderate (e.g., cat. 4) | 14.81 | 7.48 | 3.98 | 3.29 | 11.88 | 6.12 | 3.40 | 2.82 |
| | 14.52 | 7.36 | 3.88 | 3.20 | 11.66 | 6.03 | 3.31 | 2.73 |
| | 14.22 | 7.25 | 3.77 | 3.11 | 11.45 | 5.94 | 3.21 | 2.65 |
| | 13.93 | 7.13 | 3.67 | 3.02 | 11.23 | 5.85 | 3.12 | 2.57 |
| | 13.63 | 7.02 | 3.57 | 2.93 | 11.01 | 5.76 | 3.02 | 2.49 |
| | 13.33 | 6.90 | 3.46 | 2.84 | 10.80 | 5.66 | 2.93 | 2.40 |
| Fair (e.g., cat. 5) | 13.04 | 6.79 | 3.36 | 2.75 | 10.58 | 5.57 | 2.83 | 2.32 |
| | 12.74 | 6.67 | 3.26 | 2.66 | 10.37 | 5.48 | 2.74 | 2.24 |
| | 12.44 | 6.56 | 3.15 | 2.58 | 10.15 | 5.39 | 2.64 | 2.16 |
| | 12.15 | 6.44 | 3.05 | 2.49 | 9.94 | 5.30 | 2.55 | 2.08 |
| | 11.85 | 6.33 | 2.95 | 2.40 | 9.72 | 5.21 | 2.45 | 1.99 |
| | 11.56 | 6.21 | 2.84 | 2.31 | 9.51 | 5.12 | 2.36 | 1.91 |
| Untrained (non-racer) | 11.26 | 6.10 | 2.74 | 2.22 | 9.29 | 5.03 | 2.26 | 1.83 |
| | 10.96 | 5.99 | 2.64 | 2.13 | 9.07 | 4.94 | 2.16 | 1.75 |
| | 10.67 | 5.87 | 2.53 | 2.04 | 8.86 | 4.85 | 2.07 | 1.67 |
| | 10.37 | 5.76 | 2.43 | 1.95 | 8.64 | 4.76 | 1.97 | 1.58 |
| | 10.08 | 5.64 | 2.33 | 1.86 | 8.43 | 4.67 | 1.88 | 1.50 |

Reprinted, by permission, from H. Allen and A. Coggan, 2010, *Training and racing with a power meter*, 2nd ed. (Boulder, CO: VeloPress), 54.

(in fact, roughly 40 to 45 percent of the energy expended during such exercise is derived aerobically) or that such an effort fully taxes anaerobic capacity (which generally requires 1.5 to 2.5 minutes to deplete). Nor does it mean that a 5-minute all-out effort entails exercising at precisely 100 percent of $\dot{V}O_2$max (most athletes can sustain a power that would elicit 105 to 110 percent of their $\dot{V}O_2$max for this duration). But power output over these target durations would be expected to correlate well with more direct measurements of these various physiological abilities. The durations of these index efforts were also chosen in an attempt to increase the reproducibility of the data, as well as for convenience in gathering the data.

## Power-to-Weight Ratio

The power-to-weight ratio is important in cycling because of the importance of climbing, and therefore gravitational resistance, in many disciplines. Cycling speed on a flat road or velodrome is largely determined by the ratio of power to frontal body surface area, which increases only slightly between a 60-kilogram rider and a 90-kilogram rider. This fact partially explains why large, muscular riders like Fabian Cancellara and Miguel Indurain have a major advantage in flat or rolling time trials or road races compared with smaller riders like the famous Italian climber Marco Pantani. The tables are turned, however, when significant climbing is involved, which is generally the case in many centuries, long road races, triathlons, and even some criteriums. In those cases, the higher your power-to-weight ratio is, the faster you are as a cyclist. In cycling, therefore, one of the main goals is to be as light as possible in weight while producing the greatest possible wattage. The trick is figuring out at what weight you produce the most watts.

The power profile chart uses watts per kilogram, the universal standard scientific power-to-weight ratio measurement. For the metric minded, the calculation is simply the watts that you are producing divided by your body mass. For example, an 80-kilogram rider may have a FTP of 320 watts compared with a 60-kilogram rider who has a FTP of 270 watts. When normalized to body weight, the former rider has a FTP of 4.0 watts per kilogram, whereas the latter has a FTP of 4.5 watts per kilogram.

For those more accustomed to working in pounds, divide your weight in pounds by 2.2 (a pound equals 454 grams) to get your weight in kilograms. For example, if you weigh 165 pounds, you would divide 165 by 2.2 to find your body weight of 75 kilograms. Next, divide your wattage numbers at each period by your weight in kilograms. If, for example, you weigh 165 pounds and are able to hold 350 watts for five minutes, you would divide 350 by 75 (i.e., 165/2.2) to get a ratio of 4.67 watts per kilogram.

## Power Profile Test

To create your own power profile of cycling strengths and weaknesses, find a section of road where you will not be interrupted by stop signs or intersections. Use a place that you can return to periodically for retesting. The wind conditions should be similar every time you conduct the test. For maximal reproducibility, some cyclists choose to perform the test indoors. An indoor setting is especially useful for those who live in areas that have severe winters where outdoor riding and testing may be impossible, as well as for cyclists who live in major cities where safe, long stretches of road may be hard to come by. Note, however, that indoor test values may not equate perfectly to your outdoor test values or riding capabilities, so you may need to adjust your indoor results upward or downward. Your true values will be revealed with a bit of experimentation, for example, by performing a 5-minute test effort on the trainer and on the road within the same week to keep fitness fairly constant.

Each time you test, you should be at a similar place in your training block. Try to do the test right after a rest week so that you will be fresh and relatively fit. Be sure to perform the same warm-up routine each time on the way to your testing grounds. Most of your warm-up should be done at Coggan's training levels 2 and 3 (the endurance and tempo categories from table 3.2 on page 49). A fit, experienced, and rested cyclist can potentially test all four periods (5 seconds, 1 minute, 5 minutes, and 20 minutes) over the course of a single workout (table 3.4). But because the goal is to achieve your best possible test scores, you may choose to split the test into two sessions. If in doubt, do two sessions so that you are as fresh as possible for each segment of the test. For example, you may choose to test your 1- and 5-minute efforts two or three times over the course of a single test workout and then return the next day to test your 5-second and 20-minute efforts. During testing, do not worry about cadence, heart rate, or anything other than the watch, and make sure that you drive hard to the end of each timed effort. In other words, just go as hard as you can for that particular interval. Whatever happens, happens. Record your efforts as intervals on your power meter, if possible.

## TABLE 3.4 Sample Power Profile Test Protocol

| Description | Time | Intensity of effort |
|---|---|---|
| Warm-up. Include fast pedal intervals, 3 x 1 min, at 110 rpm at 80–90% FTP with 1 min easy spinning after each. | ~45 min | 65–75% FTP. |
| FTP effort. 3–5 min recovery at 60–70% FTP. | 5 min | 100% FTP. |
| Test effort. 3–5 min recovery at 60–70% FTP. | 1 min | All out! |
| Easy riding. | 10 min | 70–80% FTP. |
| Test effort. 3–5 min recovery at 60–70% FTP. | 5 min | All out! Start from rolling at about 20 mph (32 km/h) and really hammer it in the last 45 s! |
| Recovery. | 10 min | 60–70% FTP. |
| Test effort. 3–5 min recovery at 60–70% FTP. | 1 min | All out! Start from about 20 mph (32 km/h) out of the saddle and hammering. Then be seated and drive it to the finish. |
| Test effort. 3–5 min recovery at 60–70% FTP. | 1 min | All out! Start from about 20 mph (32 km/h) out of the saddle and hammering. Then be seated and drive it to the finish. |
| Hard sprint. Recover 2 min at 60–70% FTP. | 15 s | Maximal. Start from a slow speed of about 15 mph (24 km/h) and sprint from out of the saddle. |
| Hard sprint. Recover 10 min at 60–70% FTP. | 15 s | Maximal. Start from a slow speed of about 15 mph (24 km/h) and sprint from out of the saddle. |
| 20 min TT. | 20 min | All out! |
| Cool-down. | 15–60 min | 60–70% FTP. |
| Download your data and pick out the best 5 s, 1 min, 5 min, and FTP. | | |

## Interpreting and Applying Your Results

What emerges from your power profile is a unique pattern that shows your relative strengths and weaknesses in cycling. To analyze your power profile test results, simply calculate your power-to-weight ratio for the maximum power that you can generate for five seconds, one minute, five minutes, and at functional threshold power. Then find corresponding values in each column of table 3.3 (page 84). If your performance falls between two values, as will often be the case, assign the nearest ranking. The values used in this analysis must reflect your best effort; otherwise, the resultant profile could be distorted, leading to inappropriate conclusions and decisions about training. Keep in mind that performance at each duration is being evaluated in light of the world's best cycling performances. Thus, even a highly successful sprinter on the road will tend to appear relatively weak in five-second sprints in comparison with match sprinters, whereas track sprinters and kilometer riders will likely have relatively low five-minute and FTP levels relative to their high rankings at the shorter five-second and one-minute durations.

The comparison with data from other cyclists and the rankings of, for example, category 3 or domestic pro, are not meant to suggest that if your data falls within a given range, you should automatically be racing in that category. After all, racing is done not in the lab but out on the roads! The rankings indicate that your fitness is comparable with cyclists in those categories. Beyond just seeing where you stack up in the cycling hierarchy, the ability to determine your own relative strengths and limitations is where the true value of power profiling comes in. A rider who knows his relative strengths and weaknesses in comparison to others can develop a program to improve in the weak areas and make real progress. A cyclist could even use awareness of her strengths and weaknesses to identify events in which she might achieve the greatest success and thereby build on her strengths. For example, suppose that you are currently racing in category 4. Your one-minute, five-minute, and FTP values all fall within the category 4 or 5 range, but your five-second value is in the category 2 range. This profile suggests that you have the ability to compete and win in the majority of category 4 races, which often come down to a sprint. Therefore, your best path to upgrading may not be focusing on your endurance but working on bike handling or race tactics to complement your sprinting strength.

Although every power profile is unique, several patterns are typical. The cyclist who is an all-arounder will have a generally horizontal plot across all the categories. That is, all four values will fall at about the same point in that individual's range. The all-arounder does not excel at any one thing but is likely competitive in his or her category across a broad range of events. Note that this profile is common for beginning racers because of their undeveloped training; as a racer or rider trains more or targets specific events or disciplines, areas of strength often begin to reveal themselves.

A distinctly upsloping plot (especially between the columns for one minute and five minutes but also between five minutes and FTP) is typical for the classic time trialist. Most time trialists are weak in neuromuscular power and anaerobic capacity but have relatively high aerobic power and an especially high lactate threshold. Although such cyclists may be able to improve their performance by spending lots of time practicing sprints, they may decline in aerobic fitness and perform worse in time trial races. Choosing between specializing in one area versus developing and improving other skills is a classic dilemma facing many elite cyclists, and the decision should be made with a solid plan and coaching support in place.

## Q&A    With David Martin: Monitor Training and Fitness

| Current position | Senior sport scientist, Australian Institute of Sport<br>Sport Science Coordinator, Cycling Australia. |
|---|---|
| Professional relationship and background with cycling | Sport science support for Australian Olympic Cycling Teams 1996, 2000, 2004, 2008.<br>Sport Science Coordinator for Australian Cycling since 2000. |
| Personal background with cycling | Recreationally competitive as a graduate student in mountain bike and road cycling events.<br>Still compete as a member of "old farts" team for 24-hour MTB challenges.<br>Enjoy my commute to work when the sun is coming up as I ride around the local lake. |
| Favorite ride (either one you've done or always wanted to do) | I have ridden up the famous Stelvio climb in northern Italy numerous times and always wanted to have a go starting in Bormio. |
| Favorite cycling-related experience | I had a great MTB race in an event called the Chequamegon 40 held on the Birkebeiner ski course in Wisconsin. It was a muddy course, and everyone's bike was breaking down. For some reason my bike just kept working, and I ended up moving up the rankings as the race progressed. It was one of those exciting days when everything was working for me but nothing was working for those I was competing with. Isn't it fun when luck is on your side? |

*(continued)*

**David, there seem to be many ways to quantify fitness, from $\dot{V}O_2$max tests in the lab to field tests done out on the road. If you could have only one test or get only one piece of information to monitor a cyclist, what would it be and why?**

I must say, I love cycling power meters—actually it is a love–hate relationship. I love all the information that we can obtain with a well-calibrated SRM crank, but I hate trying to manage 30 to 60 SRM cranks being used by different cycling squads located around the world. Fixing broken power meters is no fun at all!

The power output–duration curve is particularly helpful when expressed in both watts and watts per kilogram of body mass. This power profile can be used in many ways, and it is a nice starting point for understanding a cyclist's capabilities in a straightforward, functional manner. How much power can the athlete sustain for 30 minutes? If an athlete weighs 75 kilograms, then 380 watts is good, 400 watts is very good, and 420 watts is world class.

By monitoring training power output and race power output, it is possible to start seeing the big picture: What is the cyclist doing for training? And what is the cyclist capable of? This information, combined with the knowledge of what the cyclist *wants* to be capable of, allows a well-formulated training progression to be established. For instance, a cyclist can sustain 350 watts for 30 minutes, but in his training he never holds 350 watts for more than 10 minutes and rarely accumulates more than 15 minutes at 350 watts during a workout. But to be competitive, he needs to hold around 380 watts for 30 minutes. This information allows a training progression to be established.

Notice that I have not even mentioned $\dot{V}O_2$max or anaerobic threshold or cycling efficiency, not because these exercise intensities are not important, but because to me power profiles and power cadence relationships have emerged as more important for managing athletes. The laboratory is still the place I go for research, but much can be learned from careful observations of power output produced in the field.

 **OK, if you're a cyclist wanting to track your performance over a season or multiple seasons, what information do you absolutely need and what would be nice options?**

Although power is really helpful for understanding when cycling form is good and not so good, it still remains tricky to know whether power output produced over a four-minute period is low because a cyclist is tired or unmotivated. A tired cyclist or an unfit cyclist may produce low power (compared with her or his personal best) for a four-minute effort despite producing a maximal effort, whereas an extremely fit cyclist may not produce high power output over a four-minute effort because she or he is unmotivated or tactically it is not the right thing to do. Determining whether an athlete's power is down because of lack of capacity versus not being committed remains a big challenge when interpreting data. We are now asking cyclists to tell us whether they gave 100 percent effort during their rides to help us understand when max efforts are occurring. Interestingly enough, in many races the professionals can finish a 160-kilometer stage and not give more than 70 percent effort, depending on how race tactics unfold. Understanding perceptions of effort as well as actual power output produced is an interesting aspect of monitoring training that we will be researching into the future.

This information is all about helping athletes learn about themselves. What makes them tick, what they find motivating, what they are good at, how long they can stay engaged in heavy training and racing blocks, what environments are motivating, and what environments are not conducive to productive training—these are all good questions that consistent monitoring can help answer. One final point: Power meters and training logs don't make cyclists faster! Some cyclists think that by monitoring their training they will somehow get faster. Unfortunately, plenty of good loggers out there will never win a race.

 **The popularization of power monitors has really revolutionized cycling and the monitoring of pace and overall training. Does it make other methods of monitoring, such as heart rate, speed and distance, and subjective sensations irrelevant or obsolete? Or are there things that a power monitor cannot tell us?**

Recently, we are seeing an entire new language emerge from dedicated power monitor users. It is not uncommon to see a professional cyclist post a comment on Twitter or Facebook such as the following: "400TSS ride today and my MMPs from 1–2 minutes were close to PBs. Not bad considering IF was .82. ATL is certainly climbing quickly, which should boost my CTL to seasonal PB levels." There's not a lot said about perceptions, satisfaction, injury, or illness in these kinds of comments.

From my perspective, I think we will see software packages bringing up questions that allow the coach and athlete to document sensations in addition to the power output and heart rate responses to training and racing. I think this will provide a more complete picture of where a cyclist is, and this information will contribute to better management of the cyclist. I am a big fan of sensations. For a while I thought I could provide advice to coaches and athletes by just looking at power meters, but unfortunately the day-to-day awareness of where the athlete is and how he or she is coping with life in general seems to be important as well. Maybe that is why Australian coaches are so good—they tend to spend a lot of time talking to the athletes and seeing them daily in a training environment. This approach is very different from training programs based only on power meter feedback.

There is a subtle but definite risk for cyclists who train with power monitors all the time but don't have a functional power meter during races. If all their hill climbing and time trialing has been guided by power output feedback, cyclists may feel lost when competing without the feedback that they have grown accustomed to. Even for those who use a power meter while racing, there's the risk that it'll become a glass ceiling of sorts, in that a cyclist will end up racing by the numbers rather than responding to the race. So, for example, let's say that the cyclist is in a quality break with a real chance for the win. If he has convinced himself that he can ride at only 300 watts in the

*(continued)*

break because that's what he does in training, then he might not race to win by taking the risk and going for 310 or 320 watts to make the break stick. Cyclists must always remember to race the race rather than be a robotic slave to the computer!

# Integration of Data Channels

Technological advances and creative thinking are focused on developing new ways to improve our understanding of how the body works and responds to exercise. Athletes and coaches must keep an open mind to such new ideas and assess where and how they can be incorporated into training and performance monitoring. Although we remain huge fans of power-based training, its optimal benefits really derive from its integration with multiple objective and subjective data channels, resulting in a holistic view of a cyclist's response to training. Wattage forms the anchor because it is the actual mechanical work that your body is producing while cycling. But data such as heart rate, speed, cadence, and perception of effort help you understand how your body produced that work, responded to that stress, and ultimately whether it got you down the road faster. Other data from emerging technology can provide even deeper insight into cycling performance.

Remember, though, that a computerized device cannot automatically track or record two important pieces of the performance puzzle: how you felt and which events happened at what time. Therefore, to get the most out of your numerical data, you need to record a detailed set of notes that you can use to make sense of the various data. Keep in mind that the times in which you fail to meet your goal are important opportunities for learning lessons that will help you succeed in later events. Therefore, try to strip away the rationalizations and give an honest account of each ride in terms of how you felt and what actually happened.

## Training Diaries: More Than Numbers

Self-knowledge is fundamental not only to smart training but also to predicting overtraining (discussed in chapter 5). The best diagnostic tool available to cyclists and coaches is a detailed training log, encompassing not only the training performed but also the subjective response to that training. If you are serious about optimizing your cycling, keep a training diary. Some terrific options are available for those who are tech savvy and computer literate, but whether you use software, a custom spreadsheet, an online training log, or just write in a blank notebook, the important thing is to record your training and be able to interpret it. Indeed, the subjective notes are at least as important as the actual training because they provide context and important between-the-lines information. Many coaches rely with equal parts on your training log and actual power files to plan your next training block. With a rich store of data within your log, you and your coach can analyze it in detail to recognize your strengths, your limitations, and your response to particular workloads. From there, you have a basis to replicate your successes and improve from your mistakes.

Be sure to include the following information in your training diary:

▶ **Deviations from your planned program.** Log both your intended and actual workouts so that you can check for ideal versus realistic training patterns. Did you deviate significantly from your original program? Did the deviations occur because of illness or family or work commitments? How effective were your adjustments to these changes? You need this information to plan for future inevitable setbacks to your new plan.

▶ **Your reaction to heavy training.** How quickly did you recover from hard workouts or heavy periods of training? How do you respond to several consecutive days of hard efforts? How did you feel mentally after a block of hard training? Everyone responds to training and recovers at different rates, so you need to program your training based on your own parameters. Such data can give you clues about your individual responses as you approach the state of overtraining, helping you to prevent its onset in the future.

▶ **Notes about your readiness to train.** Record sleep and dietary patterns, resting heart rate, mental state, and subjective notes on life events (e.g., a tight deadline or heavy stress at work).

▶ **Data related to your successful experiences.** The training diary is not just about writing down bad news or explaining why you did not perform up to expectations—if you performed well in your training or racing, analyze that too! You are looking to understand exactly what went right so that you can replicate it. If your tapering before the peak races worked or you found it ridiculously easy to bridge up to the winning break, you need to understand that strength.

## Heart Rate Integration

As we mentioned earlier in this chapter, heart rate by itself doesn't measure how much work you are doing so much as it measures how fast your heart is pumping. The same is true of other individual data channels such as speed, ratings of perceived exertion, or time. But the integration of multiple channels allows a more holistic view of the overall system at work.

We can see the value of looking at changes in heart rate within the context of data from other channels relatively simply by looking at a change of mean maximal power for a certain period, say 20 minutes, noting the corresponding mean maximal heart rate for that same period, and then comparing those values over a month's or season's worth of data. Generally, as you become fitter, your heart rate will decrease for a given power output or a given speed. As your fitness improves, your training zones shift, and although your maximum heart rate won't change much (if at all), your speed and power will change in relation to your heart rate.

Remember that identifying trends can be difficult when viewing heart rate data over time because heart rate can be affected by many factors, including hydration level, amount of sleep, and fatigue. But note the heart rate and power data illustrated in figure 3.8: A rider produces 202 watts in August with a heart rate response of 172 beats per minute and then four months later produces that same 202 wattage with a heart rate of 160 beats per minute. This result suggests significant cardiovascular improvement.

The integration of heart rate with power is sometimes challenging to interpret correctly. A lower heart rate response, when matched with power and speed, can be a good indication of fatigue and overtraining. One common observation with a state of fatigue is heart rate suppression in which, even if power can be sustained, heart rate values are lower than normal. Therefore, the data in figure 3.8 could be representative of a case of sustained fatigue rather than improved fitness. More commonly, though, such fatigue shows itself as both an inability to sustain power as long as previously and a lower heart rate. Here subjective data for that workout and the preceding workouts become critical in giving you deeper insight into how

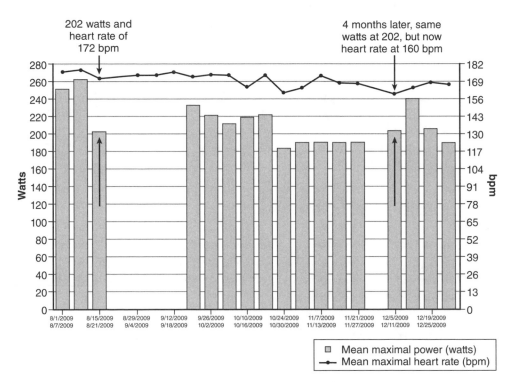

**FIGURE 3.8** A lower heart rate at the same power output is an indication of improved fitness.

the more recent workouts actually felt. If heart rate was lower than expected while perceived exertion was much higher, then the data would likely represent a state of fatigue rather than improved fitness.

## Global Positioning Systems

Global positioning systems have become ubiquitous in our lives, from the navigation system in your car that helps you find your way to a new destination to monitors from Garmin and Polar that record your track as you ride. The recording of the track is certainly interesting and has a definite cool factor. GPS can also be helpful in generating an explanation of your ride. For example, you may look at a particular data file a week or a year later and not remember why that major and prolonged spike occurred in heart rate or power. Reviewing the GPS track and seeing where you rode that day may help you recall that particular ride and what was going on at various points along the way.

Future cycling applications for GPS are intriguing and may arrive soon, especially if high-resolution GPS can be integrated with sensors on your bike that tell you how hard you were braking or leaning at a particular moment. Such technology is already being used in auto racing to help drivers and engineers improve the performance of the drivers and the cars. Applied to cycling, these combined data channels could provide invaluable knowledge for mountain bikers, cyclocross riders, or criterium riders who want to optimize cornering at speed.

## Other Data Channels

A relatively new kid on the block, the Zephyr Bio-Harness, has set out to measure physiological variables during exercise that haven't been previously measured except in a lab setting. The Zephyr Bio-Harness measures skin temperature, respiration rate, the posture of the athlete, acceleration rate, and heart rate. Each of these data channels may be useful for cycling. For example, by knowing the posture of the rider, you can correlate the increase in respiration rate, power output, and heart rate that occurs each time the athlete gets out of the saddle on a climb or in a sprint. This data may help you understand whether the rider is more economical climbing particular hills while seated or while standing, an important component of proper pacing. After some focused training, subsequent data may show that each time the rider gets out of the saddle on the steeper sections of the climb, heart rate rises by three beats per minute, respiration rate decreases, and, within one minute, body temperature decreases. This result would indicate that the athlete has learned to relax and control her breathing when out of the saddle; although the heart rate rises a little, she is still in control of the effort. Another athlete might have an increase in respiration rate when making a standing climbing effort. After they are measured and analyzed, these responses are trainable and coachable.

Body temperature is another variable that could be a factor in cycling performance. The Zephyr Bio-Harness measures skin temperature only under the chest strap, which is certainly not the same as core body temperature. Nevertheless, skin temperature can tell us a lot about how well an athlete is dressed for the ride and whether sufficient cooling is occurring on a hot day. By looking at heart rate and skin temperature, we can gauge the effects of heat stress on the cardiovascular system.

# Applying the Science

Tracking changes in fitness is a critical component of improving your cycling performance because you can evaluate your training and make changes. If you can't quickly and easily see and quantify improvements, then how do you know whether you are on track to achieve your goals? Profiling your performances over time and comparing them with your best performances, or the best performance of others, allows you to learn about your strengths and weaknesses and to monitor your overall fitness changes. But one important point to remember is that profiles of any kind are simply snapshots in time. Therefore, do not immediately assume that a single profile defines who you are as a cyclist for your whole career!

A wide range of software is available for downloading and interpreting your ride data, and each has a different focus and different features. There is no one best system for everyone. The important aspect of tracking your training remains obtaining a long-term record of how your body responds to different workloads. By analyzing the data from whichever training device you have, whether it is a GPS watch, a power meter, a heart rate monitor, or even a Bio-Harness, you can look at the cumulative effects of your training and note how your body is responding to that training. The latest breakthrough in electronic gadgetry may be a bit overwhelming at times and frustrating at others, but the effort spent gathering and analyzing the data is worth it. Even information about a recovery ride or a simple workout that you have done a thousand times helps highlight trends that can guide you to making intelligent decisions about your training. Keep in mind that the raw numbers and stats of a ride are not enough on their own. The important complementary information is how you felt during the workout. The subjective sensations provide context from which you can better interpret your training and performance. Therefore, take the time to track both your physical and mental response to training.

## CHAPTER 4

# Periodizing Your Training

**W**hat started out as a mysterious training idea from the other side of the iron curtain has become mainstream training philosophy. But periodization is much more than simply peaking for a particular race. It encompasses ideas such as progression over several years and even an entire career. A few major developments in the 1980s and 1990s changed everything when it came to our understanding and acceptance of periodization:

- The development of cycle computers, heart rate monitors, and now power monitors enabled precise quantification of effort rather than riding by feel.

- The globalization of cycling by pioneers like Greg LeMond led to new ideas, such as focusing training solely on events like Roubaix, the Tour de France, and the World Championships.

- The fall of the iron curtain in the late 1980s opened our eyes to the legal and illegal practices that enabled Eastern European countries to dominate international competition in many sports. One of the notable legal scientific theories to cross the iron curtain was the concept of periodization of training.

At its most basic, periodization is simply the idea that fitness is allowed to fluctuate throughout the year, with the aim of being at optimal physical and mental preparation at particular periods. The flip side of periodization and peaking is understanding your strengths and weaknesses, and targeting your training to maximize your strengths and minimize your weaknesses so that they don't limit your strengths. These concepts work in unison and cannot be separated from each other. What you are ultimately looking to do is to get a clear understanding of your current strengths and weaknesses and then match them to the requirements of your key races. For example, we all would love to climb like billy goats, but the reality is that the vast majority of amateur races end in field sprints. Therefore, working on your sprinting and bike handling is rarely going to be wasted time. On the other hand, if your key races have a mountain time trial and you're aiming for a high general classification, then you have to break down the requirements of that effort, assess your current abilities, and adapt your training accordingly. This idea is not earth shattering, but too many cyclists still ride to their own liking and then cannot figure out why they end up with poor or average race performances. Therefore, this chapter surveys the ebb and flow of training intensities throughout a season and career.

## Seasonal Variability in Fitness

How do we make the off-season as enjoyable and productive as possible from a fitness perspective? As always, no single template leads to success. Some riders dive straight into hard-core cyclocross training and racing for the bulk of the winter, whereas others take a more leisurely break and focus on cross-training. Still others continue with road or trainer riding as their primary activity throughout the off-season. Cyclists in warmer climes have access to year-round outdoor riding opportunities and have the tempting option of making no seasonally mandated changes in riding patterns.

©DPPI/Icon SMI

It is important to keep active in the off-season, but the activity can vary widely depending on weather, interest, and goals.

There is no single right path, because we all have personal preferences and conditions or limitations. Overall, because of our inherent love of physical activity, our off-seasons usually include a lot of activity, so few of us turn into sloths. But a common concern among cyclists is that getting off the bike for a prolonged period means losing sport-specific fitness. Therefore, one recurring question over the off-season is just how much bike fitness we can lose without severely compromising the buildup for the next season. Jan Ullrich epitomized one extreme point of view. His major drop in fitness and gain in weight necessitated that he put in a lot of extra time and effort (increasing the risk of injury or overtraining) just to get back to baseline, let alone build for a stronger season. At the other extreme, a fanatical devotion to maintaining a high level of bike fitness and optimum in-season weight throughout the off-season can be a difficult physiological and mental task, also leading to the path of overtraining and burnout (see chapter 5).

Optimal off-season fitness is obviously difficult to measure and manipulate in real-life settings, so the most realistic approach is to determine the seasonal changes in aerobic indices in athletes. In this case, the ideal is to study professional athletes to see what works for them (Sassi et al. 2008). Among a group of top professional road and mountain cyclists, $\dot{V}O_2$max was tracked over the course of a year, along with other important aerobic measures such as gross efficiency and economy. Subjects were not just highly trained amateurs or even undistinguished professionals; they were riders at the top end of the sport, including top-five finishers in the Giro d'Italia or the Tour de France, as well as current national team mountain bikers. Over the course of a season, from December, through March, to June (roughly corresponding to the rider's rest, early, and peak season fitness), $\dot{V}O_2$max increased from 69.4 to 74.2 to 76.7 milliliters per kilogram per minute, respectively (figure 4.1 on page 70). This change was matched by increases in peak power output, from 6.3 to 6.8 to 7.0 watts per kilogram during an incremental test, and greater tolerance at a set absolute workload of 17, 30, and 46 minutes.

In summary, it appears that even highly trained and successful professionals do allow themselves to lose some fitness during the off-season; their maximal aerobic capacity decreases by about 9 percent during the off-season compared with the competitive season. This finding is important in that it puts to rest the notion that any lowering of aerobic fitness is harmful. It suggests that typical amateurs can afford to decrease their aerobic capacity by at least that much during the off-season. This insight is valuable for many amateurs because they have to deal with the stress of daily life to a greater extent than professionals do, and this stress can derail even the best-laid training plan.

Taking a break helps ensure continued improvement in the coming season. We have often seen amateur master cyclists who just continue to train hard all year around and never seem to have that peak of fitness or continued improvement. Fitness stagnation is the enemy of every athlete, and two ways to prevent it are by getting proper rest (thus giving the body time to heal from, adapt to,

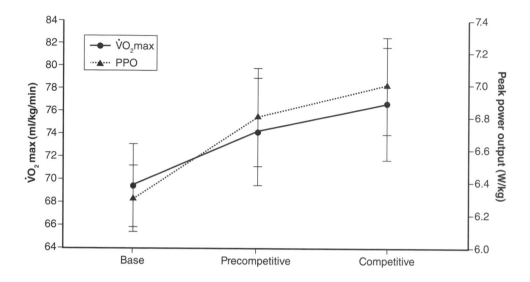

and improve from heavy training stress) and by taking on new training stimulus. Both goals can be accomplished in the off-season by spending time and effort on core training, cross-training, weight training, working on bike-related skills, or simply taking a mental break and having fun. These activities can lead to an even better season the following year.

# Training Intensity Distribution

Planning your training to accommodate the wide spectrum of energy demands that you may face is a difficult proposition. Many cyclists feel pressured to pack everything into the limited time available. Aerobic development in an endurance sport such as cycling is clearly essential, as discussed in chapter 2. Every cyclist wants to ride well all the time, and in many cases the training advice to "ride lots" is indeed constructive—the more you ride, the better you become. Up until the past 20 years or so, the predominant training philosophy for Western cyclists was simply to ride lots of base miles in the off-season and then race throughout the year. When not racing, putting in lots of bike time at the "long steady distance" pace was recommended. The theory was that racing was the best form of training. Besides, riders were all expected to perform at top levels throughout the season in all events, leaving little time for focused training. Many professionals today, who have the ability to devote massive amounts of time to training in the off-season, still maintain this general pattern to maximize aerobic development before the start of 80 to 100 days of racing throughout a season. But this approach may not be right for everyone. What approach is best for competitive cyclists with limited training time? The following sections present the scientific arguments for focusing on high-intensity, moderate-intensity, or low-intensity efforts.

## The Case for High-Intensity Training

Whether the reason for decreasing the volume of training is to taper and peak for a key event, to accommodate a busy schedule, or to work around bad weather during winter, we often worry about the loss of endurance capacity. A consistent question in the scientific literature is the potential for high-intensity training to either complement or replace traditional sustained endurance training for enhancing aerobic capacity. How much cross-transfer occurs between high-intensity training and endurance performance? Previously, it was generally assumed that high-intensity and low-intensity training were incompatible or else that they worked through different physiological systems. Recent studies, however, have demonstrated that high-intensity training may elicit the same physiological adaptations within the muscles that endurance training does (Burgomaster et al. 2005, Gibala et al. 2006, Gibala 2007).

Burgomaster et al. (2005) tested the effects of very short bouts of maximal-intensity exercise on aerobic performance. At only six sessions of four to seven maximal 30-second sprints spread out over 14 days, much less exercise was prescribed than in traditional exercise studies. Keeping in mind that every bit of training counts, the training in this study was so small that it was almost nonexistent in the way that we traditionally think of training. Before and after the 14 days, subjects were tested for their levels of citrate synthase (a key marker of aerobic metabolic activity) and the amount of muscle glycogen (another strong indicator of sustained aerobic performance). Their aerobic power ($\dot{V}O_2$max) was tested, along with time to exhaustion at a power output equal to 80 percent of the subjects' prestudy $\dot{V}O_2$peak. Somewhat surprisingly, dramatic increases in both citrate synthase activity (38 percent) and muscle glycogen content (26 percent) were seen in the experimental group despite the small dose of exercise. The increase in these metabolic indicators of aerobic capacity was impressive. But the biggest change was in the time to exhaustion at 80 percent of $\dot{V}O_2$peak power output, which jumped 100 percent, from 26 to 51 minutes. This happened despite no change occurring in $\dot{V}O_2$peak itself, a marker often (and possibly falsely) used as the key aerobic indicator in other studies.

One of the limitations of the Burgomaster et al. (2005) study was that it compared one group who did the high-intensity training (HIT) with another group who did no exercise. Although the study demonstrated that the HIT was effective compared with sitting on the couch, it did not address how HIT compared with a typical endurance training program. When comparing the efficacy of a 2-week HIT style of training (for a total of about 15 minutes of sprints in 2.5 hours of exercise spread over six sessions) with a 10.5-hour endurance training program, the total work performed was 630 kilojoules versus 6,500 kilojoules. All tested measures (muscle glycogen, muscle buffering capacity, aerobic enzymes, time trial performance) improved with both HIT and endurance training, but essentially no differences were observed when comparing the two styles (Gibala et al. 2006). Similarly, both groups improved their time trial efforts to an equal extent following the training period. Such data clearly demonstrate that cyclists can use more than one approach to achieve aerobic fitness and physiological adaptation. This conclusion is supported by the fact that higher-intensity training is being employed during rehab in clinical settings (Gibala 2007). Figure 4.2 illustrates the effects of endurance and high-intensity training.

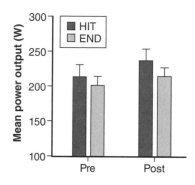

**FIGURE 4.2**   **Power capacity following endurance and high-intensity training.**

Practically, this means that you can get the same results with different methods or approaches to training and should experiment with both to see which is the most effective for your body. The HIT model is used by many athletes who have limited time to train and need to maintain a relatively high level of fitness the year around but don't have to worry about competing in longer events that might significantly tax their muscular and aerobic endurance. This HIT model might work well for track racers or masters racers who have less than eight hours a week to train. Here's what a sample week of HIT training for such an athlete would look like:

## Sample High-Intensity Training Week

**Monday:** Easy ride or rest day.

If riding, ride for 1 hour maximum and keep heart rate lower than 68 percent of functional threshold heart rate (FTHR) or 55 percent of functional threshold power (FTP).

**Tuesday:** Anaerobic capacity work on hills.

Make this ride a hilly one or simulate hills by riding into the wind. The hills can range from 30 seconds to 2 minutes in length.

▶ Warm up for 20 minutes at 69 to 83 percent of FTHR or 56 to 75 percent of FTP.

▶ Attack 10 hills, each ranging from 30 seconds to 2 minutes and keep power above 120 percent of FTP. HR should be over 105 percent of FTHR at the end of the long intervals. Your legs should be screaming for mercy at the top of each hill. Rest for 2 to 3 minutes after each.

▶ Cool down for 15 to 20 minutes at 69 to 83 percent of FTHR or 56 to 75 percent of FTP.

**Wednesday:** $\dot{V}O_2$max intervals.

Really push yourself here and do six 3-minute hard intervals holding your power at over 115 percent of FTP for the entire interval. Don't start your interval on a section of road that will include a downhill.

▶ Warm up for 20 minutes at 69 to 83 percent of FTHR or 56 to 75 percent of FTP.

▶ Do six 3-minute intervals at 115 percent of FTP (105 percent or more of FTHR). Start these off fast but pace yourself. Be sure to rest 5 minutes after each interval and keep your pace at 75 percent of FTP (85 percent of FTHR). After the intervals, ride for 20 to 30 minutes at around 80 to 85 percent of FTP (88 to 90 percent of FTHR).

▶ Cool down for 15 to 20 minutes at 69 to 83 percent of FTHR or 56 to 75 percent of FTP.

**Thursday:** Lactate threshold training.

The goal is to ride right at your threshold power or heart rate and just above to create some stress on your lactate system. These intervals are 10 minutes long—the right length to push yourself hard while being able to withstand the intensity of the effort.

▶ Warm up for 20 minutes at 69 to 83 percent of FTHR or 56 to 75 percent of FTP.

▶ Begin your four 10-minute intervals by getting out of the saddle and up to speed but pace yourself because you'll tend to push harder than a pace that you can maintain for the 10 minutes. Hold back just a little. Maintain from 100 to 105 percent of your FTP or 100 to 105 percent of your FTHR for the effort and push a little harder in the last minute. Rest for 5 minutes after each. If you have time and energy after these, then do 5 to 10 intervals of 1 minute at 120 percent of FTP (105 percent or more of FTHR) with only 1 minute rest after each.

▶ Cool down for 15 to 20 minutes at 69 to 83 percent of FTHR or 56 to 75 percent of FTP.

*(continued)*

## Sample High-Intensity Training Week   *(continued)*

**Friday:** Easy ride or rest day.

If riding, ride for 1 hour maximum and keep heart rate lower than 68 percent of FTHR or 55 percent of FTP.

**Saturday:** Group ride.

Be active at the front or repeat the $\dot{V}O_2$max interval workout.

**Sunday:** Group ride or endurance ride.

Ride at 56 to 75 percent of your FTP or 69 to 83 percent of FTHR.

When Hunter is coaching athletes, he develops a comprehensive plan for each client that works every physiological system from endurance to anaerobic capacity. Consider approaching your own training the same way. Ride in multiple training zones so that you can reap the greatest physiological adaptations.

## Indoor Trainer Volume

The HIT concept is particularly applicable in the off-season, when bad weather and darkness often limit the ability to exercise and to put in the high-volume, low-intensity training needed to maximize aerobic development. Many riders just get on the indoor trainer and drone along at endurance pace or tempo pace for much of the winter, never changing speeds or doing short sprints, hard efforts, or even threshold work. Besides being incredibly boring, training like this for long periods does not prepare riders for the rapid speed changes that occur in the peloton or the high-intensity nature of the racing season. "Racing into shape" may work for professionals who are trying to come into form for the Tour de France, but it does not work for the amateur or masters cyclist. Nonprofessionals need to be ready for hard efforts, and to do that, they have to train with a higher intensity than they might suspect.

The benefits of high-intensity training appear to extend to what is called the base training period. In a review of the existing literature on mixing high-intensity exercise into the base training phase, Paton and Hopkins (2004) found that adding high-intensity training during the off-season appeared to improve endurance performance even in elite athletes. Specifically, the survey suggested that efforts near or beyond power output at $\dot{V}O_2$max were most beneficial overall, possibly because they stimulated all the major metabolic pathways (alactic, anaerobic, and aerobic). These efforts are similar to the intense maximal sprints used by Gibala's group. Therefore, if you dread seemingly endless riding on the trainer indoors, instead do a variety of high-intensity efforts above FTP for short trainer sessions three or four times a week and focus on other forms of cross-training for endurance in the remaining time available for training.

## The Case for Moderate-Intensity Training

Cycling is largely an aerobic sport, meaning that cyclists have to produce energy from oxygen, and becoming efficient at that process is critical to success. One of the latest theories in training for cycling is that a steady diet of riding at the upper end of tempo pace, or Coggan's level 3, commonly referred to as sweet-spot training, can give you a boost in threshold fitness. This intensity roughly equates to 88 to 94 percent of threshold power or 95 to 98 percent of threshold heart rate. Why has this become a popular zone for cyclists to train in? Let's consider figure 4.3. What we see here is a chart that shows the relationship between intensity, physiological strain, and maximum duration. The chart illustrates how these factors relate to the actual training effect or increase in threshold power. As your intensity increases on the $x$-axis, the physiological strain goes up and the time that you can endure that strain goes down. In other words, the harder you go, the shorter you can maintain that intensity. Now look at the training-effect line, which represents how threshold power increases with training. Notice that the peak of this line is right in the bottom range of power training level 4, indicating that the maximum benefit of training to improve threshold power occurs in this area. This area has been named the sweet spot because the amount of time that you can ride at this intensity is relatively long and the strain is not too bad, so the overall training effect is substantial.

Riding in sweet-spot range may very well challenge the aerobic system at the best level for aerobic adaptations. As stated before, this intensity has become popular for many cyclists who have power meters because they can easily confirm

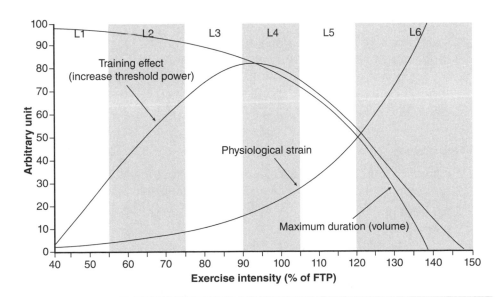

**FIGURE 4.3**  **The sweet spot spans Coggan's training levels 3 and 4.**

that they are in the correct wattage range and stay there. Although many of the scientific studies about training are polarized around low or high intensity, at this moment no hard scientific evidence indicates that training in this area works or doesn't work, although thousands of cyclists use it daily.

How much should you train at sweet-spot intensity? The answer is not clear-cut, because it depends on your goals, the length of your races, the amount of time that you have to train, and your particular strengths and weaknesses. For example, time trialists and triathletes, for whom the bulk of racing consists of sustained effort at threshold, would likely greatly benefit from lots of sweet-spot training. A good start would be to do an hour or two of sweet-spot work each week. You could do this training on separate days, incorporated into group rides or weekend races or performed on special training rides in which you do three intervals of 20 minutes at sweet-spot intensity. Most riders try to incorporate their sweet-spot work in the second hardest training day of the week, reserving the first hard day for higher-intensity work.

A typical week of moderate-intensity training would look like this:

## Sample Moderate-Intensity Training Week

**Monday:** Easy ride or rest day.

If riding, ride for 1 hour maximum and keep heart rate lower than 68 percent of functional threshold heart rate (FTHR) or 55 percent of functional threshold power (FTP).

**Tuesday:** Subthreshold or sweet-spot intervals.

Riding just below your threshold power can help you increase your threshold power because you are stressing the lactate system in this area. You will need to keep your power between 85 and 95 percent of FTP or between 95 and 98 percent of FTHR to be at subthreshold. The sweet spot is an even pace to ride at for these intervals, and that's from 88 to 93 percent of your FTP or 90 to 95 percent of FTHR.

▸ Warm up for 20 minutes at 69 to 83 percent of FTHR or 56 to 75 percent of FTP.

▸ Begin with four 10-minute intervals at sweet-spot intensity and hold your cadence and pace steady. Ride easy for 5 minutes after each interval.

▸ Cool down for 15 to 20 minutes at 69 to 83 percent of FTHR or 56 to 75 percent of FTP.

**Wednesday:** Tempo aerobic builder workout.

For this ride, choose a steady and relatively flat route where you will have to push hard the whole time.

▶ Warm up for 20 minutes at 69 to 83 percent of FTHR or 56 to 75 percent of FTP, loosening the legs for a solid 3-hour ride.

▶ Start out with two 20-minute intervals at your sweet-spot intensity (88 to 93 percent of FTP, 95 to 98 percent of FTHR) and push those to the end. Take a solid 10 minutes rest after each. Then ride for 60 minutes at tempo pace (76 to 90 percent of FTP or 84 to 94 percent of FTHR) and do a burst (pick up cadence to 120 revolutions per minute for 20 seconds) every 5 minutes.

▶ Cool down for 15 minutes at endurance pace.

**Thursday:** Subthreshold and crisscross efforts.

▶ Warm up for 20 minutes at 69 to 83 percent of FTHR or 56 to 75 percent of FTP and finish the warm-up with a 3-minute effort at your threshold (100 percent of FTP or 100 percent of FTHR). Then ride easy for 5 minutes.

▶ Now, nail it at your sweet spot (88 to 93 percent of FTP or 95 to 98 percent of FTHR) for 30 minutes. Every 2 minutes within this 30-minute set, do a hard burst of effort to 120 percent of your FTP or 100 percent of FTHR, hold for 30 seconds, and come back to your previous pace at the sweet spot. If you are feeling strong, do a second set.

▶ Cool down for 15 minutes at endurance pace.

**Friday:** Easy ride or rest day.

If riding, ride for 1 hour maximum and keep heart rate lower than 68 percent of FTHR or 55 percent of FTP.

**Saturday:** Group ride.

Be active at the front or repeat the $\dot{V}O_2$max interval workout.

**Sunday:** Group ride or endurance ride.

Ride at 56 to 75 percent of your FTP or 69 to 83 percent of FTHR.

## The Case for Low-Intensity Training

The fact that aerobic adaptations occur with both endurance and high-intensity training does not mean that endurance training should be abandoned altogether. Building a foundation of aerobic fitness is important, especially when you consider the duration and distance of many cycling events. If you have a race coming up that is over three hours long, then you will want to increase your muscular endurance to handle that duration and intensity. When examining the training programs of subelite and elite endurance athletes across a range of sports such as cycling, running, skiing, and rowing, the importance of doing low-intensity training to maximize aerobic development becomes evident.

In general, the major pattern of training distribution in endurance athletes seem to be highly polarized, featuring low intensity and very high intensity, with little time spent in threshold-type efforts (Esteve-Lanao et al. 2005, Guellich et al. 2009, Seiler and Kjerland 2006). For example, in surveying elite junior cross-country skiers, Seiler et al. (2006) reported 71 percent of time spent at less than 2.0 millimoles blood lactate, 7 percent at 2.0 to 4.0 millimoles, and 22 percent at greater than 4.0 millimoles. In junior elite rowers, this trend of polarized training intensity distribution was even more extreme; 96 percent of rowing-specific training during the base training period was performed at an intensity less than 2.0 millimoles blood lactate and the remainder was split between threshold and high-intensity efforts (Guellich et al. 2009). In the competition phase, the polarization became even more extreme. The overall distribution of volume at an intensity less than 2.0 millimoles remained similar at 94 percent, and this category saw an increase in the percentage of volume at the lowest intensities. Similarly, when dissecting the efforts above 2.0 millimoles, overall volume increased at the highest work intensities, which means that the volume of intensity was also significant. Extending this work by tracking these junior athletes three years later, the same study found that the subjects who went on to attain the most international success had a slightly higher volume of training at both extremes of the intensity spectrum.

These observational results are supported by studies that directly manipulated the proportion of training intensity distribution (Esteve-Lanao et al. 2007). In subelite 5,000-meter and cross country runners, training for five months was manipulated between predominantly low intensity in one group (80.5 percent in zone 1 and 11.8 percent in zone 2 in a three-zone model) or more volume at moderate intensity (66.8 percent in zone 1 and 24.7 percent in zone 2). The amount of above-threshold work was similar at about 8.5 percent of total volume in both groups. In a 10.4-kilometer cross country race, the group with more low-intensity training showed significantly greater improvement (–157 seconds) than did the moderate intensity group (–121.5 seconds). Such data lend strong credence to the idea that as long as sufficient high-intensity work is present, the biggest performance benefits come from focusing on aerobic development at low intensities.

What does this mean to the amateur or masters rider with limited training time? The conclusion is that when you are trying to improve you must not only train very intensely but also do active recovery rides to guarantee sufficient recovery. If you train very intensely for two or three days in a row and then ride at a moderate or tempo pace, you won't truly recover and therefore won't be ready to give 100 percent in your next intense workout. Too often riders think that they are riding slowly enough to be in the active recovery, or level 1, training zone, but in reality they are in the upper reaches of the endurance, or level 2, training zone, which isn't recovery at all. Giving yourself a measurable ceiling, using heart rate or power, on these types of rides can be extremely beneficial. The adage that when good riders ride hard, they ride really hard, and when they ride slow, they ride really slow, seems to have its basis in scientific fact.

The following is a typical week of training for a low-intensity focus. Note that this is not a rest week, but a week of lower-intensity riding. A rest week would contain much less volume.

## Sample Low-Intensity Training Week

**Monday:** Easy ride or rest day.

If riding, ride for 1 hour maximum and keep heart rate lower than 68 percent of functional threshold heart rate (FTHR) or 55 percent of functional threshold power (FTP).

**Tuesday:** Endurance ride of 3 hours.

▶ Warm up for 20 minutes at 69 to 83 percent of FTHR or 56 to 75 percent of FTP to loosen the legs for a solid 3-hour ride.

▶ Focus on the middle hour as a solid and steady hour of riding with watts from 65 to 76 percent of FTP or 80 to 85 percent of FTHR. Go nice and steady, minimizing the bursts or hard efforts. If you have to go over hills and your watts go higher, that's fine, but do your best to stay in the endurance zone for the entire ride.

▶ Cool down for 15 to 20 minutes at 69 to 83 percent of FTHR or 56 to 75 percent of FTP.

**Wednesday:** Longer endurance ride of more than 5 hours.

▶ Warm up for 20 minutes at 69 to 83 percent of FTHR or 56 to 75 percent of FTP to loosen the legs for a solid 5-hour ride.

▶ Today's goal is just to get in the time and enjoy the ride. It's fine to ride at tempo pace today for an hour or so, but not much more. Focus on riding with watts from 65 to 76 percent of FTP or 80 to 85 percent of FTHR. Ride nice and steady and minimize the bursts or hard efforts during the ride. If you have to go over hills and your watts go higher, that's OK, but try to stay in the endurance zone for the entire ride

▶ Cool down for 15 to 20 minutes at 69 to 83 percent of FTHR or 56 to 75 percent of FTP.

**Thursday:** Endurance ride of 3 hours.

▶ Warm up for 20 minutes at 69 to 83 percent of FTHR or 56 to 75 percent of FTP to loosen the legs for a solid 3-hour ride.

*(continued)*

**Sample Low-Intensity Training Week** *(continued)*

▶ Focus on the middle hour as a solid and steady hour of riding with watts from 65 to 76 percent of FTP or 80 to 85 percent of FTHR. Ride nice and steady, minimizing the bursts or hard efforts. If you have to go over hills and your watts go higher, that's OK, but do your best to stay in the endurance zone for the entire ride.

▶ Cool down for 15 to 20 minutes at 69 to 83 percent of FTHR or 56 to 75 percent of FTP.

**Friday:** Easy ride or rest day.

If riding, ride for 1 hour maximum and keep heart rate lower than 68 percent of FTHR or 55 percent of FTP.

**Saturday:** Group ride.

Make sure to get in an extra hour or two after the group ride.

**Sunday:** Group ride or endurance ride.

Ride at 56 to 75 percent of your FTP or 69 to 83 percent of FTHR.

## A Measured Approach

Focusing solely on high-intensity efforts might be tempting in light of the studies demonstrating common physiological adaptations with this type of endurance training. Equally, given that elite athletes train predominantly at low intensities, one extrapolation is that the bulk of training for time-constrained athletes may be at low intensities, but moderate-intensity workouts could prove to be valuable as well. Overall, although high-volume or high-intensity training may be interchangeable in physiological responses, neither necessarily guarantees performance improvement. Faude et al. (2008) trained competitive swimmers over four weeks with either high-volume or high-intensity programs, followed by identical tapering periods. Both programs were sufficiently stressful to elicit a similar trend toward decreased vigor, but maximal 100-meter and 400-meter swim times were unchanged following both programs.

The ideal may be a moderate compromise that considers the following items:

● High-intensity training has a place in complementing and improving endurance training, during both base and competition phase training. Therefore, we should get away from the traditional mind-set that the two are exclusive and somehow harm each other.

- Quality is not exclusive to threshold or interval workouts, and it should not be defined by how hard or exhausted you feel at the end of the ride. At the upper levels of performance, quality and quantity are often the same.

- The use of short, high-intensity efforts is especially relevant for situations in which training volume is decreased suddenly and for a short time. For example, if work or school severely curtails training volume, you may consider focusing on maintaining the intensity of your workouts and sacrificing endurance rides.

- The research on high-intensity training supports the basic idea of tapering for a big race, in which the quality of the high-intensity training is maintained while the total training volume is reduced. Overall aerobic capacity should not be affected by this decrease in endurance work over the short term.

- The big caveat is that high-intensity work is not meant to replace endurance training over the long term. Cycling is an endurance-based sport, and endurance training remains the foundation for long-term improvement and progression. You must continue to get in those long rides one or two times a month to tax your muscular endurance and create a higher level of cumulative cardiovascular strain.

- One potential conclusion of research into training zone distribution is that most time-constrained athletes likely already perform as much high-intensity training as their lifestyle and recovery capacity permit. Therefore, when an opportunity arises for a period of increase in volume, the best approach may be to concentrate on increasing the amount of low-intensity effort to maximize aerobic development rather than increase the amount of high-intensity effort.

## Q&A  With Martin Gibala: High-Intensity Training

| Current position | Professor and chair, Department of Kinesiology, McMaster University. |
|---|---|
| Personal background with cycling | Competed in triathlon for approximately 10 years during and following university; now mainly a recreational cyclist, both on and off road. |
| Favorite ride (either one you've done or always wanted to do) | Nowadays any ride that involves my kids. |
| Favorite cycling-related experience | Watching a stage of the 2006 Giro d'Italia live from a seaside cafe overlooking the course in the town of Baveno, outside Milan. |

(continued)

**Marty, your work in the past few years seem to have brought about a revolution in training focused on high-intensity efforts. Can you tell us a little bit about the research?**

We have been studying physiological adaptations to brief repeated bouts of very intense exercise. The exercise model employed in our studies is the Wingate test, which involves 30 seconds of all-out maximal cycling against a high braking force on a specialized ergometer. Our standard protocol involves subjects repeating the Wingate test four to six times—separated by 4 minutes of recovery—for a total of only 2 to 3 minutes of very intense exercise per training session, with three training sessions performed each week for up to several weeks. The unique aspect of our work has been the very low training volume, equivalent to about 300 kilojoules of very intense exercise per week. One of the most remarkable findings from our studies has been the dramatic improvement in exercise performance during tasks that rely mainly on aerobic energy metabolism (including prolonged cycling time trials) despite the very low training volume. These studies have included needle biopsy samples to investigate potential mechanisms, and we have consistently found an increased muscle oxidative capacity (assessed using the maximal activity or protein content of specific mitochondrial enzymes) that is comparable to changes typically observed after prolonged endurance training. In one study (Gibala et al. 2006), we directly compared a group of subjects who performed our standard HIT protocol versus a group who performed six sessions of continuous cycling at 65 percent of $\dot{V}O_2$peak for 90 to 120 minutes per day. Total training time commitment over 2 weeks was approximately 2.5 and 10.5 hours for the sprint and endurance groups, respectively, and total exercise volume was approximately 90 percent lower for the HIT group. The two diverse training protocols induced remarkably similar adaptations in exercise performance and skeletal muscle oxidative capacity. Other work has shown improvements in cardiovascular parameters associated with oxygen transport capacity.

 **What would be your advice to cyclists looking to apply your research about high-intensity training—especially those who are busy professionals strapped for training time?**

High-intensity interval training is clearly a time efficient way to train. This type of training can induce numerous adaptations that we normally associate with traditional endurance training, despite a lower total training volume and reduced time commitment. Although most of our work has been conducted on recreational athletes, work from other laboratories has demonstrated that highly trained cyclists can also improve performance by incorporating high-intensity intervals into their normal training regimens. In terms of specific protocols, it appears from the limited literature available that a range of interval training strategies may be used successfully. For example, one study showed similar improvements in performance when different groups of cyclists incorporated various interval strategies into their normal base training. The most effective protocols were 12 intervals of 30 seconds at a very high intensity equivalent to 175 percent of $\dot{V}O_2$max pace with 4.5 minutes of recovery, or 8 intervals of 4 minutes at 85 percent of $\dot{V}O_2$max with 1.5 minutes of recovery between repeats.

 **What do you see as the proper mix between high-intensity training and aerobic training for cyclists? Does that mix differ throughout the year?**

This is a difficult question, but I would point to work from John Hawley showing that when highly trained cyclists replaced approximately 15 percent of their normal aerobic training with a series of high-intensity intervals (repeated 4-minute efforts at 85 percent of $\dot{V}O_2$max) over a period of several weeks, simulated race performance was improved. As for the proper mix, there is no precise formula based on science, but a ratio of 80 to 90 percent aerobic training to 10 to 20 percent HIT seems reasonable. Of course, these results are based on an accurate definition of the terms *high intensity* and *aerobic*. Many people do not appreciate that the majority of energy provision during repeated sprint efforts is derived from oxidative (i.e., aerobic) energy metabolism. This is true even during the most extreme sprint protocols. What many people consider anaerobic training is actually a very potent aerobic training stimulus.

 **The eternal question in the off-season seems to be whether any high-intensity efforts should be performed or whether the emphasis should be on building a big aerobic base and keeping efforts low to moderate. What's your take on this question?**

Generally speaking, I do believe that some occasional high-intensity efforts should be included with off-season training, if only to alleviate boredom and to serve as a periodic physiological reminder of the cardiovascular, neuromuscular, and metabolic adaptations that may be unique to this type of training. The time-efficient nature of HIT should also not be overlooked, even in the off-season. My bias is that HIT can facilitate, or contribute to, the building of a big aerobic base and that these terms should not be considered mutually exclusive. The infinite variety of HIT protocols also makes this type of training attractive, and it can serve as a welcome break from the monotony of traditional base training.

# Methods of Periodization

Many excellent books have been written on how to periodize your training. We recommend Joe Friel's book, *The Cyclist's Training Bible*, as a place to investigate this topic further (Friel 2009). Thanks to Friel, many of us are now familiar with the general concept of periodization based on macro-, meso-, and microcycles. Most of us implement this concept with a mesocycle of two to three weeks of hard training followed by a week of recovery and then repeat the general pattern with a higher volume or higher intensity or both. Although this overall system remains sound, advanced training ideas can be used within the various cycles. Therefore, we will explore two methods that you may wish to incorporate into your periodized training: targeted system training and block training, with alternating microperiods of hard training and rest.

## Targeted Systems Training

In the common periodization plan, a mesocycle revolves around the basic template of several weeks of hard training followed by a recovery week. A typical training week, often termed a microcycle in training and periodization literature, can consist of a variety of training workouts such as sprints, hill intervals, long endurance rides, and time trial simulations. Many of us periodize our annual programs in this way, and most weeks consist of variations of the same basic template (e.g., recovery Monday, sprints or training criterium Tuesday, intervals Wednesday, endurance ride Thursday, and so on). This approach is the equivalent of diversifying your investment portfolio so that you minimize risk, in this case loss of overall fitness or ability in one particular area of cycling. But if you're doing hill intervals only once a week, you may not be overloading your body sufficiently to maximize training stimulus in that system and subsequent adaptation. This path may be optimal if you are already a strong all-around rider or if you are mainly aiming to maintain your fitness. But like the investor going for a maximum return by investing heavily in one stock, you may want to overload on a particular energy system over one or several microcycles so that you can maximize your fitness gains within that system. The downside is that other aspects of your riding may suffer slightly, but you can target them in turn during another micro- or mesocycle, an approach that offers the potential for overall greater gains through the concept of targeted overload.

Therefore, within a periodized annual program, an advanced concept is to target and overload one particular aspect of cycling and then move on to another component. This kind of focused training has revolutionized pro cycling. Many Tour de France contenders are racing less and training more, in essence coming closer to the racing–training split of typical competitive amateurs. For example, the purpose of the mountain reconnaissance trips before Le Tour is not only to become familiar with the nuances of the climbs but also to put in intense work specifically on climbing. As another example, if you really want to target time trials, you might plan a week or two when, while mixing in other rides, you ditch the sprint work and focus on doing two or three high-quality time trial–specific workouts each week. The caution is that this approach requires careful planning to pull off without overtraining. You need to build up to this type of training, ensure adequate recovery, and carefully note how you are reacting to the intense workload. A sample plan for four months of targeted systems training might look like this:

## Sample Targeted Systems Training Plan

**January:** Endurance focus with average rides at least three or four hours in length and longer six-hour rides on weekends.

**February:** Muscular strength and tempo focus. Rides emphasize big gear intervals and riding at tempo pace (76 to 90 percent of FTP or 84 to 94 percent of FTHR).

**March:** Focus on threshold work by riding only at threshold power, just above or below, during intervals and the majority of rides.

**April:** $\dot{V}O_2$max hill climbing. The focus this month is on doing hills from three to eight minutes in length at your $\dot{V}O_2$max power (106 to 120 percent of FTP or greater than 105 percent of FTHR).

The beauty of this type of training is that you focus on a particular system each month or six weeks, so there isn't much guesswork involved in designing your workouts. If your goal is more long term, then this approach to your training is good because your fitness improves a bit more gradually. The downside is that the training can be monotonous day after day, and you must have faith that the overall plan will come together when you want it to.

## Block Training

This type of training is a more refined and systematic version of the targeted systems training discussed previously, and it takes place over an entire macrocycle or season. Block training disregards the traditional build and rest increments. Rather, cycles are structured around training until exhaustion is imminent, resting until completely recovered, and then repeating the cycle. The length of each cycle is highly variable depending on the athlete, time of year, and specific focus. Block training is popular with elite full-time athletes but can be difficult to implement for amateur or recreational athletes because it requires the athlete to be unconstrained by the typical five-day workweek. Depending on the cycle, your recovery days could come on the weekends, when the majority of us have the most time to train, and your high-volume days may come during the week, when training time may be scarce. But for those not constrained by the traditional workweek or for those who have flexible work schedules, the block method of training is definitely something to consider.

Block training focuses on one or two specific energy systems at a time and builds from the bottom up. The endurance system is worked on first, then subthreshold (sweet spot), threshold, $\dot{V}O_2$max anaerobic capacity, and finally neuromuscular power. Viewed holistically, block training is the true embodiment of building deep fitness from the ground up. Rather than trying to build every floor of a house at the same time, this paradigm builds fitness horizontally by laying a deep foundation of each fitness system, ensuring that each floor is completely set and strong before starting to build the next floor above.

How does block training play out? For example, the athlete who is focusing on threshold work may start the block on day 1 with a solid 3-hour ride and within this ride do the equivalent of 1 hour or more of riding at 100 percent of his threshold power or heart rate. The rest of the ride will probably consist of some tempo and endurance pace riding. Then on day 2, the athlete repeats this ride, as he does on days 3, 4, and so on until he can no longer effectively do intervals at threshold power. When the athlete can't even hold 90 percent of his threshold power for 20 minutes, it is time to rest. The recovery period, consisting of either active recovery rides or complete rest, continues until the athlete recovers completely and is ready for a new block of threshold training. The duration of the recovery period could be as short as 1 day or as long as 8 days depending on the athlete's fitness level and response to the training load. The key factor here is that the athlete must be able to come back and push at his desired intensity for at least 3 more days of hard training in the next threshold training block. If the athlete cannot complete at least 3 more hard days, he did not rest enough. Careful monitoring and self-knowledge becomes paramount here. At least three threshold blocks would take place before the athlete applies the same approach to the next system (e.g., $\dot{V}O_2max$ ).

When you first think about this method of training, it doesn't seem as if it would work as well as traditional periodization, but in reality it can be much better. By focusing on one system at a time and building upward from the aerobic system, you receive the greatest training benefits from each system rather than spreading out those efforts and stimuli. The key is to completely fatigue the system being trained, recover fully, and then hit that system again. Cyclists using block training have to work extremely hard and push themselves to the limit, so this system works well with highly motivated elite athletes. Nevertheless, it can work for all cyclists. They have to completely fatigue the system being trained and then recover fully so that they can do it again. In addition, they must carefully monitor their performance and fatigue levels to know when to stop a cycle and begin another one.

Another key component of block training is assuring that each system is well developed. Putting in at least three blocks per energy system before moving to the next higher intensity can take some planning. After all the systems in each block have been trained at least three times, the cyclist can make training blocks more versatile and combine different energy systems into one block. For example, day 1 might be a combination of neuromuscular power and anaerobic capacity hill repeats, followed by $\dot{V}O_2max$ intervals and sweet-spot work on day 2, threshold training on day 3, and finally a long five-hour endurance or tempo ride with some short neuromuscular bursts on day 5. Block training isn't for everyone, but it can be highly effective if you adhere closely to the rules.

## Quantifying Fatigue and Freshness

Professional cyclists often talk about form, fitness, and fatigue. These sensations are subjective, but mathematical modeling can help describe and even predict these peaks and troughs in performance. One way to do this is by modeling the overall training stress balance, which is a function of the acute, or recent, stress and the long-term training stress accumulated by the cyclist. The training stress balance is automatically calculated in TrainingPeaks WKO+ with their Performance Manager, but the theory underlying it can be useful regardless of whether you use power monitors or computerized software.

The first task is anchoring training stress to something that makes sense both mathematically and on the road. With Performance Manager, each ride is given a training stress score (TSS) that is based on threshold power (see chapter 3); a ride of 1 hour at functional threshold power scores 100 TSS points. All other rides, from easy recovery rides through long and hard interval workouts, are then normalized and given TSS points relative to this effort through a mathematical algorithm. Chronic training load (CTL) can be viewed as a weighted average TSS over the past 6 weeks or more of training, whereas acute training load (ATL) can be viewed as the weighted average TSS over the past 7 to 14 days. Training stress balance can then be calculated as the chronic training load minus the acute training load. Thus, a declining trend, or negative training stress balance, can indicate a cyclist who has done a very hard week of training and is starting to fatigue. In contrast, a rising trend, or positive training stress balance, can indicate an athlete who is resting and tapering, and who might be fresh for a race.

For example, if a rider's CTL is 95 TSS per day, that means she has averaged 95 TSS points over the last 42 days of training, or equivalent of nearly 1 hour per day at threshold power. If a rider's ATL is 133, that means she has averaged 133 TSS points over the last 7 days and in this case would probably be fatigued. The difference between fitness (CTL) and fatigue (ATL) is the training stress balance (TSB). When the difference is a positive number (e.g., 100 CTL – 90 ATL = 10 TSB), then the athlete is said to be fresh and could have a good performance on that day. When the TSB is a negative number (100 CTL – 133 ATL = –33 TSB), then the athlete is more fatigued. People respond differently to training. Some people recover more quickly than others do, recovering from training and competing in 4 days when others might need 6 days. Some can handle greater chronic training load. Tour de France athletes have values of over 140 TSS per day for much of the season, whereas others might struggle at a chronic training load of 80 TSS per day.

Using this model, it is relatively easy to overload a cyclist progressively and rationally without much risk of overtraining. Note that training stress balance is a relative number that, by itself, does not indicate fitness or predict performance.

© Human Kinetics

**Through periodization and tapering, you can maximize your fitness and freshness for a particular goal event.**

For example, if you just sat on the couch for a month, you would have an extremely high training stress balance and would be considered very fresh, but you would have low overall fitness because of the minimal chronic training load. Also, there is no ideal number that every cyclist should aim for before an important race. Some cyclists find that they perform best with a high positive score, whereas others have their peak performances when slightly fatigued with a negative training stress balance. Finally, you can achieve a particular training stress balance score by various routes (e.g., you can have a score of −10 both when you are in the midst of a heavy acute training load and when you are recovering from a heavy training load), so the overall trend is as important as the actual number. One final limitation of the training stress balance model is that it does not account for or track off-bike and life stress.

A case study from one of Hunter's clients, professional cyclist Aldo Ilesic, leading up to the Tour of California illustrates the benefits of managing your form. One of the toughest things about using technology in training, especially with professional athletes, is just getting the data, which involves everything from making sure that their power meters work on their bikes, to the mechanics of installing it on both the training and race bikes if you're lucky enough to have multiple bikes, to finding a decent Internet connection after every race. Fortunately, Aldo and his team are very interested in this data and work hard to capture it for each training session and race, so his charts are much more accurate and predictable. If you have holes in your data set, then your predictions will be poor at best, so be sure to capture as much data as possible. Learn to estimate your training stress score for each ride, too, so that you have an estimate even if your power meter goes on the fritz.

When you first look at figure 4.4 notice the stair-step pattern that the chronic training load forms leading up to the Tour of California in mid-May. This stair stepping is something that masters riders, amateur racers, and professionals all have to do to prepare their bodies for increasingly harder training loads. Taking the big picture view, we see that his CTL, one of the best indicators of overall fitness, increases through November, plateaus in December, and then climbs sharply through January and February when the racing season starts. When his early spring campaign is over at the end of February, he returns home for a recovery break. Note this critical period from February 8th to March 10th in figure 4.5 on page 90. In less than a month his CTL falls from a high point of 132 TSS per day to 96 TSS per day. This means that he has a positive TSB (is very fresh!) for nearly a month. Although this recovery period might seem excessive for a masters athlete doing high-intensity training, it is appropriate for a professional cyclist who will race more than 80 races in a season. These rest periods allow the body to recover, rebuild critical blood values, and prepare for the upcoming stress of the second half of the spring season.

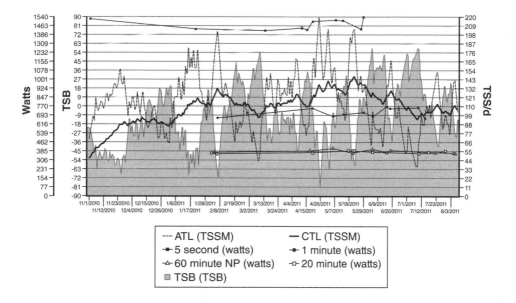

**FIGURE 4.4** The progressively harder training blocks over the course of Aldo's season form a stair-step pattern.

In figure 4.5 note that Aldo's buildup for the Tour of California (held in May) begins in earnest on March 10th. In this type of buildup the athlete should not exceed a growth rate of 8 TSS per day for CTL. A rate higher than that means that the athlete has increased intensity or volume too quickly, which could create a nonfunctional overtraining situation (see chapter 5).

Although many riders can handle this rate of increase for short periods, doing so is not desirable until closer to the event, when the athlete is prepared to handle it and is about to take a rest period. After this initial build period, a short rest is needed not because the athlete is overtired but more to make sure that he is well rested and prepared sufficiently for the final build, which will be intense and difficult. Notice that in this rest period starting on April 10th in figure 4.6, Aldo's training stress balance (TSB) becomes a significantly positive number (+34) after nearly a week of positive numbers, which indicates that he's well rested and should be able to train hard for the next three weeks beginning April 18th. During this time, he has to train harder than ever to prepare and adapt for the upcoming Tour of California. The first week, the third week of April, has a CTL growth rate of 15 TSS per day, followed by a short three-day rest period and then another CTL growth rate week of 15 TSS per day, followed by a four-day rest period. Block training allows him to train intensely until he can no longer continue. He then recovers just enough to begin another block on May 1st. He finishes his final preparation in the first week of May with a reduced week, and his CTL growth rate drops because he can't maintain that growth rate and is beginning the tapering process.

From the expanded view of the taper period in figure 4.7, it is clear that his taper was well planned because his TSB becomes positive. Another key aspect

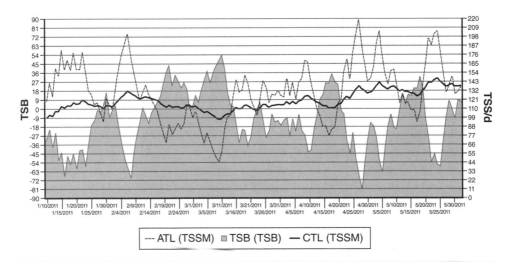

**FIGURE 4.5**  Aldo's periodized training blocks.

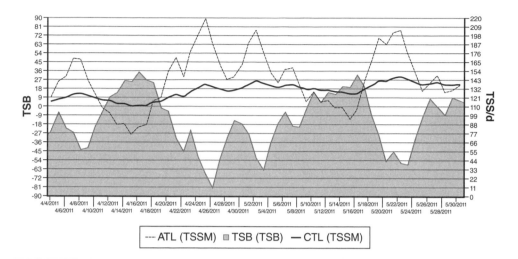

**FIGURE 4.6**  Aldo's final month building up to the Tour of California.

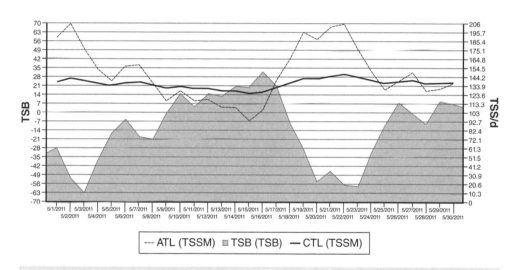

**FIGURE 4.7**  Aldo's final taper to build freshness for the Tour of California.

is making sure that he has just the right amount of freshness and can maintain it to create a peak performance. Before the Tour of California started on May 16, 2011, Aldo's taper from May 8 onwards allows him to become fresh a week before the event and maintain that freshness throughout the week. This length of time guarantees that he is well rested but still fit. If you rest too much, you lose fitness, and that's not the purpose of a taper!

The creation of form requires the proper balance of training stress and rest. That form is not always easy to create, but using an analytical approach to training can help you plan your training and resting more accurately.

Whatever you use for tracking your fitness and performance, the concepts underlying training stress balance can be a powerful tool for periodization in the hands of a well-versed athlete or coach. The key is to understand that your current fitness and form is a function of both your short-term and your long-term training loads. From that understanding, you can plan your training in a gradual and progressive manner to ensure that you are properly rested before your peak events.

# Tapering

You've trained smart and trained hard the whole year, and now your peak events are approaching. You want to hit the line in top form. You know that how you approach your physical training in these final weeks can either take you to the pinnacle of peak performance or send you falling off the precipice. This period is also mentally stressful, because your results in your peak events play a huge role in how you (or your sponsors if you're lucky enough to have them) perceive the season as a whole. You have the potential to exceed your expectations, but you also have the fear of falling flat on your face.

Preevent mental anxiety can drive athletes to destroy their carefully laid plans in favor of cramming in last-minute training. The typical result is suboptimal race-day performance. Periodization involves not just the foundation of training in the months leading up to prime time but also the intricate planning of the final week or so leading up to the event. The popular term for this phase of training is tapering, and it too has undergone a revolution in thought over the past decades.

A taper is a highly specialized training phase designed to promote an overall drop in training stress by decreasing the volume while maintaining intensity, initiated an appropriate number of days before the event. Tapering allows the body sufficient resources to recover and adapt by temporarily sacrificing aerobic capacity while maintaining anaerobic capacity. The duration of the taper and the type of intensity work during the taper vary depending on the event. So a taper for a period of track racing would differ from that for a time trial or hilly road race, and these would differ from the taper for a multiday or weeklong stage race. But these tapers would differ most significantly in the nature of the breakthrough workouts, and the remainder of the time would be devoted to low-intensity recovery efforts.

Traditionally, tapering was performed by keeping the same general weekly training plan but dropping volume and especially intensity drastically. Often, intensity would be almost completely removed from the equation during the taper. The underlying belief was that the whole point was to minimize overall training stress and thereby maximize recovery. This idea sounds fine in theory, but in practice it often led to more rest than desired, such that physical conditioning, and especially race conditioning, was lower at event time than it was at the start of the taper.

The reason for tapering is in large part physiological, in that you are aiming to give your body as much rest as possible and to conserve as much energy as possible before the big event (Mujika et al. 2004). When balancing training stress versus recovery, tapering tilts the balance by decreasing stress and maximizing recovery, thus allowing physiological adaptation. This is the general concept behind overreaching and the traditional rest week of a mesocycle, but it is taken to an extreme with tapering.

Research into optimizing tapering is fraught with difficulties (Pyne et al. 2009). First is the difficulty of recruiting appropriate subjects. Ideally, studies would use competitive athletes who are training for a major event, but these are typically the last subjects willing to sign up for studies that may mess up their training and peak event. Second, individual variability is huge in terms of response to a training load or a tapering program. Finally, the optimal tapering strategy may depend not only on the competition but also on the pattern of training in the weeks before initiating the taper (Thomas et al. 2008).

Because of the general lack of well-controlled experimental studies on tapering, the underlying physiological mechanisms behind the general improvement in performance are unclear (Houmard 2009). Similarly, any changes in physiological responses to tapering can be dramatically influenced by the amount of prior training and ultimately the state of overreaching before initiating tapering (Thomas et al. 2008). For example, $\dot{V}O_2$max may or may not change with tapering, and the correlation between changes in $\dot{V}O_2$max and performance is not solid. The same is true of many other physiological markers, including hormonal status, aerobic enzymes, muscle glycogen levels, and blood lactate response to exercise (Mujika et al. 2004).

Recently, the preferred approach to maximizing recovery while keeping the engine tuned to race pace has been to cut more from the volume portion of the program and less (or none) from the intensity of training. In other words, you should not completely remove intervals from your training or do intervals of less intensity. Instead, decrease the endurance rides and consider spending the extra free time tackling the mental aspects of tapering. Trinity et al. (2008) tracked college varsity swimmers who used a low-intensity taper one season and a tapering regimen with 50 to 60 percent more high-intensity work the following season. The high-intensity taper resulted in 8 to 14 percent higher maximal mechanical power than the low-intensity taper and permitted the maintenance of power and swim performance for a longer period (figure 4.8 on page 94). Tapering can also be quite prolonged, again depending on the prior intensity of training. For example, the mechanical power and swim performance of collegiate swimmers who were tapering for national championships demonstrated a biphasic pattern of a large initial improvement in the first week, minimal change over the second week, and a further large improvement in the third week (Trinity et al. 2006).

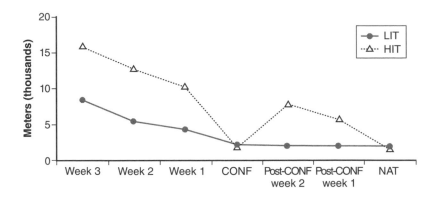

**FIGURE 4.8** **The amount of high intensity training during a low versus high intensity taper.**

Reprinted from J.D. Trinity, M.D. Pahnke, J.A. Sterkel, and E.F. Coyle, 2008, "Maximal power and performance during a swim taper," *International Journal of Sports Medicine* 29(6): 500-506, by permission from Georg Thieme Verlag.

Although the consensus is that maintaining intensity during the taper is important, the optimal timing and frequency of these higher-intensity efforts are unknown, or at least cannot be applied to everyone in every situation. So there's no generic blueprint that says that everyone must do some hard efforts on Tuesday and Thursday leading up to a Sunday race. Recording, analyzing, and correlating your training and event data in a software package like TrainingPeaks WKO+ or another comprehensive system can help you determine just how much rest or taper you need for a peak performance.

Further, the definition of tapering may need to be expanded beyond the current interpretation of continually maintaining a reduced training load all the way through the lead-up to the competition. Although not proven in human studies, mathematical models suggest that an initial taper followed by a second phase of a return to a near normal (50 to 80 percent) training load two to three days immediately before the event may initiate further adaptation and prime the body for performance on race day without adding significantly to fatigue (Thomas et al. 2009).

The length of the event plays a role in determining tapering strategy. For a longer event like a road race or long stage race, fitness is paramount over freshness, so a rider can risk being a little less fresh entering those events because fitness will win the day. No one ever won the Tour de France after resting on the couch for two months beforehand! For a shorter event like a flying 200 meter or pursuit on the track, a BMX race, or even a short time trial, freshness can win the day. Shorter events require more anaerobic capacity, and anaerobic capacity is filled to the brim with more rest. If you are preparing for a 2-minute hill climb time trial, after you have the fitness, a full week or 10 days of rest and easy riding to top off the anaerobic tank will likely be the best training.

A recent study surveyed tapering literature to draw some general conclusions (Bosquet et al. 2007). The methodology of this study was a meta-analysis, in which all available data from previous studies was pooled together and statistically analyzed. Among the questions explored were the effects of decreases in training intensity, volume, or frequency, along with the pattern and duration of the tapers. The major findings supported the current prevailing wisdom that the optimal tapering involves a reduction in training volume without any modification to the intensity or frequency of training. Specifically, optimal tapering seems to be achieved with a 41 to 60 percent reduction in overall volume. So if you're used to a 10-hour training week with 5 days of riding and 2 days of breakthrough workouts, the volume might drop to 1-hour rides, but you should generally still do five of them, and two of them should remain condensed interval or sprint workouts. Furthermore, the drop in volume does not need to be immediate; it can be a gradual drop over the first few days. In addition, the ideal tapering duration seems to be at least 2 weeks. This timeline is somewhat longer than the 1 week that many of us allot for a taper or recovery segment in the typical 4-week cycle of training. This finding highlights that a taper is a specific program, not just an extended recovery phase.

## Tapering Pitfalls

Although the physiological aspect of tapering is important, we should recognize that a mental aspect is equally important. Even if your key event is the Tour de Nowheresville, do not underestimate the self-imposed pressure that you consciously or subconsciously place on yourself. With the added stress and expense of travel that the key event may involve, not to mention the overtime at work and home to get ready to travel, trying to maintain a "normal" training routine is simply mental suicide.

You can mentally and physically mess up many weeks of work by not tapering correctly. Among the ways to spoil your preparation are the following:

▶ Not reducing overall training volume. Many of us measure success or enjoyment of cycling by the number of kilometers ridden, and the big drop in volume can lead us to sabotage our taper by adding unnecessary volume.

▶ Not practicing the taper (including nutrition, equipment, race tactics, and everything else under the sun) before less important events.

▶ Obsessing too much about the big event. Although thinking and planning for the event helps you to focus your mind on the task, you can easily become too fixated on the event, putting pressure on yourself that you may not want or be able to handle. Get away from the bike!

# Applying the Science

Most amateur cyclists have only 8 to 12 hours per week to devote to their training because they have to juggle work, family, kids, and other demands. Persuading recreational athletes with such time constraints not to hammer on every single ride can be difficult. Because they deem every minute valuable, these athletes feel almost guilty if they ride easy. But with advances in technology such as power meters, we have become more efficient with our training time. Quantity of training has been supplanted by the quality or specificity of training as the determinant of success.

To train optimally, cyclists must be able to distinguish a fun ride from a training ride. We believe that cyclists have to include both kinds of rides. If you do intervals all the time, this sport that we love becomes too hard and the fun factor disappears. One of the benefits of the advances in technology is that by using the data collected and analyzed from power meter software, you can maintain fitness and then take that base fitness level to a higher fitness level when you want. This is what periodization is all about: creating the fitness peak exactly when you want to ride the best!

## CHAPTER 5

# Preventing Overtraining and Enhancing Recovery

The human system is amazing in being able to adapt to the stresses imposed on it, and nowhere is this adaptation more profound than in response to the stress of exercise. Even a sedentary person who is overweight can become a fit athlete in a relatively rapid fashion through a carefully planned training program. Body composition changes through a reduction of adipose tissue and an increase of lean muscle, the muscles themselves become more adapted to exercise, and motor coordination eventually makes previously impossible movements subconscious and automatic. With continued training over a season or a number of years, the body becomes more refined and better adapted for exercise, getting stronger and faster.

But there is a limit to the adaptive potential of the body. When the stress imposed on any structure is too high, it will ultimately break down. In some cases, such as with a broken bone, the body may eventually heal itself and become even stronger at the point of breakage. Too much stress, however, can also cause catastrophic and irreparable damage. We see this when a wheel or frame buckles in a crash. In the case of the body, excessive stress can cause a multitude of physiological changes, such as prolonged changes in immune function, which can take months or even years to fully recover. In parallel, stress can also cause psychological burnout, turning a keen and motivated cyclist into an apathetic one who quits the sport. Cyclists who want to maximize and optimize their improvement in the sport are constantly riding the knife's edge, trying to push the body hard, but not too hard. When they cross this critical threshold, further training can become a negative force, leading to a period of underperformance that can take weeks or years to overcome.

The challenge of understanding and preventing overtraining results from the insidious nature of its onset. Unlike a physical injury such as a broken bone or a mechanical mishap like a broken wheel, overtraining rarely exhibits a clear threshold point. Rather, overtraining in cyclists is more akin to a slowly leaking tire. Unless carefully monitored, overtraining can become a slippery slope. The typical highly motivated cyclist perceives a decrease in performance as resulting from a lack of training rather than a lack of recovery. In response, the cyclist trains even harder to compensate, setting off a negative spiral of harder training, which prompts even more overtraining.

This overtraining syndrome (OTS) is a multidimensional disease that includes many contributing factors beyond a simple overload of training. In parallel, recovering from OTS requires a holistic approach that addresses these factors. This chapter surveys some of the possible factors underlying overtraining and examines potential diagnostic tools. We also examine the scientific evidence behind popular options for enhancing recovery from heavy exercise and training.

# Recognizing Overtraining

Because overtraining affects the physical responses to training and adaptation, the body must also contend with a wide array of psychosocial stressors, from sports-related (team dynamics, coaches) and environmental (frequent travel, altitude) challenges to personal (relationship, work, financial) issues. Given the multitude of potential contributing factors beyond the quantification of training load, isolating the direct cause of overtraining can be difficult. The primary determinant is likely different for each cyclist. For example, a masters cyclist who juggles training time with a demanding job and a young family may overtrain from an inability to manage these multiple responsibilities. Alternately, a keen junior cyclist just starting in the sport may overtrain from trying to ride too much too soon or may develop overuse injuries from riding overlarge gears. Therefore, the social context of the cyclist must be carefully considered in managing overtraining. In addition, underlying medical issues may predispose (e.g., history of depression) or directly contribute (e.g., injury) to the onset of OTS.

## Stages of Overtraining

The principle of overload is fundamental to the process of improving fitness (McNicol et al. 2009). A period of stress followed by recovery results in a "supercompensation" in which the body adapts to the imposed stress and becomes stronger, thus improving performance. The human body is highly adaptable to the stresses imposed on it as long as the stress is not excessive.

The European College of Sport Science, in its 2006 position stand (Meeusen et al. 2006), presented overtraining as a continuum from the desired "normal" and functional overload and functional overreaching (FOR), through to nonfunctional overreaching (NFOR), and ultimately to overtraining syndrome (OTS) and burnout. Although this representation is possibly an oversimplification—debate continues about whether the process of overtraining is a continuum or a series of distinct and independent phases—having standardized definitions as a basis of discussion is helpful (these are outlined in more detail in the interview with Dr. Romain Meeusen on page 110).

- **Training.** A process of overload that is used to disturb the body's normal state of fitness, which results in acute fatigue (one to two days at most), adaptation by the body, and ultimately an improvement in performance. This level of training is what we do most of the time, such as a few hard interval sessions followed by a day or two of easier rides over the course of a week, or two to three weeks of progressive overload followed by a recovery week of reduced training to permit the body to adapt to the stress.

- **Overtraining.** Within this paradigm, overtraining is used to describe a period in which greater than normal training stress is imposed. An example may be suddenly spending two weeks doing more and harder intervals than you have been used to doing or spending a week at an intense climbing camp in the mountains, where you put in long hours and do lots of hard climbing. As explained in the three definitions that follow, overtraining can be a normal and positive process of overload and supercompensation (see functional overreaching), or it can become a negative stimulus that is more than the cyclist can handle (see nonfunctional overreaching and overtraining syndrome).

- **Functional overreaching (FOR).** A process in which overtraining, possibly followed by a temporary drop-off in performance lasting days to at most several weeks, results in the body adapting by becoming stronger and thus being able to produce performances that exceed the previous baseline. A critical component of FOR is a period of adequate recovery following the period of overtraining. An example may be a cyclist who spends a week at a climbing camp in the mountains, recovers at home with an easy week, and then settles back into a more normal training program during which he sees his overall riding level improve.

- **Nonfunctional overreaching (NFOR).** An extreme level of overtraining, often associated with inadequate recovery, in which the drop-off in performance after a period of overload is prolonged and performance stagnates or remains at baseline or lower for weeks or even months. Besides causing physiological changes, this state is often accompanied by psychological disturbances such as irritability, increased fatigue, and decreased vigor. Hormonal disturbances also are more likely within this phase. For example, NFOR might occur if the cyclist returned from a week at the climbing camp and then, without taking a recovery period, continued to push his body by doing a few additional weeks of hard training, thinking that by doing so he could take advantage of his newfound fitness and motivation to reap even greater benefits. With sufficient rest, cyclists in NFOR typically recover over a period of several months.

- **Overtraining syndrome (OTS).** An extreme level of overtraining, in which performance becomes impaired for many months to years. A host of psychological and physiological impairments can be present, and cyclists who reach this level often burn out completely and quit the sport. In general, rarely does physical stress alone bring about a state of OTS. Rather, the use of the term *syndrome* is intentional in recognition of the numerous factors that may contribute to its onset. For example, to achieve a state of OTS, the cyclist from the NFOR example described in the previous paragraph would likely have had one or more prior instances of NFOR in addition to a period of increased stress in his home, work, or team life or a physical issue such as an overuse injury or weakened immune system. Think of OTS as the perfect storm of overtraining that you never want to come near!

Although power monitors make direct quantification of training load possible, no hard and fast equation can state that a certain amount of work defines normal training, FOR, NFOR, or OTS. First, all cyclists differ in their ability to respond to a particular workload. Two cyclists riding an identical workout will respond differently based on their number of years in the sport, their particular phase of periodized training, and even their training for the previous day or week. Just as it is pointless to expect your body composition, weight, and resting heart rate to match someone else's, it is equally senseless to expect your potential for overtraining to be similar to another's. Therefore, an individual approach must be applied to training and addressing the possibility of OTS. Even when looking at a single cyclist, predicting the effect of a particular workload can be difficult because the nature of a periodized training plan generally means a wide fluctuation in workload throughout the year, making it hard to establish a baseline for workload or performance.

## Diagnosing Nonfunctional Overreaching and Overtraining Syndrome

At the most simple and applied level, NFOR and OTS can be defined as a prolonged decrease in sport-specific exercise performance in an athlete. But even this seemingly clear-cut definition can prove frustratingly vague in practice. A cyclist, coach, sport science support team, or doctor might need to address questions such as the following:

- How can a decrease in sport-specific performance be objectively quantified?
- How long must impaired performance continue before NFOR or OTS becomes the official diagnosis?
- What is the baseline level of performance, not only for performance measures such as maximal wattage on an incremental test but also for physiological, hormonal, and immunological responses?

Currently, no clear criteria or tests exist for directly quantifying or diagnosing the various stages of overtraining. Rather, diagnosis of nonfunctional overtraining revolves around excluding other sources of underperformance (Meeusen et al. 2006). Taking a page from Sherlock Holmes, after all other possibilities are eliminated, the remaining explanation (overtraining), no matter how improbable, must be the truth. When a sustained performance drop occurs, all areas of the athlete's life should be evaluated. Table 5.1 presents a checklist of risk factors that can contribute to NFOR or OTS.

Analyses of overtraining tend to be retrospective rather than prospective or predictive, in that the possibility of NFOR or OTS is often realized only after a prolonged period of underperformance rather than calculated in advance. Given that this approach is equivalent to closing the barn door only after the horse has bolted, the utility of such analyses in a day-to-day training design is limited. Thus, the ultimate goal in overtraining research is to develop a prospective tool that can either predict the onset of NFOR and OTS or calculate its probability with a

### TABLE 5.1    Risk Factors for NFOR and OTS

| Type of stress | Risk factors |
| --- | --- |
| Work and home life stress | Sleeping pattern changes<br>Major changes at home<br>Increased work responsibilities or travel |
| Underlying medical issues | Seasonal allergies<br>Illness<br>Crashes or injuries<br>Medical conditions or predispositions<br>Inadequate or improper nutrition |
| Extreme or unusual training stress | Excessive expectations compared with realistic progression<br>Sudden jump in intensity, duration, or both<br>Lack of, or inadequate, recovery in program<br>Monotonous training routine<br>Too much high-intensity effort |

high degree of accuracy. At the very least, athletes, trainers, and coaches need a way to measure training status and to recognize when athletes may be sliding into nonfunctionality so that they can adjust their training accordingly before they progress to a full-blown state of overtraining.

One highly effective tool, the Performance Manager within TrainingPeaks (introduced in chapter 4 as a means of monitoring block training on page 87), has been developed based on power meter data. The beauty of power meter data is that by recording every workout, you record not only your cumulative training stress but also your personal bests as they occur. Understanding the relationship between your personal best power outputs at various time periods and how fresh or fatigued you are when they occur is key to understanding just how much training load you can handle. The Performance Manager is part of the TrainingPeaks WKO+ software developed by Hunter and Dr. Andrew R. Coggan. With the advent of power meters and the ability to record nearly every pedal stroke of work done by the cyclist, we can now more accurately quantify the training stress that each athlete can handle.

Let's look at a few examples of FOR, NFOR, and OTS so that you can better grasp these concepts. As a coach, Hunter has helped hundreds of athletes monitor their training status so that they can continue to improve and recognize when they need a break.

## *Example of Functional Overreaching*

For most of us, FOR is something that we are continually striving to achieve. But attaining this goal can be challenging because it requires a certain amount of hard work, which means combining frequency and intensity to create conditions to achieve FOR. Most cyclists are able to ride at sufficient intensity, which is really just a matter of pushing themselves hard in group rides, during interval days, and at races. The more difficult side is the frequency. Life, work, family, and all the outside stresses sometimes conspire to prevent us from training three to five days in a row, which could be needed to achieve FOR. The other thing that prevents us is our own perception or beliefs about FOR. Athletes, especially newer ones, often think that they are tired (and they probably are a little bit), but they haven't dug deep enough to reach true FOR. Here a coach can make a difference in assuring the athlete that it's OK to train when tired.

The following is a typical week of training in a program designed for a masters athlete to achieve FOR. Remember that this sample week won't create FOR for everyone, and a little less training may create it for some (especially athletes over 60). Nevertheless, this is a good general week of training for a typical masters athlete who has 10 to 12 hours a week to train, and it should provide enough training stress to create adaptation. In this example, our sample athlete, Bob, is focused on improving his functional threshold power (FTP) and his anaerobic capacity.

## Sample Week of Training for FOR

**Monday.** This is typically a rest day or a very easy day of training for one hour. Critical here is that if you do decide to ride, you should do a ride that is embarrassingly slow.

**Tuesday.** This is your most important workout of the week because you should be rested (if you are not, you can do the big workout on Wednesday and ride easy again today). For Bob, this workout is five intervals of 10 minutes at 100 to 105 percent of his FTP, and he rests for 5 to 10 minutes after each. Bob will complete a sixth interval if his fifth one has an average wattage within 10 percent of his third one, which would mean that he's still training with enough intensity to stress his lactate system. To challenge his neuromuscular system, Bob will finish the workout with five to eight hill sprints on the way home.

**Wednesday.** This workout, an anaerobic one, is the second most important workout for the week. In general, you want to do this workout before the threshold workout, but because it's a lower priority to Bob in terms of benefit, he places it on the second day of the plan. Bob is going to do six intervals of 2 minutes, six intervals of 1 minute, and six intervals of 30 seconds. He'll rest 2 minutes after each one. He'll do them on a slight uphill to ensure that he can create enough force to challenge his anaerobic system. Most athletes won't ever think of doing 18 intervals, much less doing them with short rest periods, but if you are in a race, just the terrain of the course might force you to do 18 intervals. Again, Bob will do some extra 30-second efforts if he has time and feels strong in the end. This breakthrough workout forces athletes to expand their beliefs about what is possible.

**Thursday.** If Bob has done the first 2 days correctly, he'll be tired today on the bike, which is perfect. He'll still be able to do some sweet-spot (88 to 93 percent of FTP) intervals, but it could be hard for him to reach a consistently higher intensity. He'll do three efforts of 20 minutes at the sweet spot, taking 5 minutes of rest after each. He'll then do five to eight hard hill sprints (or 20- to 30-second sprints) to exhaust himself completely.

**Friday.** This needs to be a rest day or a very easy day similar to Monday to create just a touch of freshness for a hard weekend of training.

**Saturday.** This workout needs to be a tough one—intense, long, and tiring. Bob should come back from the ride in a highly fatigued state and glad to be home. A group ride can be part of this ride as long as Bob also gets in some riding before and after. After the group ride, Bob should try to do as much riding as possible at his sweet spot. If he doesn't have a group ride available, then a kitchen-sink workout is perfect for today. A kitchen-sink workout has all the physiological zones in it—20-minute threshold intervals, 1-minute hard anaerobic efforts, some sprints, and some endurance and tempo work. Following is a typical kitchen-sink workout.

*(continued)*

## Sample Week of Training for FOR *(continued)*

▸ Warm-up: 15 minutes.

▸ Main set: Do three efforts of 1 minute of fast pedaling. Then do four sprints on the big ring (53 x 15) at about 22 miles per hour (35 kilometers per hour). Do a gear shift to 14 and then another to 13. Rest for 3 or 4 minutes after each.

▸ Then do four intervals of 12 minutes just above threshold (105 percent). Do your best to hold it there!

▸ Rest for 5 minutes after each.

▸ Then ride at endurance pace for 45 minutes but slow down every 5 minutes and do a big-gear burst from a near standstill. Stay seated and push that gear over until you reach 80 revolutions per minute. Then you are done and can return to endurance pace.

▸ Do six efforts of 2 minutes on the flats—2 minutes on and 1 minute off. Make sure that your watts are over 120 percent of your FTP on each effort.

▸ Pedal easy after each effort.

▸ Finish with 45 minutes at your sweet spot (SS), which is 88 to 93 percent of FTP. Do a burst every 3 minutes to watts of 200 percent, hold for 10 seconds, and return to your SS.

▸ Ride at endurance pace for 20 minutes.

▸ Cool down for 5 minutes.

**Sunday.** This is an endurance day because if Bob did his workouts correctly this week, he'll be exhibiting symptoms of FOR and all he'll be able to do is ride at a steady endurance pace for 3 or 4 hours. If he's still feeling strong, he could connect with a group ride, which will help to push him a little more.

This sample week might not seem much different from what you are currently doing, but the difference is likely in the volume of intervals and doing workouts on back-to-back days. If the workouts are done correctly, Bob will be sufficiently tired on Monday in a nice state of FOR. He'll rest on Monday, Tuesday, and Wednesday with easy rides and then resume training on Thursday through Sunday to create another bout of FOR.

### *Example of Nonfunctional Overreaching*

As discussed earlier, NFOR is hard to diagnose but not hard to create. NFOR comes about after a long time of hard training with FOR. If Bob did the previous two-week plan for six weeks in a row without taking a proper rest week, he could be in a NFOR state. Possibly, he could reach NFOR in only four weeks. As a coach, what Hunter looks for in athletes is not necessarily verbal complaints of fatigue (though as seen in chapter 3, those are helpful!) but other key symptoms of NFOR that help to confirm this negative state of training.

Most cyclists complain of a lack of sleep or poor sleep, or a feeling of injury, not just tiredness. Some of the signs that a cycling coach looks for are a rider that says she has been dropped by riders who normally would not drop her, a rider that gets muscle cramps on a ride that she has never gotten them on before, and a rider that complains that she just feels as if she doesn't have any power or strength in her legs. This feeling that the leg muscles are not strong anymore (even though that isn't the correct scientific term for what the rider is feeling) is a key confirming indicator the cyclist is truly in NFOR. The only way to respond to NFOR is to plan at least several weeks of rest, check the training diary and data in detail, and check in with a physician for possible blood tests.

## Preventing NFOR and OTS Using Performance Manager

The power meter can be a critical tool in helping to prevent overtraining because it quantifies the amount of effort expended. When used in combination with the latest software tools, the information on those recorded rides forms an important data set you can use to track performance trends. Let's look at an example that illustrates how Performance Manager modeling can help cyclists prevent overtraining and maximize training benefits (figure 5.1). Eric has been a masters rider for

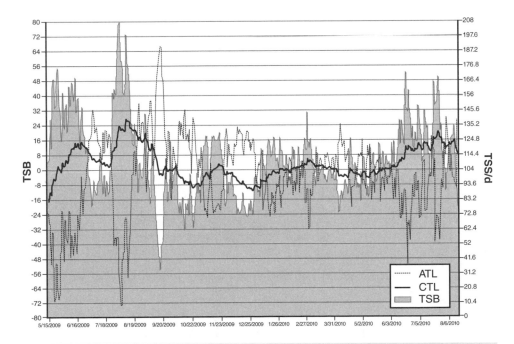

**FIGURE 5.1** Performance Manager chart for an athlete who adjusted his training after a period of nonfunctional overreaching.

*(continued)*

about 5 years now, weighs 155 pounds (70 kilograms), has a functional threshold power of 300 watts, and is a solid all-arounder. He is a typical masters rider trying to balance family, work, and cycling, so he has between 8 and 12 hours a week to train most weeks and can occasionally fit in a 15-hour week of training. In figure 5.1, the darker line on the left side of the chart shows how quickly he ramped up his chronic training load. This occurred during a hard 10-day-long training camp, and he wasn't ready for that increase in training load in such a short time. A rapid increase in training stress is a surefire way to bring on nonfunctional overreaching and then potentially overtraining. Right after this increase on August 15th, notice how the chronic training load drops from 135 to 104 and then down to 90 on October 20th so that he can recover. He can maintain a chronic training load of only 90 to 100 for the next 6 months, at which point he is finally able to rebuild it at a more gradual, rational, and sustainable rate. On the right side of the graph you can see that he is currently increasing his chronic training load at a more sane and rational growth rate of about 4 to 5 TSS per day each week and is reaching the same high value as he had during the period immediately following the camp. But now he is working at a maintainable training load. Overall, because Eric was monitoring his power printouts, he was able recognize that he had reached a nonfunctional level of training and needed to allow his body to recover before crossing over into NFOR.

### Example of Overtraining Syndrome

OTS is a syndrome that can occur in both the best professionals in the world and the average weekend warriors. Although it's more likely to occur in elite athletes, all of us must learn to recognize when it's occurring and take the appropriate actions.

In this example, the overall syndrome started nearly a year and a half before the OTS actually affected the athlete negatively. This athlete was determined to break through at the professional level (he was already a pro but had not had any significant results), and he began with an intense winter of training during which he rode on the indoor trainer for more time than normal, did some weight training, and cut his caloric intake to reduce his overall body fat and weight. He was successful in improving his sprint power, raising his threshold power, and reducing his weight and body fat, ultimately coming into the season fitter than ever. He started winning right away against professionals whom he had never beaten before. He continued his winning ways all the way through the spring season, winning eight pro races and leading a prestigious series. He continued training hard into the summer and racing hard as well, even winning some races that did not suit his natural abilities and strengths. He led this series into the fall and clinched the title as overall winner, but he was clearly riding on fumes at this point. He had been complaining of fatigue and exhibiting all the symptoms of NFOR for nearly two months, but he wanted to keep going to clinch the overall series title. This effort was the final nail in the coffin for him, and it sent him into a full-blown case of OTS. Right after the final race, he became ill. He was sick for nearly two weeks and didn't feel well for two additional weeks afterward. Unfortunately, this trend continued well into the following season. Ultimately, he wasn't able to race or train more than two hours a day for an entire year afterward.

In figure 5.2 we see his Performance Manager Chart. The solid line represents his chronic training load (CTL), and we see that his CTL increased to nearly twice the load of his previous year within a three-month period. His CTL then stayed high for the entire year without ever coming down for more than a four-day stretch (which would indicate a rest period), and it even increased toward the end of the season. The dashed line represents his acute training load (ATL), or his short-term fatigue, and it's apparent that he was fatigued much of the season despite having some short rest periods between races. The shaded curve represents his training stress balance (TSB). A negative number signifies a period of decreased ability to perform. Notice that the TSB line is consistently negative for nearly six months. When it is positive, it's positive for less than two weeks.

The most important thing to recognize in this Performance Manager Chart is the lack of significant rest for nearly 10 months of a hard training and racing season. Although to most of us resting might seem like an obvious thing to do,

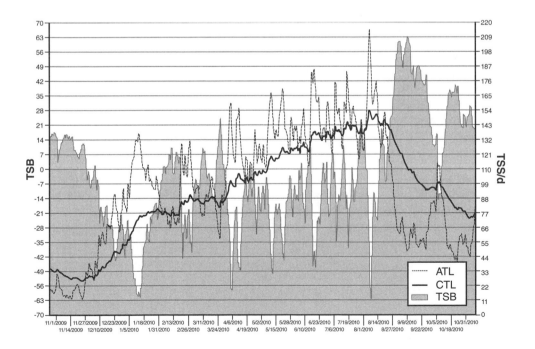

**FIGURE 5.2** Performance Manager chart for a cyclist in OTS.

professional cyclists find it hard to incorporate resting when they feel the pressures of having to perform well. As discussed earlier in this chapter, many factors relating to the entire physiological system can contribute to creating OTS, and it's not easy to identify the key thing until it's too late. Using tools like power meters and special charts and graphs can help you to identify some of these critical points and prevent NFOR and OTS. But the biggest lesson to take from this is that having a power monitor and recording the data by itself is not enough. As Dr. Martin's interview on page 59 highlighted, nobody wins because they're the best data logger! On the other hand, careful ongoing *analysis* of the data, along with honest assessment of goals and communication, may have helped to prevent this situation. For more information on the theory and general use of Performance Manager, see Quantifying Fatigue and Freshness on page 87.

## Testing for NFOR and OTS

Because the most relevant symptom of NFOR and OTS remains a reduced sport-specific performance, one diagnostic tool is a standardized test on a cycle ergometer. If standardized tests are done on a regular basis, the test responses can allow valuable longitudinal tracking of overall performance and progress. In addition, because one of the hallmarks of NFOR and OTS is difficulty in recovering and performing multiple efforts, the use of a two-bout exercise protocol has been advocated (Meeusen et al. 2010). In this protocol, two incremental maximal exercise tests (30-watt increase every three minutes) are performed four to five hours apart. The use of this protocol permits objective quantification of both performance (e.g. maximal wattage) and physiological responses, including heart rate, blood lactate, and stress markers in the blood such as cortisol and adrenocorticotrophic hormone (ACTH). A cyclist in the NFOR or OTS state will generally have both a lower initial maximal wattage than when in a normal baseline state and a much higher drop-off in maximal wattage between the first and second test. Blood lactate and maximal heart rates are also typically lower than during baseline testing. Finally, stress markers in the blood appear to spike in the second test when a cyclist is in NFOR or OTS, reflecting a lack of recovery (Nederhof et al. 2008). Even without access to blood analysis, such a protocol can provide firm quantification of performance throughout the season, and it can be performed with only an indoor trainer and a power monitor.

One caveat is that a standardized test of this type, done in the lab or at home, is a high source of training stress, so doing this test frequently (more than monthly) to test for NFOR or OTS is not advisable if these diagnoses are already suspected or if the cyclist is in the recovery phase. Another consideration is that performance will naturally decrease with prolonged rest because of the normal process of deconditioning. Table 5.2 outlines other supplemental tests and data that may help in diagnosing NFOR and OTS.

**TABLE 5.2**     Supplemental Methods of Monitoring Nonfunctional Overreaching and Overtraining

| Method | Rationale | Notes |
|---|---|---|
| Resting heart rate, heart rate variability, heart rate response to submaximal and maximal exercise | Theorized that high stress levels result in a rise in resting HR along with an altered HR response to exercise. | Survey of existing literature suggests that the amplitude of such changes is small and may fall within normal day-to-day variability. Therefore, HR measures cannot be used as a single indicator of overtraining (Bosquet et al. 2008). |
| Heart rate recovery from maximal or submaximal exercise | Theorized that a faster decrease in heart rate following exercise indicates better fitness and recovery level. | The reliability of heart rate recovery from either maximal or submaximal treadmill exercise has proved to be low, making reliance on it as a diagnostic indicator of recovery problematic (Bosquet et al. 2008). |
| Blood lactate response to maximal exercise | Cyclists in a state of overtraining typically exhibit lower peak lactate levels (Bosquet et al. 2008). | Can be problematic to interpret because both improved fitness and OTS can result in a similar rightward shift in the lactate response to incremental exercise. |
| Profile of Mood States (POMS) | Standardized psychological questionnaire for measuring various positive (e.g. vigor) and negative (e.g. fatigue, anger, tension, depression) components of mood and psychological well-being. | Case study of athletes in NFOR demonstrated high subjective fatigue with low vigor (Nederhof et al. 2008). |
| Recovery-Stress Questionnaire for Athletes | Standardized questionnaire containing questions related to general and sport-specific stress and recovery (Kellmann and Kallus 2001). | Case study suggested that control athletes have low stress and high recovery scores, whereas athletes with NFOR and athletes recovering from NFOR have high general and sport-specific stress scores (Nederhof et al. 2008). |
| Psychomotor speed | Reaction time may be slowed because of possible central nervous system etiology and similarities with depression and chronic fatigue. | Broad survey of existing literature suggests that this may be a valid marker (Nederhof et al. 2006, 2007), but experimental data is inconclusive if there isn't one, or increase size if there is (Nederhof et al. 2008). |

## Q&A    With Romain Meeusen: Getting Over Overtraining

| Current position | Full professor, Human Physiology & Sports Medicine, Vrije Universiteit Brussel. |
| --- | --- |
| Professional relationship and background with cycling | Holder Lotto Sport Science Chair, scientific institute that works with the professional Lotto-Ridley cycling team. |
| Personal background with cycling | Not that much. I like to ride the bike. |
| Favorite ride (either one you've done or always wanted to do) | Alpe d'Huez. |
| Favorite cycling-related experience | Following several stages of the Tour the France with the Lotto cycling team. |

 **Romain, living in the Belgian heartland of cycling you've conducted studies on both cycling commuting in Flanders and the phenomenon of overtraining. Can you tell us a little bit about both of those areas of research?**

We conducted a one-year lifestyle intervention study in a sedentary population. Subjects did not use their cars to commute and took bikes instead. We showed that a spontaneously selected physiological loading in cycling to work meets the requirements of health- and fitness-enhancing activity. We also showed that cycling to work has a positive influence on coronary heart disease risk factors and is likely to improve the mental health status and body composition of previously sedentary healthy adults. We are now finalizing a study in which we examine whether commuting to work in a polluted environment still has beneficial effects on health.

About 15 years ago we started a research line on overtraining. We immediately encountered the difficulty that there is no single definition for this phenomenon. We therefore wrote an expert consensus statement for the European College of Sport Science (Meeusen et al. 2006) to define the difference between functional overreaching, meaning the extra training trigger that will eventually lead to an improvement in performance; non-functional overreaching, which can be a precursor to overtraining; and the final step in the continuum, overtraining syndrome.

 **Can you differentiate overreaching and overtraining for us? Are there different outward symptoms and different underlying physiological effects?**

Our studies were conducted in various athletes, and we designed a specific double-exercise test to distinguish between nonfunctional overreaching and overtraining syndrome (Meeusen et al. 2010). The distinction between the conditions is difficult to make. Most of the time a post-hoc determination is made, meaning that the length of recovery from the symptoms indicates which phase the athlete was in. But athletes who have difficulty recovering and show underperformance that cannot be explained should consult a sports physician who specializes in the topic as soon as possible. The physician will be able to discover the possible cause of underperformance or if not can perform a double-max test to see how various blood hormones behave to distinguish between the two states.

It is important to emphasize that training is only one of the triggers that needs to be considered. Other elements, such as immunological, hormonal, and psychological disturbances that occur simultaneously with an imbalance in training and recovery, can lead to symptoms. Overtraining syndrome is called that because it has a *combination* of symptoms.

 **So where does nonfunctional overreaching or overtraining syndrome occur? Is it in the muscles, the nervous system and brain, both, or somewhere else entirely?**

Both conditions can have their origin at several places. Therefore, the first action of an athlete should be to visit a sports physician who can exclude other possible causes of underperformance. Many causes of underperformance can have their origin at the muscular level, with muscle cell destruction, inflammation, and general fatigue followed by a sympathetic disturbance or change in resting heart rate. One of the symptoms often present before physical problems occur is a psychological disturbance. Most athletes will show symptoms of depression, irritation, fatigue, lack of vigor, and so on. A simple psychological test such as the Profile of Mood State can be a good test for early diagnosis of nonfunctional overreaching. That something goes wrong in the brain is underscored by the fact that psychological symptoms are present and that a disturbance occurs in the pituitary hormones that are controlled by several neurotransmitters, especially serotonin. This is one of the signal transducers between brain cells, and the concentration decreases in depression. We conducted an animal study in which we chronically stressed rats and then provided an acute stress; we found that there was a suppression of the serotonergic systems in these chronically stressed animals.

 **How does a cyclist pull out and recover from overreaching or overtraining?**

*Rest!* Nonfunctional overreaching and overtraining occur when there is an imbalance between training and recovery. Total rest is the cure! We should try to detect the cause of the overtraining, including social aspects such as just having a baby and getting very little night rest; experiencing problems at work; or dealing with a minor illness, a virus or bacterial infection, or psychological stress. After a period of recovery, a gradual return to training can be started. But it is difficult to make a standard recipe for recovery because overtraining is different in every athlete we've seen. Do not compare one case to others because every athlete is unique.

# Preventing and Recovering From Overtraining

If little is known about the mechanisms underlying overtraining, even less is known about the process of recovery from nonfunctional overreaching or overtraining syndrome. Designing scientific studies with the specific intention of producing a state of severe overtraining in subjects is logistically difficult and ethically problematic. But because overtraining is fundamentally an imbalance of too much stress with insufficient recovery or regeneration, it is intuitively obvious that rest and the removal of training and other stress is key to the process of recovery.

## Prevention Strategies

Ideally, athletes go through a continual process of functional overreaching to enhance their overall fitness level and performance. Staying within the range of functional overreaching without straying across into nonfunctional overreaching is the challenge, and such fine control of training stress and recovery requires intimate self-awareness. Ultimately, the basic habits of adequate rest and sleep, hydration, and well-balanced nutrition remain the most important components of athletic preparation and fatigue management at all performance levels. These points remain the key recommendation even to Olympic athletes (Robson-Ansley et al. 2009).

Several other training and psychosocial factors will help prevent nonfunctional overreaching and overtraining (Meeusen et al. 2006, Robson-Ansley et al. 2009):

- A well-periodized training plan that follows progressive overload with recovery phases to permit physiological and psychological regeneration

- Challenging but realistic goals that push the cyclist without placing unattainable expectations

- Support from family and friends

- A positive team atmosphere that includes regular communication within the team and with coaches and administration

- Maintaining training logs with both quantitative and qualitative data and regularly analyzing them for patterns consistent with overtraining

- Avoiding monotonous training of the same workouts, routes, or pattern of workouts

- Individualizing training programs rather than assigning generic templates

When there is even a remote chance that a cyclist has progressed to nonfunctional overreaching, the immediate prescription must be the severe reduction or complete termination of training. A premature return to training will negate much of the gains made throughout the recovery process and may set the athlete further back. Therefore, erring on the side of more rather than less rest is the best approach. Doing this can be difficult with cyclists because their motivation for training and returning to the sport can be high. Only with extreme overtraining syndrome and burnout do athletes experience strong apathy toward the sport or any physical activity.

During this period of rest, a thorough analysis of factors such as those included in table 5.1 on page 101 must be performed to examine other potential causes and determine the role of training stress. Where available, a multidisciplinary support team, possibly consisting of a coach supported by a sport psychologist, exercise physiologist, and sports physician, can be extremely effective for an athlete in the process of recovery. One consistent theme, though, is that although the members of the support team may have differing opinions, they must present

The potential for OTS is a risk for highly motivated cyclists of all types and at all levels.

a consistent and unified front to the athlete (Gustafsson et al. 2008). The benefit of going through a regular and detailed retrospective analysis of training data, performance, and overall training and competition experience is that it provides a valuable springboard for an athlete and coach or support network to discuss other potential factors that contribute to general or sport-specific stress, such as team dynamics, personal issues, or relationship issues. Furthermore, the analysis provides regular reminders to the cyclist about the need for self-awareness and proper recovery habits.

Just as the etiology for NFOR and OTS is different for every cyclist, no single template can guide the process of recovery, and individualization is required in planning the timeline and nature of recovery. After a sufficient period of complete rest, only mild training should be initiated after several weeks, and the cyclist must be discouraged from trying to make up for lost time by jumping right back into normal or extra training. In conjunction with the resumption of training, the cyclist should regularly use standardized questionnaires or subjective notes to track his or her perceptual responses to training. The cyclist should also seek to correct or balance non-training-related factors that may have contributed to NFOR or OTS.

## Can Motivation Overcome Burnout?

Whatever its cause, OTS undeniably includes a psychological component. We all likely know people who, in both everyday life and cycling, are incredibly motivated and ambitious. But the sources of their motivation surely differ. Some are self-motivated in that the motivation comes from their own free choice and tends to be internal. In contrast, others are motivated by external factors such as family expectations or financial pressures. Although these externally motivated individuals may be high achievers, some research suggests that they may be less likely to sustain enthusiasm and more likely to burn out eventually. One interesting theme in the field of overtraining research has been the influence of motivation and its role in predicting the potential for OTS and burnout. Lemyre et al. (2007) tested the quality of self-determined motivation in a cohort of 141 elite winter athletes in Norway and then tracked them over the course of a season for OTS symptoms. A third of the subjects were 2002 Winter Olympians, and the remainder were elite junior national team members in popular and high-pressure Norwegian sports such as Nordic skiing, alpine skiing, biathlon, speed skating, and Nordic combined. Before the start of the competitive season in September, a questionnaire to ascertain the athletes' internal motivation or self-determined sport motivation index (SDI) was given, and it was followed by questionnaires geared toward assessing both overtraining and burnout at the end of the winter competitive season.

Overall, the Olympians had much higher SDI scores than the junior and elite athletes did. It is tempting to suggest a cause-and-effect relationship in which a high

SDI is a requirement for being an Olympian. But this relationship could exist simply because the Olympians had crossed the psychological threshold of making it to the ranks of the truly elite, thus reinforcing their self-motivation (i.e., being an Olympian is actually the reason for their high SDI). In the junior elite athletes, higher SDI was not significantly correlated to overtraining but was negatively correlated to symptoms of burnout, such that higher levels of self-determined motivation appeared to protect against the risk of burnout. But no similar relationship was found in the Olympians between SDI and either OTS or burnout symptoms, possibly because athletes in this group were all highly self-motivated and therefore exhibited a small range of differences. In summary, in athletes working to get to the top, motivation for the "right" reasons, especially those based on self-improvement goals rather than external rewards, appears to be important.

## Recovery Modalities

The process of training involves stressing the body and then permitting it to recover and adapt to become stronger. At the level of the muscle fiber, the repeated contractions at high force cause a buildup of metabolites and a cascade of microcellular damage. A common response to this muscle trauma is an increase in fluid buildup—edema—and inflammation, leading to the feeling of heavy and sore legs. This result is traditionally viewed as a negative and counterproductive result of exercise, impairing muscle regeneration and adaptation while possibly exacerbating further muscle damage (Toumi and Best 2003). High-impact sports like running are associated with high levels of exercise-induced muscle damage or delayed onset muscle soreness (Howatson and van Someren 2008) because the muscles absorb the force of the body landing on the ground, causing the muscles to lengthen even though they are contracting and producing force (eccentric contractions). Although cycling does not have the same impact forces and involves concentric contractions, in which the muscle contracts and shortens as it creates force, muscle damage can occur with any large increase in training volume or intensity. As will be seen, research on recovery modalities as it applies to cycling is severely limited by this difference in exercise modes.

Of course, the body is amazing in its ability to adapt fairly rapidly to almost any load placed on it. So after the first few days of hobbling around, the next similar bout of exercise doesn't cause the same aches and pains. This outcome is commonly ascribed to the muscles and connective tissues building themselves up to become stronger to resist further damage. But the physiological nature of the recovery process is unclear, as is the effectiveness of various recovery modalities. Even so, the importance of recovery cannot be overstated. Simply put, too many athletes train too hard and recover too little, ultimately steering themselves toward the hazy world of overtraining and suboptimal performance. A look at two of the most common recovery interventions, cryotherapy and compression garments, highlights some common themes in recovery research.

## Inflammation—Friend or Foe?

The process by which muscles recover, repair, and ultimately adapt to become stronger remains unclear. Although many athletes believe that muscle inflammation is a negative consequence of training that should be minimized or avoided, it is possible that the inflammation is a critical stimulus for adaptation within the muscle. Therefore, reducing the symptoms of hard training, including the fluid buildup in the legs and the sensation of heavy legs, may be counterproductive because it impairs the microcellular or hormonal process of adaptation. For example, one paradigm asserts that the production of oxygen radicals and hormonal changes that accompanies inflammation is not a pathological or negative condition but is actually required for eliciting protein synthesis and optimizing muscle repair. Therefore, the emerging question in recovery research is whether decreasing the amount of initial inflammatory response to exercise-induced muscle damage decreases the rate of subsequent adaptation and ultimately decreases the long-term training benefit by altering the stimulus to the muscles. Currently, studies into this paradigm are limited but are becoming more important and feasible given the advances in technology, such as gene expression analysis, and the increasing cellular and mechanistic approach to sport science.

### Antioxidant Consumption

Reactive oxygen species, normal by-products of metabolism and exercise, have been under investigation in the scientific community for their role in a range of physiological processes and clinical conditions, from causing different diseases to being a cause of aging. For athletes, reactive oxygen species production increases with hard exercise and may therefore contribute to muscle damage. Because antioxidants are thought to scavenge these reactive oxygen species, the inclusion of antioxidants such as vitamins C and E has become increasingly popular in recovery drinks. Admittedly, research into antioxidant supplementation is difficult to interpret because of the wide range of subject populations, exercise protocols, dosage, and timing used in the various studies, but scientific data on athletic populations does not seem to support clear efficacy. In a survey of the existing literature on vitamin C and E supplementation, two popular antioxidants used in recovery drinks and as standalone supplements by athletes, McGinley et al. (2009) concluded that taking either vitamin alone or in combination may reduce the levels of indices of oxidative stress, although this did not appear to result in any protection from muscle damage. Indeed, analysis of data from multiple studies suggested that high dosages of vitamin E, which is fat soluble and therefore can be stored for a prolonged period in the body, may lead to a slight increase in all-cause mortality (Miller et al. 2005).

Another common reason for vitamin C supplementation is to improve immune function and minimize the risk of illness. Ultramarathon runners appeared to develop fewer upper-respiratory-tract infections in the 14 days following a 160-kilometer race when given 600 milligrams of vitamin C (Peters et al. 1993). Few cyclists, however, would have such high levels of exercise on a daily basis or even as a peak event. When studying more realistic levels of exercise, such as 2 to 3 hours of moderate-intensity cycling in the heat, 1,500 milligrams of vitamin C supplementation over 12 days decreased slightly the rise in the stress hormone cortisol but did not alter the levels of inflammation marker interleukin-6 nor protect against developing upper-respiratory-tract infections compared with placebo (Carrillo et al. 2008). Thus, antioxidant supplementation may positively affect immune response only when an athlete is participating in extreme exercise or is near the state of overtraining.

Such reports highlight that antioxidants are not a panacea and that athletes should not blindly take vitamins or other nutritional supplements without full knowledge of the potential benefits and risks (see chapter 9 for an overview of the pros and cons of athletic supplements).

## Cryotherapy

Cryotherapy, or body cooling, whether through cold packs, cold showers, or cold-water immersion, has gained great popularity as a recovery tool in the world of team sports such as soccer and rugby. Of these, cold-water immersion, in which the athlete sits up to the waist or torso in a tub of cold to near-freezing water for brief periods, has become especially popular. Sometimes, athletes alternate repeatedly between cold-water immersion and warm-water baths. The general theory behind such a recovery method is that the cold water acts like an ice pack to reduce swelling and inflammation following hard exercise and muscle damage. Warm baths may then promote blood flow and accelerate recovery. Despite the seeming logic and popularity of cold-water baths and contrast baths, the use of such regimens is based largely on anecdotal reports rather than solid scientific evidence (Howatson and van Someren 2008), and only recently have well-designed and controlled scientific studies tested their efficacy in reducing exercise-induced muscle damage and enhancing overall muscular adaptations.

A series of research studies from the Australian Institute of Sport on exercising humans reported a significant benefit for cold-water immersion (head-out immersion in 15 °C water) and contrast water therapy (alternating between 1 minute in 15 °C water and 1 minute in 38 °C water) as recovery interventions, compared with either hot-water immersion (38 °C immersion) or passive recovery. This improved recovery was observed over the 72 hours following muscle damage from a bout of hard resistance training (Vaile et al. 2008c); a smaller increase in midthigh circumference indicated less swelling or edema within the muscles. Contrast baths also lowered the perceived pain compared with passive recovery. The efficacy of cold and contrast baths was also suggested by less impairment in squat jump performance and isometric force compared with passive recovery.

A parallel study, also from the Australian Institute for Sport, investigated the efficacy of hydrotherapy interventions on recovery from daily sessions of hard cycling workouts (Vaile et al. 2008b), using a research design analogous to either a hard training block or stage racing (figure 5.3). For 5 consecutive days, subjects performed an intense 105-minute cycling protocol, consisting of 66 maximal sprints ranging from 5 to 15 seconds in duration along with two time trials of 2 minutes and a 5-minute time trial, followed by 14 minutes of cold-water immersion, contrast water therapy, hot-water immersion, or passive recovery. Sprint power had trends toward decreasing following passive and hot-water immersion but trended toward a slight increase following cold and contrast baths. Although not statistically significant, the same pattern of results was evident with subsequent time trial performance; a slight decrement occurred in average power with passive recovery, but maintenance or a slight improvement occurred with cold and contrast baths.

In addition to day-to-day recovery, cold-water immersion appears beneficial to rapid recovery and repeated competition within a single day, such as may happen during heats of track racing or multiple-stage days on the road. Four different cold-bath interventions, ranging from continuous to intermittent head-out immersion in 10 to 20 °C water, were compared with active recovery of 40 percent of $\dot{V}O_2$max workloads (Vaile et al. 2008a). Each intervention was for 15 minutes and was followed by 45 minutes of passive recovery. Each exercise bout consisted of 15 minutes of steady cycling followed by a 15-minute time trial. All four cold-bath

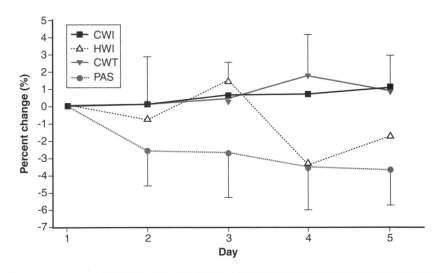

**FIGURE 5.3**  Changes in time trial performance following various recovery methods (PAS = passive recovery, CWI – cold water, HWI – hot water, CWT = contrast between hot/and cold).

Adapted from J. Vaile, S. Halson, N. Gill, and B. Dawson, 2008, "Effect of hydrotherapy on recovery from fatigue," *International Journal of Sports Medicine* 29(7): 539-544, by permission from Georg Thieme Verlag.

interventions prevented any decline in time trial performance, whereas active recovery resulted in 4.1 percent less total work in the second time trial.

These studies suggest that cold-water baths have a strong potential for improving recovery in testing that is realistic for cyclists. But no clear consensus has emerged on the effectiveness of cold-water immersion, because other recent, well-controlled studies were unable to find any benefit. Howatson et al. (2009) sought to compare the use of cold-water immersion with passive recovery following two bouts of damaging exercise from drop jumps. Equal levels of damage and recovery were observed between the control and cold-bath group in all responses, including inflammatory markers, thigh circumference to determine swelling, subjective sensation of soreness, range of motion for knee flexion, and maximal voluntary contraction force of the quadriceps.

Current evidence suggests that cold-pack therapy is not as effective as cold baths. Fu et al. (1997) reported that applying cold packs increased rather than reduced muscle damage compared with passive rest in rats that were undergoing seven weeks of endurance training. In exercising humans, Yamane et al. (2006) systematically trained subjects for four to six weeks of cycling training and six weeks of forearm resistance training, and investigated the use of cold packs as a means of posttraining recovery. Overall cycling performance on an incremental ergometer test improved after training, but single-leg cycling performance increased significantly in the control leg, although not in the cooled leg. In addition, the diameter of the femoral, or leg, artery was measured as an indication of blood vessel adaptation to training; a statistically significant increase in diameter of .3 millimeter was observed in the control leg, whereas no perceptible change was found in the cooled leg. A similar pattern was reported in the brachial, or arm artery; greater improvement in muscular endurance and an increased diameter in the control arm occurred after training, but lower muscular improvements and no changes in arterial diameter occurred in the cooled limb.

Mechanistically, any benefit from cold-water immersion appears to result largely from the cooling rather than any benefit from water immersion itself. The finding of essentially no benefit from hot-water immersion (Vaile et al. 2008b, 2008c) suggests that the decrease in inflammation and edema brought about by hydrostatic pressure and compression from water immersion is not a primary mechanism of benefit. Second, it suggests that the main benefit of contrast bath therapy (alternating cold and hot baths) comes from the cold immersion rather than the hot immersion. Finally, core temperatures following hot-water immersion were higher than at the completion of exercise, compared with similar values following contrast bath and passive recovery, and lower core temperatures with cold-water immersion. Thus, another limitation of hot-water immersion as a recovery tool is that it would not benefit cyclists exercising in hot environments because the slower cooling of body temperature can result in greater risks of heat illnesses during subsequent exercise.

Overall, then, the efficacy of cold-water immersion and other forms of cryotherapy as a recovery modality is somewhat equivocal. Well-controlled studies using both muscle damage and cycling-specific protocols report both beneficial and detrimental effects to training recovery and performance. Cold-water immersion can provide symptomatic reductions in perception of pain, and this positive psychological effect may help elicit a greater time trial performance. More research is required to understand the actual cellular process of response and repair, particularly the inflammatory response.

## Compression Garments

Another popular form of posttraining recovery for cyclists is the use of compression garments, especially compression tights and socks. Such compression garments have long been used in clinical settings for patients who have circulatory problems or who are facing prolonged bed rest. They have also been used during long-distance flights to minimize circulatory problems from prolonged sitting, sometimes called economy class syndrome.

Blood leaves the heart at high pressure and circulates throughout the tissues, slowing to extremely low speed and pressure at the capillaries to enhance nutrient exchange. The challenge is moving this blood back to the heart with such reduced pressure, especially against the force of gravity when standing or sitting. The skeletal muscle pump of the rhythmic contractions of the leg muscles normally aids this movement during standing or walking by compressing the veins and squeezing blood back to the heart. When this process is impaired by prolonged sitting or circulatory disorders, blood can pool in the legs, causing fluid buildup (edema) and eventually tissue damage. The rationale behind compression garments is that the increased pressure around the limbs may improve circulation, reduce inflammation and edema, and improve removal of waste products and venous return. Such garments have proven effective in clinical settings, but despite heavy commercial promotion, minimal research has been conducted in athletic or cycling-specific applications until recently. As stated by Barnett (2006) in a review of recovery modalities, "No studies appear to have investigated wearing elastic tights during posttraining recovery alone."

To date, no controlled scientific studies have been able to demonstrate a clear performance benefit of using compression socks or tights either during exercise or as a recovery modality. As with cooling, the difficulty in compression garment research is understanding the physiological versus perceptual responses. What limited positive data exist have been largely restricted to perceptual sensations of muscle soreness. In recreational runners, wearing knee-length compression socks during a 10-kilometer paced run resulted in lower perceptual muscle soreness 24 hours later compared with control (Ali et al. 2007). In another study, Bringard et al. (2006) found that wearing compression tights versus regular elastic tights did not alter the energy cost of running at various speeds during a graded maximal exercise test, nor did it affect perception of sweating or thermal comfort (figure 5.4). But when worn during a steady-state 15-minute run at 80 percent of $\dot{V}O_2$max, the compression tights condition had a minor improvement in lowering the energy cost.

The balance of experimental data currently points towards no strong effect on physiological or performance responses from compression garments. In a companion pair of studies, Maton et al. (2006a, 2006b) used surface recordings of muscle activity and concluded that compression garments did not improve force patterns or muscular endurance when worn during a recovery period between static contraction tests. Similarly, Davies et al. (2009) found that wearing compression tights may decrease the production of muscle damage markers such as creatine kinase and decrease perceived muscle soreness 24 and 48 hours following drop-jump exercise. But wearing or not wearing compression tights for 48 hours had no effect on subsequent 5- to 20-meter sprinting performance; both conditions resulted in a similar level of impairment. Duffield et al. (2010) found a similar pattern of reduced perceived muscle soreness but no change in subsequent performance when testing intermittent sprinting and plyometric jump performance 24 hours after an initial exercise bout.

Overall, the wearing of lower-body compression garments during recovery from exercise does appear to reduce subjective sensations of muscle soreness. One school of thought argues that this decreased perception of pain may provide a stimulus for higher self-paced performance. But this notion has not been supported

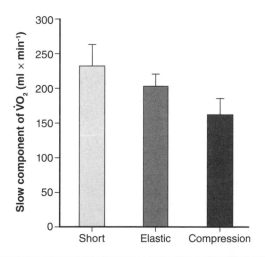

**FIGURE 5.4** **A slight lowering of oxygen demand may result from wearing compression tights while running compared with wearing shorts or noncompression tights.**

Adapted from A. Bringard, S. Perrey, and N. Belluye, 2008, "Aerobic energy cost and sensation responses during submaximal running exercise: Positive effects of wearing compression tights," *International Journal of Sports Medicine* 27(5): 373-378, by permission from Georg Thieme Verlag.

by any data demonstrating improved isolated muscle response or better sprinting and plyometric performance. Currently, there is a gap in the literature on research using cycling-specific efforts or exercise protocols that do not deliberately induce muscle damage. A good example of relevant research design might be that of Vaile et al. (2008b) on cold-water immersion, in which responses to hard cycling efforts over repeated days were tested.

# Applying the Science

The foundations of optimal recovery are passive rest or mild activity coupled with quality nutrition and adequate sleep. These practices appear to provide the body with the basic building blocks and hormonal responses that it needs to repair itself from the stress of exercise and adapt to become stronger. The current scientific consensus is that most popular recovery interventions, such as compression garments and cold therapy, can provide symptomatic relief from pain and discomfort resulting from heavy exercise. But only a few studies have demonstrated clear performance benefits with subsequent exercise. This dearth of evidence should not be taken as a blanket dismissal of these recovery interventions for cyclists because current experimental models are limited in their cycling relevance. Many cyclists use a little bit of each of the recovery modalities, and the individual nature of the athlete plays a large role as well. Some athletes claim that soaking in the hot tub after a ride is the best recovery method for them, whereas others believe that soaking in a tub of ice water helps them recover more quickly. One well-known and successful professional cyclist is so superstitious about recovery that he is typically found after his races laying on a magnetic pad, wearing compression pants, resting his legs up on the wall, wearing special biofeedback glasses, and listening to classical music only, much to the bemusement of his teammates. You should understand each of these modalities and then try each one to see which might help you the most.

Much remains unknown about the process of recovery from hard cycling training because the dominant experimental model has focused on acute muscle damage, usually a single intense bout of eccentric contractions, which is far different from the effects of consecutive days of hard cycling efforts and concentric contractions. In addition, little is known about the physiological process of adaptation to training itself, especially relating to whether inflammation from hard exercise plays a positive or negative role in stimulating such adaptations. As noted by Barnett (2006) in his review, further investigation is needed in several areas:

- A comparison of the effect of each of the commonly used recovery modes (stretching, massage, cryotherapy, compression garments) when included as a regular component of training recovery rather than after acute damage.

- Whether the decreased perception of pain or soreness from recovery interventions enhances subsequent exercise performance. Further, does the symptomatic relief from discomfort and pain elicit a higher subsequent capacity for training, and if so, is this a positive training effect or does it enhance the risk of overtraining?

- Interactions, both positive and negative, in combining multiple recovery interventions and the interaction with nutritional strategies for optimizing recovery and glycogen resynthesis.

- The positive or negative role of inflammation and reactive oxygen species formation from hard training and muscle damage on adaptation to training.

## CHAPTER 6

# Finding Your Perfect Pace

At its most basic, the human body is a machine. Unfortunately, it is not a perpetual motion machine, but rather a finite system that will eventually tire and fatigue. The factor that can make the big difference in race performance is how we distribute that finite store of energy over the course of the race. Despite tactical nuances and racing dynamics, the essence of cycling and many other endurance sports is the individual effort needed to complete a set distance in the fastest time possible. One of the critical determinants of success is how well you gauge your efforts along the way. Nothing is worse than misjudging your pace and blowing up well before the line—well, nothing except the bitter feeling of crossing the line knowing that you have plenty of juice to spare.

In time trials, as in mountain biking and cyclocross, athletes have a high level of control over pacing their effort. Is it best to try to maintain constant speed or power over the course of a 40K time trial, or is it preferable to start easier and then try to push harder during the latter stages? What is the best way to approach a time trial that involves one or more big climbs?

Road races may also be affected by pacing. The main strategy for most road races is to conserve as much energy as possible for the majority of the race and then at a decisive moment throw caution to the wind and put all that saved energy into play. But should you maintain an even pace and stay steady in the peloton before that moment, or should you make repeated efforts to move up and down the pack? What is the best pacing strategy in breakaways? After you get off the front, you have to pace yourself when you take a pull at the front and be careful that you both keep ahead of the pack and make it to the finish line with enough energy to beat your competition.

How you prepare for the competition itself is a huge factor in how much energy you have available at the start line. Precompetition warm-ups have become as much an ingrained ritual as a physiological necessity, and many cyclists now spend an hour or more to warm up before the race starts. Although preparing your body for the effort to come may be beneficial and important, the tradeoff is that you are expending energy that you might need later. So, the question is, how much warm-up is a requirement rather than just a tradition, and what is the optimal warm-up for you?

At the macro, or long-term level, periodizing your training (chapter 4) and recovering properly (chapter 5) have delivered you to the start line with the optimal level of energy. In this chapter we explore the scientific evidence for pacing your effort in a variety of cycling competitions, from warming up to crossing the finish line.

# Warm-Up

Many cycling events require a hard effort right from the gun, such as in the opening minutes or laps of a criterium, mountain bike race, or cyclocross race. Track events require huge power outputs right from the start, and many last for only a brief time. Even sustained events that are more moderate, such as a time trial, require a high power output right away. Road events can set off at a relatively easy pace from the line, but an attack can come right at the gun. Even if you don't join in on the attack, the whole pack can start to hammer and force you to dig deep. If you aren't physically ready for this hard effort, you can quickly go off the back and you will have to spend a lot of energy to chase back.

These hard efforts are certainly mentally difficult to do right off the line, and they can feel horrible, with or without preparation. For this reason, one of the traditions in cycling is a thorough warm-up before the race. The sight of riders warming up on trainers or rollers is common at velodromes and at many road and off-road events. Warming up has been proposed to elicit a host of positive physiological benefits:

- Elevating body temperature to enhance metabolic and muscle function, which may occur by speeding up chemical reactions, enhancing the transmission of nerve signals, and increasing the viscosity and flexibility of muscles and joints. The higher body temperature may also cause the body to start sweating to remove heat, priming the body for heat release during exercise.

- Raising the metabolic rate to prime the body to release fuel and the muscles for aerobic metabolism.

- Increasing the nervous and hormonal activity in the body to prepare the body for exercise.

- Increasing heart rate and priming the cardiovascular system to enhance blood flow.

- Increasing mental arousal.

©Anna Gowthorpe/PA Archive/Press Association Images

**Mountain bike racers need an explosive starting effort to reach the trails in good position.**

But everything has a downside, including warm-ups. An intense warm-up may end up fatiguing the body and being counterproductive. A warm-up that is too strenuous, in either intensity or duration, may begin to deplete glycogen stores and decrease the already small amount available. Even in relatively cool temperatures, warming up on a trainer or rollers can quickly elevate body temperature beyond comfortable levels because of the lack of air circulation and convective cooling (see the interview with Dr. Lars Nybo on page 234). Many professional cyclists now experiment with wearing special cooling vests during time trial warm-ups to achieve a metabolic and muscular warm-up without overheating. The sweating that accompanies warming up may also increase the likelihood that dehydration will affect performance and decrease the amount of blood flow available to the muscles. Therefore, two important questions need to be answered in terms of developing an optimal warm-up schedule before competition.

1. Is warming up even necessary?
2. How long and intense should the warm-up be, and does it need to be adjusted based on the nature of the competition?

Surprisingly, despite a popular consensus that a warm-up is beneficial, the systematic investigation of this question and the related question of what constitutes an optimal warm-up is relatively sparse in the scientific literature. Existing studies differ greatly in subject, sport, and test selection as well as the duration and intensity of the warm-up. With a lack of scientific consensus, warm-up protocols in many sports appear to be based largely on the athlete's or coach's trial and error or simple tradition. Consider the common advice that a warm-up should simulate the event (e.g., a number of sprints are typically done in the warm-up for a criterium) and the seemingly conflicting belief that a shorter competition requires a proportionately longer and more intense warm-up. Similarly, Tour de France riders routinely spend hours preriding the time trial circuit and then do another hour or more of intense warm-up on the trainer before hitting the start ramp.

Bishop (2003a, 2003b) prepared two thorough reviews on the effects of both passive (body warming without exercise) warm-ups and active (exercise) warm-ups on exercise performance (table 6.1), and presented three major conclusions and considerations:

1. **In general, a consistent benefit was observed as long as the warm-up was of at least moderate intensity.** A hard warm-up, however, does not necessarily improve performance above that of a moderate warm-up. Over a 3-kilometer cycling time trial, a moderate warm-up and a hard warm-up provided equal improvement in performance time compared with no warm-up, and the bulk of the benefit was from higher power output during the first 1-kilometer segment of the time trial (Hajoglou et al. 2005).

2. **For short-term, maximal-intensity exercise such as sprint or kilometer efforts, the primary benefit of a warm-up appears to be increasing muscle temperature.** This temperature increase appears achievable with three to five minutes of moderate-intensity exercise and may even be achievable with passive warming (e.g., heating blankets around the legs). Light-intensity warm-up or calisthenics and stretching that do not raise muscle temperature by 2 °C or more do not seem to be sufficient. Care must be taken to ensure that the warm-up is not too intense or that the recovery period is so brief that the ATP-PC system is depleted before competition.

3. **For intermediate-duration exercise or longer events in which high-intensity starts are required, the primary benefit of warming up appears to be in raising oxygen uptake in the body.** This increase in oxygen uptake decreases the reliance on anaerobic metabolism. In fact,

you will hear many cyclists comment that they need to "open up the pipes" before competition, which means that experientially and intuitively they believe that a strong warm-up helps to increase their oxygen uptake for intense races. Therefore, this kind of warm-up should be timed to end shortly before the start of competition. At the same time, care must be taken to ensure that the warm up is not so intense that glycogen depletion occurs or that the body gets too hot.

**TABLE 6.1    Summary of Study Results on Structuring Cycling Warm-Ups**

|  | Short-term exercise (mainly track sprint efforts) | Intermediate- to long-term exercise (cycling efforts >10 s) |
|---|---|---|
| Intensity | Low-intensity warm-up (e.g. stretching, calisthenics) is generally ineffective.<br><br>Warm up at 40–60% of $\dot{V}O_2$max or at a moderate level of perceived exertion. | Low-intensity warm-up (e.g. stretching, calisthenics) is generally ineffective.<br><br>Warm up at approximately 70% of $\dot{V}O_2$max (moderate to slightly hard perceived exertion). |
| Duration | As short as possible for muscles to increase temperature, approximately 3–5 min. | 5–10 min if at moderate to heavy intensity to permit oxygen uptake to elevate to a steady state. |
| Recovery | 5–15 min to permit PC regeneration while not allowing muscle temperature to drop back to baseline. | <5 min to prevent oxygen uptake from returning to baseline. |

Some recent studies suggest that, by and large, athletes were quite successful in self-selecting a warm-up duration and intensity that enabled optimal performance even when they had minimal feedback (Mandengue et al. 2005). When given free choice of intensity, duration, and recovery before a ride to exhaustion at 100 percent maximal power obtained during an incremental test, fit but non-trained cyclists self-selected a warm-up of just under 13 minutes at an intensity of approximately 62 percent maximal power (150 watts or approximately 2.1 watts per kilogram), eliciting 78 percent of maximal heart rate and 75 percent of $\dot{V}O_2$max. Recovery time before the test was self-selected at slightly over 6 minutes. When warm-up intensity was increased by 10 percent beyond this self-selected effort, time to exhaustion during a subsequent test ride decreased compared with the self-selected warm up (figure 6.1 on page 130). Indeed, the performance time with the harder warm-up was as low as it was with no warm-up at all (Mandengue et al. 2009). Therefore, an extremely intense warm-up can have the same negative effect on performance as no warm-up at all.

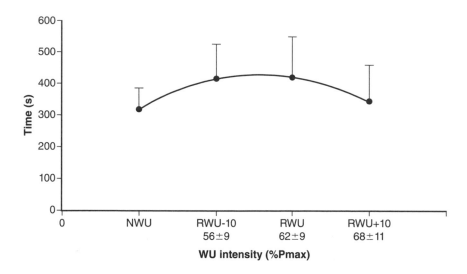

**FIGURE 6.1** **The effect of warming up on tolerance to 100 percent maximal power effort.**

NWU = no warm-up; RWU = freely selected warm-up; ± 10% intensity from RWU.

Adapted from *Science & Sports* 24(1), S.H. Mandengue, I. Miladi, D. Bishop, et al., "Methodological approach for determining optimal active warm-up intensity: Predictive equations," pp. 9-14, copyright 2009, with permission from Elsevier.

Experience seems to be the best teacher, and here you will need to do some experimentation to find out what works best for you for different events. Besides noting the guidelines outlined here, you should consider a host of individual factors when designing a warm-up. These factors are summarized in table 6.2. The extent to which each variable should be considered when planning your warm-up depends on how well you tolerate the anticipated conditions and challenges. Keep a log of your experiences, noting the type of warm-up, how you felt before and after the warm-up, and how you fared during your event.

On pages 132 and 133 are some sample warm-ups grouped by type of event that you can try for yourself (figure 6.2). Typically, the shorter the event is, the more intense it is. Make sure that you consider all relevant factors when planning your warm-up.

**TABLE 6.2     Considerations for Designing a Warm-Up Protocol**

| Factors | Impact | Recommendations |
|---|---|---|
| Hot temperatures | Increases the risk of overheating and dehydration | Decrease the duration of the warm-up or possibly eliminate it. <br><br> Employ cooling strategies during the warm-up (stay out of the sun, warm up on the road rather than on a trainer, use a fan if on a trainer, drink cold water). |
| Cold temperatures | Increases the rate of cooling after the warm-up | Prolong the warm-up or decrease the time between the warm-up and competition. <br><br> Keep on as much clothing as possible before the competition. |
| Intensity of the event | Affects the ability to perform at a high level at the start of the event because of a lack of oxygen uptake | An event with an intense start (criterium, mountain bike race, cyclocross, and so on) necessitates an intense warm-up to overcome the fight or flight response (sympathetic or parasympathetic nervous system). <br><br> Finish the warm-up close to the start of the event. |
| Fitness level | Affects the rate of heat storage and fatigue resistance | Fit cyclists may need a longer warm-up to raise body temperature and prime the aerobic metabolism. They can also endure a longer warm-up without depleting fuel stores but may dehydrate faster because of greater sweating. Less-trained cyclists should err toward a shorter warm-up to prevent undue fatigue. |
| Technical nature of the event | Affects the time and effort needed to preview the course | For events such as mountain biking and cyclocross, the previewing time needs to be incorporated when choosing the duration and intensity of the warm-up. A tough course that becomes a "race to the trail" necessitates a more intense warm-up for the initial sprint, although the race might be a long one. |

FIGURE 6.2

## Sample Warm-Up Plans

### SHORT EVENTS

Track racing, short hill climbs of <3 km, BMX racing, and so on.

▶ **Goal**

To warm up the muscles; to avoid taxing the anaerobic system because short events place heavy demands on the anaerobic system, which can be easily depleted.

▶ **Warm-up**

10–15 minutes of easy pedaling in a light gear.

3 × 1 minute of fast pedaling (over 120 rpm) but with little force on the pedals.

Rest period is 1 minute after each.

One or two short sprints of 75–100 meters at approximately 80 percent of maximum sprint pace.

Rest for 3–4 minutes after each sprint.

5–10 minutes of easy pedaling and possibly light stretching so that the warm-up ends less than 5 minutes before the start of the event.

### MEDIUM LENGTH

Criteriums, short-track mountain bike (MTB) races, hill climbs of <8 km, cyclocross, and so on.

▶ **Goal**

To warm up the muscles for high force output and to increase oxygen uptake; to work intensely enough to overcome the fight or flight response; to induce moderate sweating if the temperature is not too hot.

▶ **Warm-up**

10–15 minutes of easy pedaling in a light gear.

5 x 1 minute of fast pedaling (over 120 rpm) but with little force on the pedals.

Rest period is 1 minute after each.

2 x 5 minute "ramps" to functional threshold power or functional threshold heart rate. Each ramp starts at 80 percent of FTP or 85 percent of FTHR and ramps to 100 percent of FTP or 100 percent of FTHR for the last minute of the 5-minute effort.

Rest period is 5 minutes after each.

## LONGER EVENTS

Road races, MTB races, longer hill climbs >8 km, and century rides.

### ▶ Goal

To make sure that the bike is functioning correctly; to warm up the muscles a tiny bit; to clear the mind and mentally finalize the strategy.

### ▶ Warm-up

10–15 minutes of easy pedaling in a light gear.

5 minutes at tempo pace (80 percent of FTP or 85 percent of FTHR).

5 minutes of easy pedaling in a light gear.

## ULTRAENDURANCE EVENTS

MTB and road events longer than 5 hours.

### ▶ Goal

To make sure that the bike is functioning properly; to review tactics and strategy; to confirm that adequate nutrition and hydration are on board; to remember to hold back the pace in the first hour.

### ▶ Warm-up

10 minutes of easy pedaling in a light gear.

# Pacing Strategy Options

A number of research studies have either modeled ideal pacing strategy or analyzed the effort of elite athletes during their time trial events (Abbiss and Laursen 2008). Many athletes and coaches may subconsciously think that an even distribution of power is ideal in terms of the fastest race times. Let's look at the various strategies that athletes have used or that scientists have studied.

## Even Pacing

The constant, even pacing (sometimes referred to as iso power, because *iso* is Greek for "equal") strategy shown in figure 6.3 is the simplest to visualize but the hardest to do, because you attempt to go for a constant speed or power output throughout the race. If the course is hilly, maintaining an even speed means having a power profile full of spikes. Conversely, maintaining an even power profile means a variable speed on an uneven course.

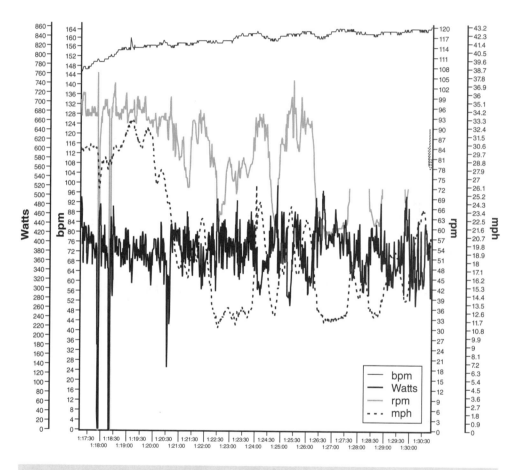

**FIGURE 6.3**  Even pacing profile.

## Negative Splits

Another pacing technique that is difficult to pull off is known as negative splits (figure 6.4). This term describes the strategy of starting slow and then getting faster as you go. Essentially, you break the distance down into segments and try to increase your pace a little bit with each one. Carrying out this plan can be difficult because you need a lot of discipline to avoid going out at max effort (you feel almost guilty because you're not killing yourself). Then you have to be able to kick it up a gear as the event progresses despite accumulating fatigue. Probably the greatest example of this strategy was the effort of Norwegian speed skater Johan Olav Koss in the 10K event at the 1994 Winter Olympics. At his home track in Lillehammer, Koss systematically decreased his lap times over the course of the 25 laps, smashing the existing world record in the process. An example of applying the negative-split approach to a 20K to 40K time trial might be to start out at a pace just below goal pace, bring up the intensity to goal pace after five minutes, and then raise the pace a little more after completing each successive 20 or 25 percent of the event distance.

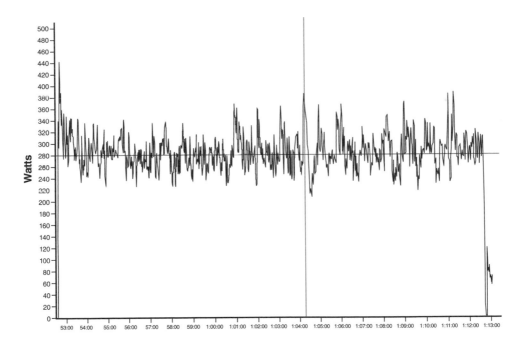

**FIGURE 6.4** Negative-split pacing profile. The first half is at 270 watts and 10:40. The second half is at 286 watts and 9:20.

## All-Out Start

In the all-out start pattern, the cyclist starts at a pace that is well beyond his sustained power output level (figure 6.5). The rider flies like a bat out of hell right out of the starting gate and then attempts to hang on. But the cyclist may ride at such a high pace that his heart pounds out of his throat and his legs turn to lead, such that he can barely sustain a decent pace. The cyclist often has to struggle at a greatly reduced pace simply to get to the finish line. This strategy may be appropriate for a short and hard effort such as a track pursuit. In the pursuit, the rider's power is highest in the first minute and drops all the way to the finish as he struggles with mounting muscular fatigue.

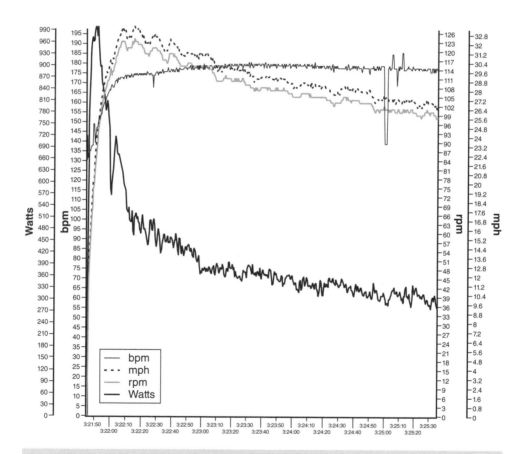

**FIGURE 6.5** Fast-start pacing profile for a track pursuit.

## J Pattern

The J-shaped strategy appears a bit more sophisticated than the go-for-broke pattern, and it is likely the default pattern that most of us fall into (figure 6.6). Namely, we start out a bit harder than our sustainable workload and then drop below that workload for most of the event because of accumulated fatigue from the early effort (and likely from lack of focus and other psychological obstacles). Then we realize that the finish line is close and we still have a lot to give, so we try to make up for lost time by pushing hard during the final quarter or so of the event.

At the start of time trials especially, the perception of exertion lags behind actual exertion, which leads to the mistake that many of us make of starting too intensely. About five minutes normally passes before perceived exertion catches up to actual exertion, and by then it's too late; having maintained too high a level for that time, you have little choice but to reduce your intensity and underperform.

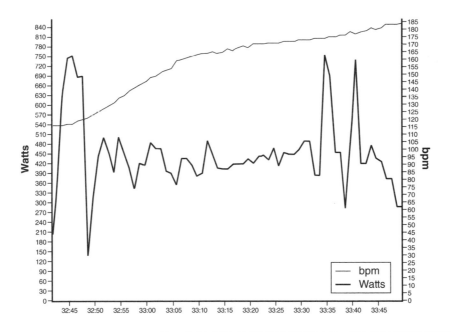

**FIGURE 6.6  J-curve pacing profile.**

## Double Peak

Perhaps the best pacing strategy is what we call the double-peak strategy, so named because when you download a power file from a power meter, the graphic shows an initial peak of wattage in the beginning and a second peak at the end (figure 6.7). This strategy is a combination of the negative split and J-shape pattern. It differs from the negative and J-shape strategies in that initially you must restrain your effort to prevent your perceived effort from underestimating your actual effort, but you still have to keep your effort a little bit above your known sustainable goal pace.

Suppose that you want to average 300 watts for a 40K time trial. In the double-peak strategy you start strong in the first two minutes of the event but hold your watts below 330. You may have peak wattage of only 600 watts just off the start line rather than your maximal five-second record of 900 watts. Although 330 watts is not sustainable for the entire time trial, it is just a touch higher than your goal pace, and by maintaining it for only two minutes you do not dig yourself into a deep hole. After two minutes, you reduce your power to your goal pace of 300 watts and maintain that effort until the last five to seven minutes of the event. Then you bring up your pace gradually to a near-maximum effort in the last minute so that you explode right on the finish line. This strong finishing effort is what creates the second peak of our double-peak strategy. You should use this strategy when you are trying to perform your absolute best in a competitive event or even in an interval workout for efforts longer than three minutes.

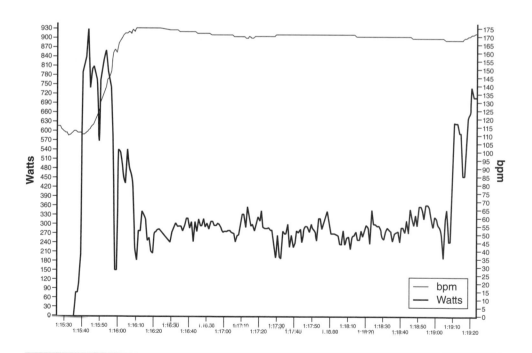

**FIGURE 6.7** Double-peak pacing profile for a track pursuit.

## Comparison of Starting Strategies

A recent study on a time trial of approximately five minutes, equivalent to a track pursuit, aimed to compare slow, even, and fast starting strategies (Aisbett et al. 2009a). The primary results of this study are simple and clear. Namely, the slow-start condition resulted in the slowest overall time (5:09) and average power (333 watts). This time was slower than the overall time for the even-start strategy (5:04, 338 watts), which in turn was slower than the overall time for the fast-start strategy (4:53, 350 watts). Although self-selected power output was higher in the slow-start condition after the initial one-minute section when the power output was clamped, the increase never made up for the time initially lost by being conservative. Similarly, no differences in self-selected power were found between the even- and fast-start conditions, such that the only substantive difference between these two pacing strategies was again the time lost with the relatively slower initial portion in the even-start strategy.

Taking a fast-start strategy one step further, a subsequent study then compared a fast but even starting pace (constant higher than average initial pace for the first 60 seconds) that you might use with a J-shape or double-peak pacing versus an all-out starting strategy (15-second sprint and then 45 seconds at higher than average pace). The all-out strategy resulted in an improved overall result in a 5-minute time trial (Aisbell et al. 2009b). The finding that a fast-start strategy produces optimal performance has also been observed in 1,500-meter cycling time trials; the fastest of three self-paced time trials was marked by the highest power output during the first 300 meters (Hulleman et al. 2007). Currently, the scientific jury is still out on the efficacy of a fast start for efforts longer than about 5 minutes. We recommend that you use this strategy only when you have an effort or event shorter than 5 minutes. In longer efforts, the fast start may cause you to fatigue yourself unnecessarily.

## Q&A    With Paul Laursen: Laying Out the Watts

| | |
|---|---|
| **Current position** | Physiologist, New Zealand Academy of Sport Performance; professor, Auckland University of Technology. |
| **Professional relationship and background with cycling** | Academic supervisor for doctoral students working with Cycling Australia and the Australian Institute of Sport. |
| **Personal background with cycling** | Triathlete, category B cyclist. |
| **Favorite ride (either one you've done or always wanted to do)** | Ironman Canada Bike Course: Penticton, Osoyoos, Richter Pass, Keremeos, Yellow Lake. |
| **Favorite cycling-related experience** | Team Race Across America 1995, 1997. |

*(continued)*

**Paul, your research in the past few years has focused on pacing strategies in cycling. Can you tell us a little bit about the research?**

My interest in this area began shortly after I finished my PhD in 2003. In search of an area to focus my research attention for my first academic job, I remember reading a paper by Tim Noakes titled "Physiological Models to Understand Exercise Fatigue and the Adaptations That Predict or Enhance Athletic Performance." This intriguing paper laid out the multiple reductionist theories that we scientists often use to explain why we fatigue during various exercise tasks. For example, we often blame high levels of lactic acid as the cause of our fatigue during exercise, but we now know that fatigue can occur under low lactic acid levels also. Tim outlined what is to me a more plausible model to explain fatigue, called the central governor hypothesis. This model predicts that some central governor exists to control the body's exercise intensity so that catastrophic levels of any one variable are never reached and organs like the brain, heart, and such are protected. The research I have led in this area was conducted predominantly by my outstanding PhD student at the time, Dr. Chris Abbiss (see page 26 for his interview), who tested these theories on fatigue and pacing using both laboratory and field-based studies

 **One of the things that is often heard in cycling time trials and many other sports is that you should aim to start slow and then increase your pace throughout the event. Is this negative split the best strategy to adopt?**

The answer is, I think—it depends. For a short-duration time trial of less than about 10 minutes, like a Tour de France prologue, for example, more of an all-out pacing strategy is thought to be best because you need to get your energy into the bike and bring it up to speed to give it kinetic (moving) energy. If you leave any kinetic energy in the bike as you are crossing the finish line, it is essentially wasted energy. So for these types of time trials it is best to apply your energy earlier on and hold on. But for longer-duration time trials of greater than about 10 minutes, it does appear that a negative split is optimal. That is, you start slower relative to your average speed but increase your pace during the back half. This strategy is thought to improve performance over longer-duration time trials by reducing the rate at which you use carbohydrate as a fuel and limiting accumulation of fatigue-related metabolites, such as lactic acid, early on in the exercise task.

 **What about a time trial that has a flat portion and then a big climb to the finish? What's your advice in terms of pacing?**

In the case of the flat portion on this course, you'll be working mostly against the force of air resistance. On the climb section of the course, however, you'll be working mostly against the force of gravity. This change in the predominant forces working against you lowers the bike's kinetic energy and causes you to lower your cadence. Just think about your own riding and how it's much easier to spin on the flats, but when you go up a hill, you generally drop your cadence and grind it out. The lower cadence forces you to increase your power output. Because these higher power outputs are metabolically challenging, you should therefore conserve energy during the flat portion before the climb. For example, if your FTP is 250 watts, you might want to ride a bit more comfortably at say 220 watts before the climb.

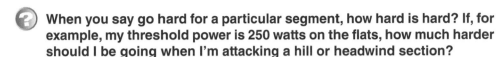 **When you say go hard for a particular segment, how hard is hard? If, for example, my threshold power is 250 watts on the flats, how much harder should I be going when I'm attacking a hill or headwind section?**

You've identified another situation in which pace might be altered to improve overall performance. So here, if your threshold power is 250 watts, you might raise it to 270 to 300 watts for a while on a climb and then recover after it flattens. A headwind versus tailwind situation is the same. Going into a headwind also reduces bike stiffness and lowers kinetic energy. Therefore, it makes sense to go 270 to 300 watts into the headwind and then recover during the tailwind section.

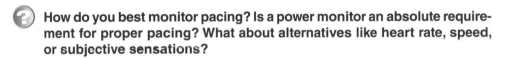 **How do you best monitor pacing? Is a power monitor an absolute requirement for proper pacing? What about alternatives like heart rate, speed, or subjective sensations?**

To me a power monitor is best. I find it's a really great way to keep on track during a time trial—either to get that extra cue to push harder or to hold back. Speed will fluctuate with the conditions, as will heart rate. Nevertheless, these variables are nice to keep track of because usually they will all correspond, and you'll get used to knowing where your heart rate should be for various time trial distances. If I were to focus on only two variables during a time trial, however, they would be my subjective sensations of how hard I can go and the odd glance at the power monitor. Both types of feedback can either tell you to keep it real or help you push your boundaries.

# Plotting Your Pace

What is the ideal starting strategy for a middle-distance cycling effort? Traditional advice for time trials is to start slow and under control and then get faster as the time trial unrolls, similar to how a rolled-up carpet unrolls faster and faster until it slaps on the floor. This approach is the traditional negative-split pacing strategy. But in most cases when riders are free to select their pace, even with a bike computer for feedback, they seem to adopt a J-curve strategy. Many cycling events, such as criteriums, mountain biking, and cyclocross, place a huge emphasis on a massive initial effort in getting the "hole shot" through the first few minutes or laps. Without this initial surge, you may end up completely off the back or stuck in traffic, ultimately causing you to expend a lot more effort or be unable to catch back on. The same may be true of time trials, in which a lower initial effort may leave you with too much distance or time to make up in the latter stages compared with a higher initial pace. In a time trial, having a power meter can really help you ride at your best pace. You can use your power meter to regulate your watts in the first part of the event, pace yourself over hills or climbs correctly, and help you know how much more intensity you can handle near the end of the event. Time trials can vary from dead flat to rolling to hill climbs, and they can be different lengths as well. The type of time trial and its length affects how you pace yourself throughout the event.

Among the key rules in time trialing, two are paramount:

1.  Get to your start time on time!*
2.  Don't start too hard, don't start too hard, and don't start too hard!

If you start too hard in your time trial, you will likely ride a slower time than you would if you had started a bit more realistically. A power meter can really help here, because the power meter doesn't lie. When it says that you are doing 1,000 watts off the starting ramp and down the first 300 meters, it's not telling you that to make you feel good. It's telling you that because you are putting out 1,000 watts!

There is no reason to go that hard in the start of a time trial that is longer than 5 minutes. If your goal wattage is 250 watts for the time trial, then use the first 15 to 30 seconds to get up to speed. Nail your wattage at 260 to 270 for the next 2 minutes (to create the first peak of the double-peak strategy) and then reduce power to 250 to 260 and hold it there as best you can. Begin to push a little harder in the last 5 minutes to finish strong, and then you can blow up on the finish line.

Pacing by heart rate is inherently problematic because it takes 30 seconds for the heart rate to respond to a hard effort, so you will be constantly raising and lowering your power to chase after a response that comes 30 seconds later. You want to avoid being like the sailboat skipper who has to make constant corrections to stay on course instead of driving straight to the destination.

The length of your time trial determines how much you should hold back in the beginning of the effort. If your time trial is longer, like a 40K TT, then you should probably hold back a little for the first five minutes of the event. If it's shorter, say a 10 miler (16 km), then you can't afford to hold back so much. You might hold back for only the first two minutes of the effort. The shorter the event is, the less you hold back. If you are doing a short hill climb or track race, then you must use the fast-start strategy to ensure that you give it your absolute maximum and hold nothing back.

*The first rule is also known as the Pedro Delgado rule because the 1988 Tour champ missed his 1989 Tour prologue start by about three minutes and ended up placing third overall behind Greg LeMond by about the same time!

## Adjusting for Course Conditions

How do you pace for different courses? How will wind affect your pacing strategy? How will a hilly course differ from a flat course? In a flat time trial without much wind, the constant power pacing strategy is the simplest. Ride at a constant speed or power until three to five minutes to go and then bring up your pace until you reach the finish line. This even pacing strategy is the default strategy for any time trial. Ride as smoothly and consistently as you possibly can at your goal pace while maintaining a hard perceived exertion.

A headwind on the out leg of a flat time trial could change your pacing. When you encounter a headwind, you will also have a tailwind. One feature of a tailwind is that it normalizes some of the fitness differences between riders, such that a weaker rider will be able to maintain a speed similar to a faster rider in a tailwind because of the lower resistance on the pedals. In a tailwind, achieving even your FTP wattage is difficult. Typically, either your gearing is too small and you can't spin the gear fast enough to compensate for the lower torque and resistance or you have a big enough gear but your muscles are not accustomed to producing high power when pedaling so rapidly. This latter effect is the specific reason that so many professionals use motorpacing to simulate the race speed and intensity that they cannot replicate riding solo.

The net effect of wind is a marked discrepancy in speed between the headwind and tailwind sections. A rider with an FTP of 340 watts can perhaps put out 320 watts and ride at 32.5 miles per hour (52.3 kilometers per hour) in the tailwind, and a cyclist with a FTP of 320 watts can put out about 300 watts in the tailwind and ride at an average speed of 32.1 miles per hour (51.7 kilometers per hour). In a 40K TT the high average speed combined with this small speed difference for 20 kilometers will result in the faster rider gaining only 17 seconds on the slower rider. On the headwind section of the course, the rider with 340 watts FTP can ride at 340 watts and 22 miles per hour (35.4 kilometers per hour) for the entire 20 kilometers, and the rider with 320 watts FTP averages 320 watts but does only 20.5 miles per hour (33.0 kilometers per hour) for the same section. This difference gives the rider with 340 watts at FTP a 194-second advantage on that portion of the course. Make hay while the sun shines (or the wind blows, in this case!) and create the race-winning time gaps in the harder headwind sections.

What does the scientific literature have to say about wind? Replicating a 16K TT with an 8-kilometer headwind and an 8-kilometer tailwind segment (8.05 kilometers per hour direct wind), Atkinson and Brunskill (2000) reported that a self-selected strategy resulted in an average power output of 235 watts with a strong J-curve profile. Indeed, power exceeded this average only during the first and final 1.6-kilometer segments, including a large initial overshoot of 14 percent higher than average power output. Notably, this strategy produced a slightly slower time than a strategy of maintaining a constant 235 watts throughout both the headwind and tailwind legs. But a variable strategy that used a less dramatic power output 5 percent higher than average during the headwind segment coupled with a power output 5 percent lower than average during the return leg resulted in a faster overall completion time than either an even or a completely self-selected pacing strategy. With the 5 percent faster and slower power conditions, the subjects had a difficult time scaling back the wattage during the first portion of the tailwind leg, going only 2 percent slower than average for the first 3.2 kilometers. This effort forced them to drop wattage to 8 to 10 percent lower than average during the final 4.8 kilometers of the tailwind to maintain the overall average of 235 watts for the entire TT. Therefore, these subjects likely could have maintained a higher overall average power and a faster time by holding an initial higher pace into the headwind. Extrapolation from these data suggests that the same strategy of a variable pace could be optimal for hills. The tradeoff would be higher than average power during the hills and recovery and lower than average power on descents and perhaps the flats.

©Nico Vereecken/Photo News/Icon SMI

**Preriding the course is an invaluable step in planning your pacing strategy.**

How should you approach a hilly time trial? How should you pace the hills? Should you use a different strategy for a short, steep hill versus a longer, more gradual hill? How should you ride hills that plateau on top versus hills that have equal descents on the backside?

As suggested by Dr. Paul Laursen in the interview in this chapter and the Atkinson and Brunskill results, the goal may be to conserve some energy during the flats and then aim for a higher average wattage during the hills. When you encounter a hill followed by a downhill, you should aim to push a little harder on the uphill section and then recover on the downhill side. The downhill will allow you to recover because even if you pedal as hard as you can, reaching your threshold will be difficult. Overall, we recommend that you be conservative in your pacing before approaching the big hill on the course. If you are already riding at the absolute limit when you hit a hill, then the higher power output required by the hill can result in quickly cooking yourself. You might not recover quickly enough on the downhill, causing you to mess up your pacing for the rest of the race.

How much harder than FTP you pedal on the uphill depends on the length and steepness of the hill. For a hill that is less than one minute long and quite steep, you can pedal much harder than you can for a hill that is five minutes long but more gradual. The reason is that a long effort on the uphill will take longer to recover from on the downhill, whereas a short, hard burst of power will not accumulate the same volume of fatigue.

Your personal power profile can give you a clue about how hard you can attack hills of various durations. For example, if you are attacking a five-minute hill and know that you can hold 113 percent of your FTP for that period without cracking when you are fresh, then you could consider knocking off perhaps 5 or 10 percent of that and trying for 105 percent. Hill pacing can also depend on the nature of the subsequent downhill. If the descent is extremely steep, you have less time to recover than you would with a longer, more gradual descent. With a steep descent, you might therefore need to be more conservative going uphill. Also, if that same five-minute hill flattens out at the top or plateaus, you might want to be even more conservative because without a downhill to generate speed, you will need to get back on the gas to get back up to speed. In that case, you would maintain just FTP or just a hair above it on the uphill portion.

This detailed pacing preparation is one of the benefits of preriding a course and knowing your power profile! Unless you've performed a recon of the main hill on a TT course, you may under- or overestimate your pacing. Even if you are not able to travel to test a circuit before competition, the wonders of Google Earth and the easy availability of GPS data mean that you can preview the course virtually. Also, with CompuTrainer and other virtual reality stationary trainers, you can program the course and use the simulation to test various pacing strategies.

Translating to the road, the discrepancy in power and actual speed over various course conditions demonstrates the adage that the best place to attack and separate yourself from the pack or other breakaway partners is in the hardest sections of the course (e.g., uphill, headwind, or crosswind), where small differences in power output can result in much more distance earned than in tailwind or downhill sections. The same strategy can be seen in well-drilled sprinter trains that keep the speed so high near the finish that it becomes nearly impossible for a solo rider to generate sufficient power to make a gap off the front.

## Learning Curve

Another interesting question is how rapidly a cyclist can learn a pacing strategy and how resistant that strategy is to external factors. Recent research from the United Kingdom suggested that a particular effort can be learned rapidly and is highly repeatable when external feedback such as speed, heart rate, or power is available. No differences were observed in performance of four time trials of 4 kilometers (Mauger et al. 2009). Even without external feedback or knowledge of the distance to be ridden, it appears that athletes can quickly learn a performance solely through internal cues. Cyclists who were provided no knowledge that they would be riding a 4-kilometer time trial and were given no feedback throughout improved their times exponentially with each performance, such that their performance was identical to the full-feedback group by the fourth time trial. Stable performance of a learned strategy is also difficult to disrupt, even when subjects were enticed with financial rewards for a faster performance (Hulleman et al. 2007).

The rapid learning of a performance appears to occur even with longer time trials, in which day-to-day motivation and variability may be greater. A rapid plateau in performance occurred in 30K (Abbiss et al. 2008) and 40K time trials (Laursen et al. 2003) following a familiarization trial. A delay of six weeks between efforts, however, resulted in a slower performance again (Abbiss et al. 2008), suggesting a constant need to remind the body and brain.

The studies on learned pacing highlight the importance of race simulations and gaining as much experience with a particular event and course as possible before the competition. Through experiencing the physiological strain associated with a particular effort, the brain seems to be able to develop an internal map of how much discomfort the effort entails (Craig 2002) and use this map to develop a performance template for subsequent similar efforts (Foster et al. 2009). When cyclists were not aware of the distance to be ridden in the Mauger et al. (2009) study, they by necessity started with a conservative strategy of an easier pace to avoid blowing up and not being able to complete the time trial.

## On-Site Postevent Performance Analysis

Using the information from your power meter for immediate on-site analysis of your performance can be helpful because you and your coach can make quick adjustments in your pacing or racing strategy, or even in your gearing combination. At a velodrome track event, for example, you might be competing in eight different races, and in those events you would have heats, qualifiers, and then a final. You could have up to 30 minutes of downtime between events, leaving you with ample time to download your data and make adjustments before your next race. You could apply the same strategies to any event with multiple laps, such as during prerides of a mountain bike, cyclocross venue, or a triathlon course with multiple laps for a bike leg.

From training and testing with a power meter, you would know what cadence you generally use in your best performances. But you might discover when looking at your data that your cadence in the first qualifying round was faster. The track could be quicker than you anticipated, or the air density could be radically different (from altitude or humidity) from what you are used to in your training. With the power-meter data, you would know immediately how to adjust your pace and gearing. At a mountain bike or cyclocross venue, on-site power analysis during a preride either before or on race day can help you plan how to tackle the circuit, how long you can sustain an attack over various parts of the course, or even the power requirements for different tires or tire pressures.

Adapted, by permission, from H. Allen and A. Coggan, 2010, *Training and racing with a power meter*, 2nd ed. (Boulder, CO: VeloPress), 246.

# Applying the Science

Training, periodization, and proper recovery all have the ultimate goal of getting you to race day with as much energy and power as possible. How you go about expending that energy while warming up and racing is the final piece of the racing puzzle, and this is where detailed preparation and self-knowledge can have a major effect. Warm-up protocols are highly individual and can vary greatly depending on the nature of the race and the conditions of the day. Take the scientific advice and then add to it your own experience by trying various options and seeing what works best for you. As we have seen, a time trial or mass-start race is not always won by the rider with the highest average power. Although a high average power output is never a bad thing in a time trial, the same average power can result in drastically different times based on who is the smartest in parceling out those watts over various parts of the course. A power meter is definitely a huge advantage for achieving your optimal pace because other feedback such as heart rate and RPE do not respond rapidly enough to serve as the sole indicator of effort, although they can provide important supplementary feedback. At the end of the day, although there is a lot of science behind proper pacing, racing is a sport, and the optimal strategy may be a blend of trying to be physiologically efficient, to fight the clock, and not to concede time or distance unnecessarily.

## CHAPTER 7

# Optimizing Bike Fit

C yclists such as "il campionissimo" Fausto Coppi are revered for their beauty on the bike and their smooth pedaling. By contrast, others such as Sean Kelly seem to have become champions in spite of how they looked on the bike. What is it that accounts for this difference of appearance on the bike?

One factor is how they fitted their bikes—or more accurately, how their bikes were fitted to their unique anatomies and physiology. As with all aspects of training, each rider is completely individual in terms of makeup and needs. Each has a unique biomechanical constitution. This point applies even to identical twins, who may have the same genetic makeup but completely different levels of flexibility or history of injuries. The differences that you do not see might be in their skeletal systems, the effect of their segmental torques, and the location of the center of gravity of their bodies.

A good bike fit is the single most important cycling-related purchase you can make. You can have the fastest set of wheels and the most aero bike in the world, train with the best coach in the world, but without a proper fit you will be unable to generate maximal power on a bicycle and consequently will be unable to ride to your full potential. An improper fit is not just a hindrance to your speed and power on a bike but also a risk factor for developing a repetitive-use injury and for creating muscular imbalances because of the constrained nature of the pedaling stroke that can in turn lead to other problems. Indeed, we would argue that most new riders leave the sport of cycling because of pain while riding that is directly related to poor bike fit.

This chapter is not meant to tell you which is the best fit or which might be best for you. It is meant to educate you about the importance of bike fit, point out critical things to consider in your bike fit, and briefly review some of the bike-fitting systems out there today. As with all things related to sport and science, be sure to consider the objective data and ask questions.

# Benefits of a Proper Fit

We all want to optimize our cycling and make sure that we are riding the fastest that we can with whatever watts we have at our disposal. Efficient, effective cycling is what every competitive cyclist wants. But why is fit so important? Why can't everyone ride the same bike, adjust the seat and handlebars, and be done with it? The answer to this question starts at the hip. Everyone's hip is different, and the hip is the key pivot point in cycling. Despite its bony structure and the ligamentous stability that it provides, the hip is a major weight-bearing joint that plays a critical role in the application of force on the crankarm of the bicycle. The hip is the cornerstone of the pedal stroke. It is related to almost every element of the pedal stroke, including the path of the legs and posture. Movements such as flexion, extension, abduction, adduction, medial and lateral rotation, transverse abduction (extension), and transverse adduction (flexion) all rely on the hip. If you don't have the hip positioned correctly, you don't stand a chance of repeating the best pedal stroke millions of times.

Cycling is different from endurance sports such as running and swimming, which are also repetitive but allow more body movement. Cycling keeps the body fixed in one plane of motion, and both cyclists and bike fitters must adhere to this constraint. The three contact points on a bicycle (hands, feet, and buttocks) and the length of leg bones, torsos, and arms combine to define individual fit. Of course, the rider has some wiggle room to deviate from the set position by moving about on the bike, whether it's riding out of the saddle, sliding back on the saddle, shifting weight forward and backward for a better grip, or using all manner of body maneuvers to stay in balance and ride quickly. You can adjust your fit and change the style of your pedaling by simply moving up on the saddle, if the saddle allows you to! The ability to make such minor adjustments aside, a proper fit allows you to ride more economically and more comfortably.

The best fit is the one that is correct for you and your unique anatomy as well as the circumstances in which you will ride your bike. For example, the fit will differ for mountain biking, road biking, and triathlon. Your particular goals will affect your fit as well. If you are a recreational rider who never will race, your bike fit needs are different from those of a cyclist who competes in 30 races a year.

On the bike, you have to learn how to play at pedaling. The process is like learning to play golf, in that proper alignment is just one aspect of achieving a smooth pedal stroke and balancing the total human linked chain. There is no one ideal position to maintain, only movement in and out of balance. Your weight shifts on the saddle from one side to the other, fore and aft, and even up and down as you cycle. Remember that

- every human has top and bottom balance,
- every human has right and left balance, and
- every human has front and back balance.

The crucial component of bike fit is accounting for and integrating these balance points to produce an overall balance point that gives you control over the bike and stability in the majority of your cycling. Although body English and movement on the bike are required and often desired, you should not have to deviate greatly from your natural position simply to ride. In other words, you should not have to work or deliberately move consistently out of your natural position to feel balanced and in control.

The common goal and claim of most bike-fitting systems is that an optimal bike fit improves power, economy, and comfort on the bike. Methods vary. Data-driven approaches to bike fit such as those used by Wobble-Naught, Specialized, and F.I.S.T. bike-fitting systems start with body and flexibility measurements. From there the bike is set up based on your numbers, and in the case of Wobble-Naught, those of thousands before you. "Experience-based" fits are sometimes offered by people such as the local bike shop employee who has been racing for 20 years and can tell you what you need just by looking at you. Motion-capture fits such as the system offered by Retül and video analysis done with software tools and the Serotta size cycle are available. Each fit and fitter will put you in a slightly different position based on your body size, level of flexibility, type of bike, and so on. If you went to five bike fitters in the same week, each would give you a different fit. And each would be touted as the best!

So how do you choose the system that's right for you? We recommend that you develop and use your knowledge of the available systems and your own needs to select a bike-fitting system. In the balance of this chapter we examine some of the popular commercially available bike fits on the market today. We also ask pointed questions that you can use to guide your decision.

# Wobble-Naught

Wobble-Naught was developed by Thomas Coleman, a former elite ski racer and expert kinesiologist. He is considered one of the world's experts in teaching riders to pedal more effectively. The Wobble-Naught fit is designed to eliminate the wobble in movements on the bike because any wobble is ultimately an inefficient movement. This fit is called a precision bike fit because a quantitatively precise system of measuring the length of the bones between the joints is the heart of the fit. Coleman is adamant about this aspect and says

> You can't just cross over a joint (e.g., knee) to find a length (e.g., inseam height) as if you were simply measuring inseam length and determine saddle height from that. For instance, two people may have the same inseam length but the length of their lower legs and upper legs may differ.

Each measurement is inputted into a computer software program that was developed with more than a thousand cyclists as alpha and beta testers, along with data on muscle function from measurements of the electrical activity of muscles (electromyography or EMG) and from computer-aided design.

The primary aim of the bike fit developed by Coleman is to provide techniques that support and provide protection to soft and hard tissues without limiting their function. Up-to-date technology is used in the creation of the system. For example, data gathered from force plates positioned under the foot, along with EMG images of the muscles at rest and over the course of the pedaling stroke, yield information about how each muscle interacts with others throughout the pedal stroke. Wobble-Naught claims that EMG recordings reveal the performance of each muscle, allowing superior assessment of effort, and that these analyses have shown that even subtle changes in position or pedaling technique can have a large effect on inclusion or exclusion of major muscle groups. This is the key difference that Wobble-Naught claims to have over other bike-fitting methods. They have studied the movement patterns of thousands of cyclists at different intensities and in different positions to understand how best to customize each fit to maximize muscle energy at exactly the right time. We asked Coleman a few questions about his bike fit.

## Q&A   With Wobble-Naught

 **Tell us more about your development of the Wobble-Naught fit and other tools that you use in your bike fits.**

The Wobble-Naught fit was developed on the latest kinesiological and biomechanical backing, using measurement tools such as EMG and force plates on a lot of riders to get a big database of how cyclists actually ride. In conjunction, we use the Dartfish video analysis program to give real-time feedback to help the riders see what the changes are doing and what they need to work on. Almost all of our fitters use this video analysis because we don't see our job as just doing the fit itself. We are teachers, and putting the cyclist in the best position is just part of the job. Then we actually get them to understand how to "address" the bike and how to produce the most power in their new position. We almost always see an improvement of movement, and we always see them make more watts.

**Talk through some of the nuances. For example, why not just use a plumb bob?**

There are many ways to "make the pedal stroke," and to apply the rule of the knee over pedal spindle plumb bob doesn't refine the issues that can take a person out of the game, such as compression, shearing, or tension. Many segment lengths affect the best line-of-pull of the muscles. Think of a stringed instrument: Knowing the tension and where it makes contact is going to help you play it better. Many things can affect the pedal stroke—a partial list includes foot arch, length, and cleat placement; hip height and width; and femur length and tibia shape. Understand also that a human doesn't have to be the same on both sides!

 **Tell us about cleat position; we know that each Wobble-Naught fitter spends a lot of time making sure that the cleat is in the correct place.**

The foot brings the person into direct physical contact with the pedal environment, so an error here can greatly increase susceptibility to injury throughout the entire body. Any waste to the foot link, no manner how small, is also a waste of energy. But many people never learn to use them because they just place the cleat wherever they wish. We place the cleats to use all the foot muscles, not just part of them. If the foot is too deep into the pedal, given all its constraints, it will seem more powerful, but then it loses the much-needed suppleness, and that lack of suppleness induces stress up the human linked chain. In the long run, this can tire the muscles prematurely! On the other side of balance, if the foot is too far back, you lose the muscle strength of the lower links, and then it's harder to climb, start, and push big gears to go fast. This position places too much tension within the foot, and you have to fight more mass behind the supporting pedal, resulting in more work.

The old theory that the big toe must be in line with the pedal axis of rotation is not quite correct. Using our computer-aided design we go beyond a truss, or the framework, typical for supporting your foot. The cleat placement needs to provide the best range of motion and best line of pull. The longitudinal arch, the transverse arch, and the bony anatomy of the foot and ankle are only the part of the measurement solution. We find a range of motion that involves more than a single joint, so the basic ankle and foot motions are therefore not used. We take a podogram of the foot, taking note of any gross restriction as we test both feet for dorsiflexion while we grab the greater toe. This is a critical step in setting up the cleats.

 **What is the relationship between bike fit and actual muscle function? What's the issue if you can still generate the same wattage with a "non-optimized" position?**

The obvious response is that you're increasing your risk for injury, but you're also handicapping yourself by not allowing your body to function to its

*(continued)*

capacity. If your saddle, cleats, and stem are in the wrong place, the movements are restricted—or more correctly they are constricted from their optimal motion. Every time a muscle is contracted, a number of forces are acting on your tissues and joints: compression, shearing, and tension. Another critical thing that you must address and understand in bike fitting is the length–tension relationship. This is the amount of tension that can be developed by a muscle fiber, which is critically dependent on the length of the fiber relative to its optimal length. Consider a saddle that is set too low. This placement can cause the pedaling segments to be more flexed throughout the full stroke, causing the muscle to become flat or sharp like the strings of a musical instrument. This noise is then transmitted throughout the rest of your instrument, your body, into muscles in places such as the lower back. The appropriate choice of saddle and its amount of deflection, the right shoes, the right footbeds, and so on allow the muscles to contract through a range of lengths near maximal segment attachments, and this adjustment is equivalent to tuning your instrument before playing music!

Clearly, the Wobble-Naught bike-fitting system has been well thought out and is very successful. Wobble-Naught boasts national champions and world champions among the thousands of cyclists who have used their fit. Wobble-Naught has brought the latest technology together with solid biomechanics and an incredible understanding of the kinesiology of the body.

# Retül

Let's look at one of the most recent additions to the bike-fitting marketplace and examine how it has brought technology and science to the art of bike fitting. Retül claims to be the most advanced bicycle-fitting system available. Their system incorporates a three-dimensional motion-capture technology, immediate report capability, and a millimeter-specific digitizing tool to provide an accurate, dynamic fitting solution. Retül's claim to fame is that it looks at a cyclist's position dynamically, while the rider is actively pedaling, reading the body in longitudinal, vertical, and horizontal planes. Small LED sensors are placed at key points of your body—wrist, elbow, shoulder, hip, knee, ankle, heel, and the ball of the foot—and then a special motion-capture device tracks these positions in three-dimensional space as you pedal, relaying the information to a computer that the fitter uses to analyze the data. The system flashes an LED every 2.1 milliseconds—or 476 times a second. The system takes a full set of body measurements every 34 milliseconds, or 29 full sets of body data per second.

The Retül software processes all that data in seconds and provides output in intervals ranging from five seconds to five minutes, synchronizing the eight data points and tracking them across longitudinal, vertical, and horizontal planes. In

Courtesy of Retül.

**A cyclist uses Retül bike fit sensors to analyze movement on the bike.**

this way a fitter can see just what works and what doesn't as you actually ride rather than sit stationary atop the bike. A typical Retül fit starts out with the fitter asking the normal fitting questions about riding style, experience, goals, and injuries and then assessing flexibility. Afterward, the fitter places Velcro tabs for the various LEDs, which align on the joints of the body. One side is done at a time. Doing both sides can give the cyclist and fitter a better understanding of any asymmetries that might exist. After each change in position, the fitter can compare the before and after data to see whether there was a positive effect on the athlete's position. Retül has robust software that gives the fitter target numbers for certain positions and angles to achieve the best results.

The Retül system has three strengths:

1. It views the rider in three dimensions rather than two (as in video analysis).

2. It gives the fitter a broader snapshot of the rider's biomechanics on the bike and allows the fitter to analyze a data set of averaged pedal strokes from the rider rather than rely on a single frame of video.

3. It uses accurate and repeatable measurements rather than measurements subject to inaccuracy and human error.

Still, the information is just a tool, and the Retül system does not replace qualified fitting technicians. Retül allows the fitter to see data that he or she could not see with a standard fitting system, giving the fitter the information necessary to provide the most accurate fit possible. The fitter still has to understand the core aspects of anatomy and cycling to maximize the capabilities of Retül. The Retül system can be used alongside any sizing or measuring system and with traditional video analysis.

One other unique aspect of the Retül fit is a tool called the Zin, a wandlike device that essentially digitizes your bike's geometry into the Retül program. The Zin allows the fitter to measure your bike digitally at 13 to 15 points, depending on the bike. The Zin can measure fixed points, contours, and curves to provide a complete digital map of the bike, which can be uploaded to the Retül software and combined with your biomechanical fit data. After your bike fit, the fitter touches the Zin to various points on your bike, and a stick-figure representation appears on the computer screen. With the exact measurements of these reference points, this representation captures your precise position, allowing you to refer to it should something change or you decide to experiment later. Using the Zin, Retül has catalogued thousands of fits and bicycles, amassing possibly the largest database of bicycle frame geometries in the world. After the fit has been done, the client receives a list of all the bike frames that would fit her specific anatomy. Cyclists have long asked, "Which is the best bike for my body?" Retül is the only company that can help answer that question directly.

We asked Todd Carver and Cliff Simms, two of the founders of Retül, to answer some questions about Retül:

## Q&A    With Retül

 **What was the impetus for starting Retül? How did it come about? Give us a little history on the company.**

CS: Well, I was working in the optical measuring field and was an amateur cyclist. I saw an opportunity to bring together measuring hardware that was capable of providing body measurements dynamically, accurately, and economically enough to support a bike shop business model. I put together an initial system and software product and began testing. Then I got Todd, a 3D motion expert, involved as a partner. We refined the system and really were able to show that using it could provide faster and better data than what was currently available on the market. We continue to advance the product every year with software and hardware enhancements to stay on top of the growing field of bike fitting and bike-fitting technology.

**How do you make sure that the fitter puts the markers in the same place on each person? How critical is that part of the bike fit?**

TC: For a given fitter, the variability is low because of proficiency with the palpation technique. Between fitters, the variability is huge. We have developed Retül University so that we can teach this hands-on part of the process. We have also added a view camera to our system so that marker locations can be seen. This really helps as one fitter attempts to make sense of another fitter's data.

 **Doesn't the skin move on people, and doesn't that introduce an error into the movement patterns recorded?**

TC: In the lower extremity, the bone actually moves under the skin. In running and other impact sports, the ground reaction forces cause actual skin movement, so we've used rigid body kinematics for the calculation of joint centers with these activities. But in cycling there is no impact, so this method was not as valuable. In cycling, the knee and hip are the markers that are problematic. The rest of the markers are quite stable on the skin. For the hip and knee, first and foremost, we teach consistency. That means that each marker is placed on the rider with the pedal at the same place in the pedal stroke. We have chosen to use the pedal position that estimates peak hip and knee extension, with the pedal somewhere near the bottom of the pedal stroke. Second, we teach proper palpation of the knee and hip axes of rotation.

For the knee, we mark the distal end of the lateral femoral condyle. As you track that marker throughout the pedal stroke with manual palpation, you will see that the marker maintains contact with the joint line of the knee—it is just that a different part of the femoral condyle is in contact with it. I believe this is because the knee joint center glides as it flexes and extends. For the hip, we mark the greater trochanter. This bone moves in a small circular motion in cycling. We teach the fitters to mark the center of that rotation point. I have been working on these marker placements for nine years and believe that we have a pretty good technique that minimizes error. And this technique is much more practical for the current industry of bike fit than more advanced methods that require considerably more time and expertise.

 **Why not use the old plumb bob and knee over pedal spindle methods?**

CS: The answer is, why not? We actually take two of our markers, the knee joint center and the fifth metatarsal head on the foot, and compare them horizontally when the foot is forward. This is actually like a dynamic plumb bob. The positions are slightly different, but they accomplish the same thing. Our comparison is arguably better because we don't care about the thickness of the knee and patella combo; we are concerned with joint center instead. The system seeks out foot forward position every stroke and averages all the strokes together for the recording automatically. The measurement reads differently and is useful even for triathlon positions where the goal is a forward knee compared with the foot.

*(continued)*

**What's the greatest strength of the Retül system?**

CS: I believe that the greatest strength is the ability of the Retül system to provide a lot of accurate and dynamic data quickly. The system has full knowledge of where each marker is during capture, so the software can find and average all the Retül report measurements automatically in seconds. To re-create all the data of a single Retül report using just a video clip and analysis software would require manually clicking out measurements and taking averages of multiple video frames for hours. It is just not possible to get the same results manually when you need these measurements 20 times during a fit while you are making small changes to the client and trying to get useful data fast. Also, our ability to measure the bike geometry setup in 3D before and after the fit allows for quick archiving of bike positions, as well as automatically generated reports.

 **How does Retül compare to video analysis?**

TC: Video analysis is two-dimensional, whereas motion capture is three-dimensional. A small error is introduced to measurements by not including all three dimensions in the calculation process. Small errors make big differences in bike fit. Video cameras have a narrow field of view. Retül sensors have a wide field of view. This means that the video camera must be 1 to 2 meters farther from the rider to capture the full view of the rider. Video analysis places measurement markers on a small 2D computer screen. Retül places measurement markers on the rider's body using easy-to-find skeletal landmarks. Video analysis requires that you manually trace each measurement after it is recorded with your mouse. Retül automatically performs all the measurements instantly, with no manual work. Video analysis takes measurements from one frame of video, which may or may not be a typical position of the rider. Retül automatically averages the measurements from each pedal stroke, creating a highly refined model of the average movements of the rider.

 **What's the biggest limitation to the Retül System?**

CS: The cost of such advanced technology is often a barrier for fitters, although the Retül is a revenue-generating device. We have many stories of fitters successfully getting a return on their investment in a very short time, many in less than half a year. The other limit on the system is that the infrared nature of the tracking system prohibits use of the system outside, where infrared light is too abundant for the system to operate. We experimented with IR filtering versions of the Retül, but they become too complicated and expensive to be practical.

**Can you give me an example of the experiences of one or two people before and after Retül fitting, including their wattage? Have you captured wattage before and after and seen big improvements or small improvements?**

TC: We do capture wattage and RPE. We standardize all the motion data that way because workload can have an effect on kinematics. In the past, I have also recorded metabolic rate at steady-state workloads using oxygen uptake, heart rate, and lactate levels and did not see much improvement throughout the course of most bike fits. It just leads to a *very* expensive fit! And most times the riders have to adapt a bit before they see the improved economy. In my opinion, the claims of increased power production being given during a fit do not take metabolism into account because they are not recording it. In most situations that claim power improvements, the rider is simply working harder during the second, or post, bike fit test, rather than working at the same metabolic rate and then seeing whether wattage increases.

 **Tell us about saddle height. What happens in the Retül software when you see a low saddle or a saddle that's too high? What are the characteristics of a properly placed saddle? What do you see in the software that tells you that saddle height is correct?**

TC: A properly positioned saddle offers a rider a pedal stroke that operates within the range-of-motion limits of the knee and ankle without compromising pelvic stability (quiet hips). We teach fitters to assess the flexion and extension pattern of the knee and ankle. With the ability of the Retül system to measure both joint actions at the same time, Retül fitters can accurately and quickly diagnose a saddle that is too high or too low. In the case of a high saddle, the software may show overextended angles of the knee at the top or bottom of the pedal stroke or both. It may show excessive ankling range, in the form of plantar flexion, as the rider subconsciously attempts to accommodate the long reach. In the case of a low saddle, the software may show excessive flexion angles of the knee throughout the pedal stroke. It may also show excessive ankling range, this time in the direction of dorsiflexion, as the rider attempts to accommodate the shortened reach.

 **How does Retül address cleat placement? Does cleat placement change for a road rider versus a mountain biker or other type of rider?**

TC: For fore and aft we follow the industry neutral standard: The pedal spindle bisects a line connecting the first and fifth metatarsal heads.

For medial and lateral positioning, we adjust as needed for hip width in the rare cases of excessively large or small pelvic structures. For the normal cycling enthusiast, stance width seems appropriate when centered.

*(continued)*

For internal or external rotation, we advocate beginning with a cleat rotation that sets the foot axis perpendicular to the pedal axis. This is appropriate for the 80 to 90 percent of cyclists who do not excessively rotate either way during our observation of their walking gait. We also advocate a cleat that offers four to six degrees of float to ensure that the rider has the ability to alter foot position while moving in and out of the saddle or seated position.

For inversion or eversion, we advocate using varus heel wedges to correct for overpronated feet only. We teach our fitters to use the wedges to correct for ankle mechanics, not to change the knee tracking. We teach fitters that knee tracking problems often originate in the hip, not the foot.

Retül is an impressive tool and what it claims to do is nothing short of revolutionary. Assuming that the fitter places the markers at precise points, measurement error is all but eliminated. Further, by averaging your position over time, the system captures your true pedal stroke. Moreover, Retül goes further than merely measuring your body position with precision. What they also measure, with stunning accuracy, is your bike. If you plan to keep your current bike for the rest of your life, this is unnecessary, but if you ever want to buy a new bike, having accurate bike measurements is critical. It will ensure that you purchase a bike that fits you, and it will help you get it set up properly after you have it. Where the Retül system is lacking is in its dependence on the expertise of the fitter. Retül does have a fitting school, which is critical to producing good bike fits, but in the end Retül remains a tool that must be used properly by qualified practitioners to get the best results.

# Serotta Personal Fit System

Serotta's fitting system has been around longer than most. From the time Ben Serotta first started building bike frames in his garage, he dreamed of finding a way to make sure that he built exactly the right frame for each of his customers. He built the first "size cycle" in 1979. Arguably the father of dynamic bike fit, Serotta has built hundreds of his size cycles and trained over 1,000 bike fitters through the Serotta International Cycling Institute (SICI). Serotta believes that bike fit is personal and should be based on you, as a unique cyclist, on your style of riding, on the individual way you move as you ride, and on the way your bike should move with you. Although technology is part of it, the system is grounded in years of experience. We interviewed Paraic McGlynn, then director of SICI, about the Serotta bike fit.

## Q&A    With Serotta

 **What was the impetus for starting Serotta Personal Fit System? How did it come about? Give us a little history on the company.**

Ben Serotta built his first sizing device in 1979 out of frustration with algorithm-based systems of arriving at a frame design. CONI, the Italian cycling federation, created a body measurement system, which was the standard that most frame builders used. When Ben was riding with clients he was making regular observations about how he'd have changed the top tube or seat tube. These fitting observations were based on seeing the rider in motion, so Ben decided to make a device to analyze the person in motion and design a bike from that. Soon afterward the first Serotta size cycle was created. We believe that it is accurate to say that Ben Serotta was a pioneer of dynamic bike fitting. Ben began supplying dealers with the same knowledge and tools soon afterward. The first Serotta fit school was held in 1998, and the Serotta International Cycling Institute now educates about 200 students a year.

 **Do some people do better with the Serotta fit than others?**

I think that there is a general tendency for certain fitting systems, schools, or tools to claim competence in fitting certain cycling populations. We believe that a fitter's competence in any area of fitting is a function of his or her fitting ability and attention to detail, and how seriously the business treats the fitting function. There are five key components of being a top bike fitter:

1. Training is the first factor to be considered in becoming a great fitter. Our institute offers 10 days of fitting education that gives a fitter all the information needed to deliver at a world-class level. We do not advise taking all the courses in one block, because practice between courses assists the learning process.

2. People skills are the most underestimated attribute of a bike fitter. Great fitters help their customers achieve their goals by giving respect and great customer service, not stories of their personal athletic accomplishments or knowledge.

3. Integration and infrastructure is the next factor. Fitting is a business that requires time, space, and specialized tools that must be correctly integrated into the business in which it is situated.

4. Advocacy is a key element of bike-fitting excellence. Professional fitters need to promote the difference that a fitting can make and help the manufacturers produce equipment and products that fitters believe in.

5. Repetition is the fifth factor. Fitters improve greatly after 50 fittings, and even more after 500 fittings. There is no substitute for taking great training and applying it over and over again.

*(continued)*

Although our institute controls only one of these elements of bike-fitting excellence, the world's best bike fitters pursue all five elements, and the results speak for themselves.

 **Do you integrate power into bike fitting?**

Power highlights differences between the start and end of the fitting in most but not all cases. Individual cyclists experience changes in very individual ways, and it is important that fitters do more than just chase the most powerful position in a bike fitting. This fact is particularly relevant in working with triathletes, when riding with the same or slightly more wattage but in a more comfortable position can often mean being dramatically faster when the effect on running splits is taken into account. Also, immediate power feedback is not always present even after significant changes—many cyclists need time to adapt to what will become their most powerful position. Overall, we advocate following up with clients and focusing on the performance and comfort improvements rather than strictly power output numbers.

Before any changes are made to a cyclist's position, a baseline analysis is performed, which involves a standardized load and cadence, with video in the frontal and sagittal planes. We frequently capture heart rate to see whether there is a difference in later iterations of the position. If heart rate is not appropriate or not desired by the fit client, we use ratings of perceived exertion for the baseline analysis. Typically, two to five wattage-based loads will be used in a fitting, each with a set cadence range and RPE guidelines. Occasionally there will be more specific wattages or simulations of specific situations, depending on the needs of the individual.

Torque is also observed using a CompuTrainer to see, in gross terms, where force is being applied during the power phase on the left- and right-hand side of the cyclist. We often see significant positive changes as the fit progresses, particularly when there is a leg-length discrepancy, injury, or other factor that contributes to asymmetric pedaling. Heart rate, power, left and right power, cadence, and so on are recorded throughout the fitting, and the data can be replayed if needed.

The degree of improvement in the pre- and postfitting data is situation dependent; a cyclist who begins in a very poor position can often perform similar workloads at a heart rate that is 10 to 30 beats lower after fitting. At higher-intensity efforts, modest power improvements are usually visible and measurable. Fit clients regularly report a significant difference in the length of time that they can maintain higher workloads. The ease of maintaining higher workloads is usually reported as being significantly different in postfitting follow-up. Ultimately, the final power and performance gains are attained weeks or months later, depending on the degree of change in position. Athletes frequently produce power relatively well in their current position, even if it is not biomechanically ideal. After they have adapted to the new position (postfitting), they generally see additional performance benefits. This change, of course, is difficult to measure given the differences in training fatigue and fitness levels.

**How does Serotta address cleat placement?**

Cleat placement is one of those areas of fitting that promotes debate; you cannot look at cleat alignment as a simple matter that has clear guiding principles. The foot is one area of the body that can produce different results in seemingly identical situations. Each person's foot is different and has different muscular, ligament, tendon, vascular, and neural properties. Other foot-related considerations that are relevant to cleat placement include shoe selection, width selection, internal and external wedges, metatarsal pads, lifts, and the assistance of (if necessary) a physical therapist, podiatrist, or pedorthist.

The Serotta cleat placement process begins with a conversation designed to give the fitter an understanding of the history of the individual and the individual's body. After the customer interview is complete, the foot is examined in detail. Eight individual measurements of the foot are taken while bearing weight and eight while not bearing weight. Then the fitter performs a gross assessment of the symmetry of the height of the medial arch of the cyclist. A full flexibility evaluation follows. The fitter evaluates tibial torsion, a difference in alignment of lower leg to upper leg, as part of the flexibility evaluation. Before the cyclist mounts the bike, the fitter marks the first and fifth metatarsals so that their position can be observed.

After warming up, the cyclist pedals in his or her normal position and pedaling style while the fitter places the pedal axle between the first and fifth metatarsals. In triathlon fit, the cleat can be placed in a more aft position, which is also done for cyclists with consistent forefoot discomfort. The initial step in cleat alignment is just fore and aft cleat placement, and the fitting continues.

Fitting is really an iterative process. After the initial cleat adjustment is made, the fitter determines optimum saddle height, saddle setback, reach, and drop. When those steps are complete, cleat placement is revisited, followed by all the previous fit elements, to ensure that there is no undesirable change. Then the final power analysis and 2D analysis take place.

 **What are the characteristics of a properly placed saddle? What do you see in the software that tells you it is right?**

Saddle selection is the first part of determining the location of the saddle. After the contact points with the saddle are correct, the saddle height and fore and aft positioning are easier to identify. Dartfish allows fitters to choose and mark the knee landmark that they wish to use. After the markers are in place the fitter can use a tool that essentially functions as a digital plumb bob. Dartfish provides a tool for the fitter to measure, to within 1/100th of a millimeter, the distance from the knee marker to the center of the pedal axle. After the correct relationship with the knee is created, the fitter examines the consistency of the ankling patterns, because this also influences the position of the knee in relation to the pedal axle—heel up knee forward, heel down knee rearward. Dartfish is frequently used to coach cyclists on correct pedaling technique because most cyclists are unaware of how they actually pedal.

*(continued)*

**Tell me about saddle height. What happens when you see a low saddle or a saddle that is too high?**

Saddle height range recommendations are based on cycling discipline, goals of the athlete, flexibility, injury history, asymmetries, performance level, age, and cycling experience. The Serotta International Cycling Institute uses an interview, foot assessment, flexibility assessment, and a 2D preliminary motion analysis to determine what is ideal. In general, if a saddle is too low there may be discomfort in the front of the knee, but this is not true in all cases.

A low saddle height may create a tendency for elaborate ankling patterns to increase leg extension, which usually results in less power. A saddle height that is too high may result in discomfort at the back of the knee. The most important principle of any fitting system is that it is standardized and repeatable. Serotta fitters are trained to address each issue in a specific sequence that we believe produces the best outcome. That training is backed by hundreds of thousands of fittings performed using Serotta protocols.

Dartfish aids in the determination of the ideal leg extension. Two key measures are closely examined. Leg extension is largely irrelevant if it is not looked at in relation to the ankling pattern at the appropriate point in the pedal stroke. Given that a Serotta fitter with Dartfish is not selecting a single hypothetical point to measure, the video can be advanced until the maximum leg extension value is reached. This maximal leg extension point will be evaluated several times to ensure that it is a consistent value at a consistent point in the pedal stroke. Leg extension is always examined in relation to the ankling pattern. The correct leg extension values can be produced with poor ankling patterns. Therefore, extension and ankling are interdependent.

 **Finally, how do you integrate technology with the art of fitting?**

All great fitters have good visual skills, and the honest ones are often somewhat shocked at the depth of information that a great video analysis solution provides. Dartfish is central to Serotta education, and we have learned that fitters and consumers benefit from the clarity offered by seeing a person from multiple views with kinematic data in full high-definition video.

As an example, static measurements with a plumb bob are not performed under the correct load and cadence conditions. It is challenging to visually duplicate the ankling position of the cyclist while the fitter attempts to see where the plumb bob is relative to the pedal spindle. Given that different ankling positions influence the position of the knee over the pedal, the measurement can be inaccurate. The bottom line is that measuring the knee over the pedal spindle with a plumb bob is not as accurate or as specific as using a motion analysis solution with the appropriate load and cadence.

The Serotta bike fit is one of the most respected and established bike fits in the country. Ben Serotta could even be called the father of bike fitting because he was the first to create the "fit cycle" and build a system around fitting the bike to the athlete. The Serotta fit is clearly comprehensive and integrates all the key factors involving bike fit, from motion analysis to proper cleat placement based on the exact shape of the rider's foot. An important aspect to the Serotta fit is the fact that Serotta has embraced change over the years and has continued to improve, adapt, modify, and innovate as new technologies, methods, and studies have come about. This vision of continual improvement makes the Serotta fit one of the best choices on the market today.

# BikeFit

The last bike-fitting company that we interviewed was started by Paul Swift back in 1995 when he helped develop a product called Big Meats, known today as Cleat Wedges. Paul is a multiple national champion cyclist who saw many of his teammates experience knee problems or injuries. He believed that knee tracking was an overlooked area and began to develop products to ensure that the knees tracked properly, regardless of the force being produced by the rider or the presence of a leg-length discrepancy. He also examined how cleat placement affected the knees. BikeFit was created to fit riders from the feet up. Knee alignment is one of the keys to the fit, and all the contact points between athlete and bicycle are addressed.

Based in the Seattle, Washington, area, BikeFit has achieved a global reach with the recent addition of its European distribution center. The company's products are used throughout the world by the most influential and recognized bike fitters, as well as in the medical community. We asked Katrina Vogel, the head of education at BikeFit, and founder Paul Swift about their fit.

## Q&A   With BikeFit

 **What was the impetus for starting BikeFit? How did it come about? Give us a little history on the company.**

PS: While training at the Olympic Center in 1982, I was fit using the original Fit Kit System with originator Chris Farrell. At the time I was also working with Eddie Borysewicz and the late Dr. Ed Burke. They all noticed that one side of my pelvis kept dropping *a lot* more than the other. Dr. Burke and Eddie questioned this and asked what should be done, but the system provided no answer. I later found out that I had a quarter-inch (6 mm) structural leg-length difference. Finally, I added a lift at the foot pedal interface around 1983. Voila!—my hip didn't drop anymore. From this experience, it became apparent to me that the foot–pedal interface was basically being ignored

*(continued)*

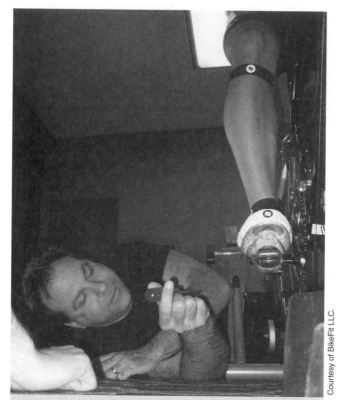

Courtesy of BikeFit LLC.

**Paul Swift of BikeFit fine-tunes a cyclist's cleat position.**

within bike fitting throughout the world. This became the cornerstone for BikeFit. In addition, in 1982 I saw a picture of 10 people standing in a row side by side, facing forward. The people were of many ages, shapes, sizes, and heights, but all of them had the same inseam length. I recognized that no formula, such as seat height being a set percentage of inseam height, would be capable of providing everyone with his or her best possible bike fit.

In 1995 there was still no system that addressed the front-view foot–pedal interface or its interlinking relationship with the side-view sagittal mechanics. Fore and aft and rotation were sometimes addressed in a bike fit, but no other system addressed medial and lateral cleat placement, canting, or leg-length differences. After I started working with recreational and competitive cyclists to make them comfortable on their bikes, doors started opening all over the place. This led to various patents and technologies, including the cleat wedge, that are now used throughout the world by cyclists of all levels, including national, Olympic, and world champions, in addition to Grand Tour winners. Additionally, most the major bike-fitting companies today are our customers and are using our products and technologies—Specialized, Andy Pruitt at Boulder Center for Sports Medicine, Serotta, Fit Kit, Retül, Steve Hogg, and many more.

### What's the greatest strength of BikeFit?

KV: BikeFit educates, develops, and mentors bike fitters to be skilled in problem solving and critical thinking. These skills are used in conjunction with the most technical video and data capture technology, but our fitters are not dependent on technology to perform a great bike fit. Our goal is to make the bike disappear so that the cyclist can enjoy the ride.

### What's the biggest limitation to BikeFit?

KV: The BikeFit system's biggest limitation is the lack of knowledge and misconceptions in the cycling world regarding the importance of the foot–pedal interface. Would a person build a house on a faulty foundation? No, yet many bike fits ignore the foundation of bike fit, which is the foot–pedal interface. For example, BikeFit is sometimes labeled as the wedge company. This is a misconception because the wedge is one small part of a comprehensive approach to bike fitting.

### How does BikeFit address cleat placement?

KV: The cleats and pedals are two of the five contact points on both road bikes and mountain bikes. Therefore, the foot–pedal interface is often the most important part of the bike fit. It affects the mechanics throughout the spine and both the upper and lower extremities of the cyclist, especially if there is a leg-length discrepancy. Incorrect cleat placement creates a ticking time bomb for repetitive use injuries, even in healthy cyclists. Each cyclist is assessed individually and is fit to her or his biomechanical and architectural needs with appropriate use of medial and lateral, fore and aft, rotational, canting, and elevation changes to the cleat and pedal system. Spindle length is an important but often overlooked consideration because stance width is variable. Some people need a longer or shorter spindle length to address their natural stance width beyond the range provided by the cleat's medial and lateral range. This concern can be especially problematic with cleats that cannot really be adjusted medially or laterally.

### What are the characteristics of a properly placed saddle? What do you see in the software that tells you the placement is right?

KV: Objectively, knee angle is within a range of about 30 to 37 degrees of knee flexion at dead bottom center. But this angle may vary according to the length–tension relationship of the cyclist's hip flexors, hamstrings, and so on. Knee angle may also be measured at the angle of the seat tube, which is typically about 2 degrees less than dead bottom center. Fore and aft position is placed to protect the patella from harm; this position is relative to each cyclist. This answer assumes that the person has the proper length and angle of stem and handlebars, so that the cyclist can sit comfortably on the saddle, and that the saddle being used is the correct one for the cyclist as well.

*(continued)*

**How have computers and technology helped you in bike fitting?**

PS: The frank answer to the first question is, Hmmm . . . not a lot. Our high-tech tools include the human brain because knowledge and critical thinking are the most important tools in bike fit. The biggest change over the years has been the progression from the use of the stroke viewer to the use of a self-leveling laser for front views and for assessing fore and aft position of the knee. From our times using Dartfish, we learned that most fitters were focusing on how to use the software and were not focusing on the fit. The fitting became the secondary focus, and the software was the primary focus.

BikeFit has been developed by the keen mind of Paul Swift, one of the leading innovators in bike fitting since the development of the wedge for cleats. His bike fit has developed from a philosophy of problem solving. Whenever Paul recognized a problem with an athlete, he studied that problem extensively and designed a solution for it. Cleat placement and seat placement fore and aft have been highly tuned within BikeFit, and this focus clearly identifies and corrects many imbalances within the riders' skeletal and muscular structure.

# Applying the Science

The fits differ from each other in a number of ways, not only in how they conduct their fit and the tools they use but also in the philosophy of the fit. From Retül's reliance on cutting-edge technology to measure dynamic motion to BikeFit's focus on the foot–pedal interface, each has a unique way of getting you in the best position possible on your bike. The proper fit on the bicycle evolves as you evolve, and a fit that worked for you in your 20s might not be the best fit for you when you reach your 40s. Two things are clear:

1. To be the most economical on a bicycle, you have to fit it extremely well.
2. Every person is different, and a bike fit done well is almost entirely custom-made for you.

These two points are really the driving factors in bike fit and should be considered throughout the process of any fit. As we start to see more technology coming into the bike-fitting industry, we see more data-driven approaches. Although we would always agree that more data is better, we also understand that computers are only as smart as the person programming them, so we caution you not to get just a computer bike fit. Some of the most interesting ideas from the bike-fitting industry have spawned companies that produce new pedal systems, saddles for different-sized pelvises, and even shoes. Clearly, the science of bike fitting is important not only for racers but for all cyclists.

One point worth noting is that when you do get a fit, be cautious in how quickly you try to adapt to it. Any change in the biomechanical relationship in the joints of the lower body can have a profound effect in cycling given that they are locked into the position and move literally millions of time in the same pattern. This learned pattern of movement causes muscles to develop in certain ways, bones to be strengthened at highly focused points of stress, and even joints to be molded. If this pattern is quickly changed and used to ride 100 miles (160 km) (easily 27,000 total pedal revolutions), trouble is likely. This warning pertains not only to bike fit but also to a change in any part on your bicycle that might affect the joints in the legs and hips. Even a change as small as replacing worn-out cleats can have a big effect and produce knee pain. The danger of making changes too quickly is real, but many cyclists haphazardly change the seat, the angle of the seat, the pedals, and other factors without much thought about what might happen.

Even Hunter has a tale of personal injury. Right before he left for a 2-week bike tour in the Alps and Pyrenees of France, he saw that his seat, which he had been using for more than 2 years, was bent heavily to the left side. Hunter, being young and naive at the time, decided to buy a new seat a couple of days before this epic 2-week ride. Big mistake! Because he had grown accustomed to that particular pattern of movement, the bones in the knee joint, along with the kneecap, had developed calcium deposits in a small area to handle the particular stress in that learned pattern. With the new seat, the pattern of movement changed ever so slightly, but after 10 days of riding 8 to 12 hours a day, Hunter developed major knee pain. It turned out to be a massive inflammation of the bursa, and Hunter was off the bike for over 6 months afterward to recover and heal. So, heed the lesson. When changing your bike fit, your components, or anything that alters that learned pattern of movement in the lower body, rider beware! Take it slow and don't be afraid to move back into your old position for a while if necessary to make a smooth transition.

We also suggest that you consider your goals before getting a bike fit. Whether you are trying to win masters nationals or the next pro race or just be comfortable while riding on a long bike tour, your goal can affect the way that the fitter approaches your final position. Other factors also matter. An older rider will not be able to achieve the same comfort and economy in an aggressive and aerodynamic position as a younger rider can. We believe that comfort should always be considered when getting a bike fit—if you are not comfortable, then it's hard to be economical. That being said, you must find the balance between economy and comfort and the best solution for your particularly morphology. Finally, as you think about bike fit, remember that improvement related to the new fit might not happen right away; in most cases, you will need some time to get used to a new position. Only after you have retrained your muscles in that new movement pattern will you be faster and more comfortable.

## CHAPTER 8

# Pedaling for Peak Efficiency

The phrase *like riding a bike* is often used in North America to denote an activity so easy that anybody can learn to do it and will never forget how. On the face of it, the act of riding a bike is indeed simple. Most riders limit their consideration of pedaling to setting their saddle height before they jump on the bike. But the inherently unnatural act of pedaling (compared with walking or running) as smoothly and efficiently as possible requires a hugely complex coordination of multiple joints and muscles (Bini and Diefenthaeler 2009, So et al. 2005). When you consider that the action of pushing the pedals is repeated thousands of revolutions on each ride, it becomes obvious that even simple and apparently miniscule improvements in form or technique can result in major performance gains and minimize the risk of injury.

The interest in improving cycling efficiency is not new, as evidenced by a 1934 study that compared the metabolic cost of cycling of a former British professional to the information then available on the efficiency of recreational cyclists (Garry and Wishart 1934). But since Lance Armstrong's recovery from cancer and his metamorphosis from a classics and stage-hunting specialist to the dominant Tour de France rider of his generation, much has been made of his pedaling style, marked by reliance on extremely high cadences (more than 100 revolutions per minute) in both climbing and time trialing. His history has revolutionized the thinking behind cadence, representing a dramatic switch from the traditional advice to use lower cadences. The basic theoretical argument behind this new thinking is that, with a higher cadence at any particular power output, less demand is placed on the muscles with each pedal stroke, thus enhancing efficiency and delaying fatigue. Many elite riders have attempted to employ a high-cadence style, with varying degrees of success. The typical endurance cycling cadence of 90 to 100 revolutions per minute, Armstrong's high-cadence road style, and the extremely high cadences currently used in track cycling all fly in the face of various scientific studies that have demonstrated that the highest metabolic efficiency results from cadences of 50 to 60 revolutions per minute.

Pedaling dynamics can be improved in a number of ways. The first obvious method is to improve the pattern of muscle recruitment during the complex task that is pedaling. Much of the old advice and new equipment developed recently revolve around this idea. Examples include specific drills such as one-legged pedaling or riding a fixed gear, training with nontraditional cranks that are not offset at the usual 180 degrees, and nonround chainrings. Another approach is to alter cadence, assuming that there is indeed an optimal cadence from a physiological or tactical perspective.

In this chapter we attempt to answer whether an optimal cadence exists, and we review the methods of optimizing cadence that have recently been proposed. We examine the scientific evidence for the current approaches to improved pedaling and summarize some of the latest ideas concerning the science and art of pedaling.

# Gross Efficiency and Economy

Two terms commonly used in defining the concept of how well we use our energy for propelling a bicycle are gross efficiency and economy. Although often used incorrectly and interchangeably, these two terms define related but distinctly different concepts. Therefore, we need to ensure that we use the correct term in the context of cycling.

## Gross Efficiency

Gross efficiency is generally defined as the ratio of mechanical work performed to the overall energy expended. So a power monitor output of 200 watts refers to the mechanical power that is going into turning the cranks. That number, however, is just a small fraction of the overall energy that the body has processed in the act of metabolizing stored fuels (carbohydrate, lipid, and protein). Most of the energy contained in the nutrients that we take in is instead converted to heat, such that the gross efficiency of the body is only 20 to 25 percent on average. To calculate gross efficiency, we would take the mechanical energy (1 watt equals 1 joule per second, so this is simple to convert) and divide this by the total energy that the body consumes (calculated by measuring oxygen uptake and then converting this to the standard energy unit of joules; see chapter 2 for more information on basic energy units). For example, requiring 1,000 watts of overall metabolism to generate 200 watts on your bike means a gross efficiency of 200 divided by 1000, or 20 percent. Therefore, the term *gross efficiency* refers more to the internal metabolic economy rather than the overall economy of the human–bike system. In other words, the term *gross efficiency* answers this question: How much overall food energy did it take for your muscles to generate 1,000 kilojoules of stored energy? Most often, the only way to calculate gross efficiency accurately is to perform a laboratory test with equipment that measures your oxygen consumption directly.

Hence, gross efficiency is the part of economy of movement that refers to your metabolism of food energy into stored energy that your muscles can use. Gross efficiency is somewhat hardwired and is determined by muscle type. Evidence indicates that people with a greater percentage of Type I slow-twitch fibers have higher gross efficiency values (Coyle et al. 1992). Gross efficiency is somewhat analogous to the baseline fuel efficiency of a vehicle. We can increase fuel efficiency in a car by tinkering with the mechanics of the engine, such as by adjusting the carburetor, burning cleaner fuel, or switching out the engine completely. Extending the analogy, although we can't switch out cardiovascular systems, we can enhance aerobic capacity by tinkering with our training and nutrition.

## Economy

Often used incorrectly to refer to efficiency, economy is a related but broader term that focuses more on the overall cost of movement. In physiological terms, economy refers to the total metabolic, typically oxygen, cost of sustaining a particular power output or speed. Heart rate is sometimes used as a surrogate when oxygen measurement is not possible. Therefore, gross efficiency, the biochemical ability of the body to convert food energy to mechanical energy, can also be thought of as the quantity of overall food energy needed to generate 1,000 kilojoules of stored energy for the muscles. Gross efficiency is just the first component of overall economy of cycling. In contrast, economy incorporates gross efficiency but focuses on how many kilojoules of that stored energy were used to ride a set distance such as a 40K time trial. At its most basic, even if your gross efficiency never changed, if you did a ride that required 600 kilojoules one day and then rode the same course with a tailwind another day and used only 500 kilojoules, then your economy greatly increased (figure 8.1 on page 174).

In keeping with the automobile analogy, economy can be thought of as the actual fuel mileage that you get out of a car, which can be affected by factors such as driving style, whether the miles are driven in the city or on the highway, whether you have a roof rack and bikes on top of the car, and the tire pressure. For cyclists, economy is affected by choice of gearing, cadence, and crankarm length. A huge factor in improving economy is better aerodynamics, from riding in the drops rather than on top of the handlebar through to optimizing an aerodynamic position for time trialing. Finally, improving economy also incorporates a number of technical skills on the bike, from maximizing draft protection in a pack to minimizing deceleration through corners, thus reducing the energy required to accelerate back up to speed.

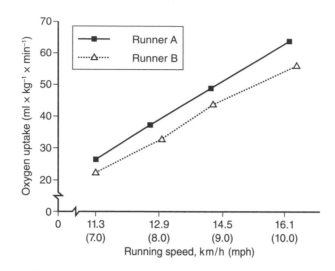

**FIGURE 8.1** **Cycling economy is a function of many factors, including weather, equipment, and technical skills.**

Reprinted, by permission, from J.H. Wilmore, D.L. Costill, and W.L. Kenney, 2008, *Physiology of sport and exercise*, 4th ed. (Champaign, IL: Human Kinetics), 111.

As should be evident, for most cyclists the parameter of interest is generally economy rather than efficiency, which is somewhat more specialized in referring mainly to metabolism and is difficult to change systematically. Thus, the more relevant term when discussing the ability of a cyclist to use as little energy as possible to achieve a set power output or speed is economy. Fortunately for cyclists with a power monitor, economy is simple to measure. All currently available units record work or the actual kilojoules of mechanical energy performed. Thus, assuming that environmental conditions such as wind and temperature are similar, cyclists can relatively easily test, in realistic field conditions, the effects of different gearing, pacing, bike positions, cornering and braking strategies, and other items on economy of movement.

## Can Efficiency Be Altered?

Although the foregoing section demonstrated that many factors not involving training can alter economy, a contentious debate has erupted over the past five years about the role of efficiency in determining performance and the possibility of improving efficiency by training. A high degree of consistency in gross efficiency was reported in trained cyclists (Chapman et al. 2006), who in turn were significantly more efficient than novice cyclists (Chapman et al. 2008). But whether higher gross efficiency is a predictor of performance potential is unclear. Lucia et al. (2002) studied 11 top-level Spanish pro cyclists, ranging from climbers and general classification Grand Tour riders to time trial specialists, each of whom had world championships or stage wins in the Grand Tours on their palmares (racing resumes). They performed a ramp test to exhaustion to determine their $\dot{V}O_2$max (maximal aerobic capacity, an excellent indicator of endurance fitness), and a 20-minute ride at a constant workload near their time trial pace. These pros exhibited a wide range of $\dot{V}O_2$max values, ranging from 65.5 to 82.5 milliliters per kilogram per minute. Furthermore, these elite professionals exhibited a wide range in gross efficiency, from 20.9 to 28.1 percent. Methodological concerns have been raised because of the high values for gross efficiency, but the elite status of these subjects makes it somewhat difficult to compare their data with that previously collected on less accomplished athletes. Also, the testing occurred in February, during the early season, when the athletes may have been at various stages in their seasonal periodization.

A closer examination of the data from Lucia et al. (2002) suggests that maximizing efficiency may indeed be crucial in optimizing performance. Independent of factors such as body mass, age, and cycling specialty, a very strong inverse relationship was found between $\dot{V}O_2$max and cycling efficiency in this group. That is, riders with relatively low aerobic capacity seemed to be able to compensate for this handicap by being much more efficient, resulting in their requiring less energy to generate a particular power output. Also worth noting is a study that profiled Lance Armstrong's laboratory testing between 1993 and 1999; although significant scientific controversy arose because of methodological concerns and alleged calculation errors, the study generated great media interest by reporting a significant increase in gross efficiency of nearly 8 percent in an already elite athlete (Coyle 2005).

Scientists continue to debate whether efficiency can be altered or improved in less accomplished athletes (Hopker et al. 2009b). A study of a cross-section of trained and untrained cyclists demonstrated a systematically higher gross efficiency across a range of workloads when subjects pedaled at their preferred cadence (Hopker et al. 2007). A high degree of variability in efficiency was also observed in trained competitive cyclists over the course of a season. Numbers increased over the precompetition phase from 19.3 to 20.6 percent, stayed at that level over the competition phase, and then decreased again afterward (Hopker et al. 2009a).

So what does all this mean? First, don't get too hung up on your genetic potential or comparing your test results with anybody else's. The reasons and mechanisms behind changes in efficiency are still being explored. Physiological, mechanical, aerodynamic, and strategic factors affect economy, and smart and dedicated training can help you exceed your perceived limits. Finally, the smoother and more economical your pedaling stroke is, the less energy you require to maintain any given power output or speed. Who wouldn't benefit from that?

# Analyzing the Neuromuscular Demands of Cycling

Although a watt is a watt, not all watts are created equal in terms of meeting the demands of the event! One of the most important guiding principles of training is to train to the demands of the event, and dedicated cyclists apply this principle to every aspect of training. Although cross-training with basketball is terrific in the off-season for fun and general cardiovascular fitness, it is not going to improve your ability to put power to the pedals on the bike. Similarly, subtle mismatches between the type of cycling performed in training and the type called for during events can limit your progress if you are not aware of them and do not adapt your training accordingly. For example, the road training that you like to do for a change of pace may not be specific enough to the demands of mountain biking. Likewise, racing 60-minute criteriums all summer may not be the most specific preparation for 60-minute cyclocross races, even though the duration and the frequent accelerations are similar on the surface. Taking the principle of specificity one step further, we should strive not only to pedal efficiently but also to pedal in the manner and pattern called for in the event that we are training for.

Consider that power files from a mountain bike race are characterized by periods (typically one to five minutes) of high power followed by coasting or easy pedaling. The technical demands of riding over rocks and roots through rough single track necessitate periods of coasting, which show as rest on a power file download. But in reality, the athlete is dancing all over the bike to maintain momentum and avoid falling off or even hitting a tree—and not actually resting. Thus, although building overall aerobic fitness is a critical goal for all cyclists, greater specificity is required. To reflect the pedaling action of the cyclist during a particular event, intervals must mimic not just the duration and frequency of intervals typical to the event but also the particular cadence and gearing.

Toward that end, Hunter and Dr. Andrew Coggan developed a tool known as quadrant analysis (see Allen and Coggan's *Training and Racing With a Power Meter* and the Q & A with Dr. Coggan on page 178 for more information). Quadrant analysis helps cyclists clearly understand the type of power generated and used, allowing them to match their training more closely to their event. Figure 8.2 presents a scatter plot of a power file from a mountain bike race overlaid on a typical hard training ride done on a road bike. The $x$-axis reflects circumferential pedal velocity, which translates to cadence, and the $y$-axis shows average effective pedal force. From this perspective, QI represents high force and fast cadence, QII is high force and slow cadence, QIII is low force and slow cadence, and QIV is

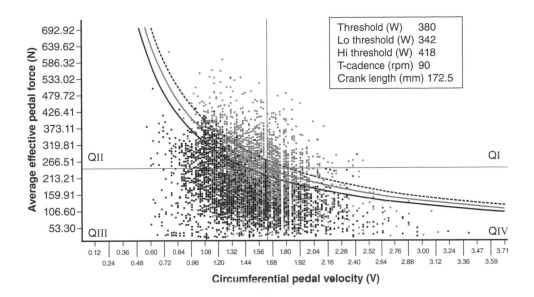

**FIGURE 8.2** Differences in neuromuscular demands between a mountain bike race and a road ride.

low force and fast cadence. The crosshairs are defined by the athlete's T-cadence, which is the cyclist's self-selected cadence at her or his functional threshold power. The plot of the mountain bike race (darker points) shows that over 33 percent of the race was done in QII, using more force or muscular strength than endurance. This plot is in stark contrast to the plot from the road training (lighter points), in which the cyclist tried to emulate a mountain bike race but spent little time creating watts in QII (less than 19 percent).

The demands of the event should largely dictate the type of training that you do. If you are training for an ultradistance road bike ride, then riding for 20 minutes each day on the velodrome will not adequately prepare you. If your event requires bursts of hard effort as short as 5 seconds and as long as 30 minutes, you need to train for that intensity and duration. As you prepare an overall yearlong training plan, consider when to include more high-intensity efforts within the plan and exactly how you will implement those workouts. If you start your intense efforts too soon in your training plan, you risk reaching your peak fitness too soon as well. Keep in mind that high-intensity intervals aren't just a matter of producing the most watts you can for short periods; how and when you create those high-intensity watts can make the difference between being fully prepared or partially prepared for your event.

## Q&A    With Dr. Andy Coggan: Quadrant Analysis

| Current position | Senior scientist, Mallinckrodt Institute of Radiology, Washington University School of Medicine, St. Louis, Missouri. |
|---|---|
| Professional relationship and background with cycling | Exercise physiologist. |
| Personal background with cycling | Cycling since 1974, racing on and off (now mostly off) since 1975. |

 **Andy, one of the big contributions from power meters and analysis software is that the cyclist can analyze the neuromuscular demands of cycling out on the road. What information can we gain from that, and how can we benefit from it?**

At least at present, none of the on-bike power meters on the market provides data on the pattern of force application within the pedal stroke. From data for power and cadence, however, it is possible to calculate the average effective pedal force and circumferential pedal velocity across pedal strokes or across time, depending on how the particular power meter in question records data. This information can provide insight into the neuromuscular demands of generating a particular power output.

 **Can you briefly explain the concept of quadrant analysis?**

Quadrant analysis is a graphical tool for analyzing power meter data to provide insight into the neuromuscular demands of a particular race or training session. It consists of plotting pedal force versus pedal velocity in a scattergram and placing crosshairs centered on the points of intersection corresponding to the individual's sustainable power and self-selected cadence at that power. This approach divides the chart into four quadrants, with significant recruitment of Type II (fast-twitch) motor units being more likely to occur in either quadrant I, where relatively high force and high velocity is used, or in quadrant II, where relatively high force but low velocity is used. Significant recruitment of Type II units is less likely to occur in quadrant III, where low force and low velocity is used, or in quadrant IV, where low force but high velocity is used.

**How does quadrant analysis and its data differ for a triathlete, a criterium rider, a century rider, and a mountain biker?**

Quadrant analysis plots reflect how power is generated during a particular workout or race, and thus they reflect both the characteristics of the individual and the nature or demands of the event. In general, though, the data are more tightly clustered when someone is riding alone, at a steady pace, or on flat terrain and are more widely scattered when someone is riding in a group, at a variable pace, or where it is hilly. The biggest variation occurs when riders are forced to pedal outside their comfort zone in terms of pedal force and pedal velocity, such as when racing in a velodrome or riding a single-speed mountain bike over rugged terrain.

 **How can a cyclist use quadrant analysis to improve fitness and performance? Is it more of a reactive monitoring tool, or is it also a predictive tool that can guide training?**

The most effective way to use quadrant analysis is to apply it both descriptively and prescriptively. That is, you should analyze races to determine their specific neuromuscular demands and then design training sessions that match those demands as closely as possible. Although performance in most cycling events is determined primarily by actual power output (especially aerobic power production), precisely how the power is produced in terms of pedal force and pedal velocity can also play a role. Used in this way quadrant analysis ensures that you are training as specifically as possible for your event.

 **Can you suggest one drill or tool that cyclists can use to improve their pedaling stroke and its efficiency?**

Based on multiple lines of evidence, I do not believe that cyclists can gain any significant benefit by performing specific pedaling drills. Rather, cyclists should focus on maximizing their power output while pedaling at a cadence that is appropriate for the cyclist's individual characteristics and the nature and demands of the event.

# Pedaling Asymmetry

Pedaling is such a simple thing that most cyclists never think about it. Any small improvement in biomechanics, however, can go a long way to improving overall comfort and efficiency and decreasing the risk of injury. Most of us learn at an early age that we have a strongly preferred throwing arm, but do we recognize that we may also have a preferred pedaling leg? Understanding the contribution of each leg is important not just for optimizing cycling performance but also for minimizing the risk of injury.

Externally, our right and left sides look pretty much alike, but they are not built equally. Each of us possesses varying degrees of dexterity, from our preferred eating and writing hands to whether we are right- or left-handed batters or hockey shooters. Such preferences are amply evident in the physiques of extremely side-specific athletes such as baseball pitchers, who have dramatically higher bone thickness and muscle strength in the dominant arm. Over time, the repetitive use of the dominant hand or side logically must cause differences in the balance of the skeleton and muscles between the two sides. Such marked side dominance can eventually emerge in the form of muscle imbalance and even injury.

Scientists have begun to ask and answer questions about side dominance and cycling. Does the same side dominance hold true for the lower body and legs? Does a significant pedaling asymmetry exist in cycling? And if so, does it present a risk of injury or cause a decrease in efficiency? Are corrective exercises in order?

In a study by Carpes et al. (2007), six competitive but non-elite cyclists performed a 40K laboratory time trial on a flat course with a normal racing position and a simulated 53 by 15 gearing. Although subjects received feedback about power, cadence, and so on throughout the trial, they were not told that the specific purpose of the test was to analyze pedaling asymmetry. This information was withheld to ensure that subjects didn't consciously or subconsciously alter their riding. One difficulty that the authors faced was how to quantify whether a subject was asymmetrical because no previous study had been able to establish an objective number or threshold for this question. The authors ultimately settled on a threshold value of 10 percent difference in torque between the right and left legs as a threshold for significance. All subjects demonstrated significant asymmetry (greater than 10 percent) at some point during the time trial. On average, the middle portions of the time trial featured both significant asymmetry of greater than 10 percent and lower overall mean torques. Therefore, in a time trial setting anyway, pedaling asymmetry does exist, matching previous findings (Daly and Cavanagh 1976, Smak et al. 1999). Each of those studies also noted a high degree of variability in the degree of asymmetry both between cyclists and within the same cyclist with repeated trials, although the general tendency was for the dominant (kicking) leg to generate higher forces.

Another interesting finding is the apparent effect of pedaling rate and workload on asymmetry. Carpes et al. (2007) reported that the higher mean torque values at the start and end of the time trial correlated with lower and nonsignificant asymmetry values (8.9 and 0.3 percent, respectively) and a decrease in asymmetry at higher cadences (Smak et al. 1999). Therefore, moderate endurance and tempo power outputs resulted in higher asymmetry. But when the torque and power output increased, the imbalances seemed to disappear. The reason for the decreased asymmetry at higher power outputs remains unknown; it's possible that the dominant leg becomes more fatigued and unable to respond at higher workloads.

Clearly, pedaling asymmetry exists, suggesting that we spend much of our riding time with the dominant leg performing a greater percentage of the overall work of pedaling. Riders with a CompuTrainer can see leg imbalances in real time with the SpinScan feature. But at this stage it's unclear what role reducing imbalances can play in improving performance or decreasing the risk of injury. We simply don't know whether asymmetry during lower-intensity cycling is detrimental in the long term. One avenue for further research is whether and how this imbalance might be considered when trying to optimize bike fit. Whether a relationship exists between asymmetry and efficiency remains unknown.

# Ankling Technique

When we think of some of the classic stars of the sport, what often springs to mind is the ease with which they seemed to pedal. Think of Fausto Coppi or Jacques Anquetil, who were famed for their elegance and lightness as they climbed or tore up time trials. These qualities arose from their pedaling action, which was marked by an aesthetic fluidity. In contrast are the monster gear mashers—the guys who seem to will their bodies and bikes to success, style and grace be damned. Think of Sean Kelly or Santiago Botero, hunched over their bikes cranking massive gears—it's hard to tell whether they're torturing their bikes or vice versa!

One key ingredient in a cyclist's style of pedaling seems to be the degree of ankle movement through the 360-degree rotation (figure 8.3). Studies on the biomechanics of cycling reveal that, although the hip and knees go through a complex movement, the ankles generally stay fixed throughout the pedal stroke. But surprisingly little research has been conducted on whether there is an optimal angle. The traditional view is that the ankle should be relatively neutral throughout the entire stroke, neither extremely toes down (plantarflexed—Lance Armstrong was a prime example of this) nor heels down (dorsiflexed—Santiago Botero was a prime example). A recent study attempted to train 11 fit masters cyclists to pedal at angles approximately 7 degrees more plantarflexed or dorsiflexed from their freely selected ankle joint angle for a week (Cannon et al. 2007). No major changes in muscle activity and recruitment patterns were observed when

**FIGURE 8.3** Although ankling technique can differ greatly between cyclists, these differences have not been shown to greatly affect performance.

©Tim Ireland/PA Archive/Press Association Images

comparing the plantarflexed position (toes down) to the self-selected position. The dorsiflexed position, however, resulted in much greater electrical activation of the calf (gastrocnemius) muscle, required a higher oxygen uptake for the same power output, and consequently exhibited lower gross efficiency.

Note that one of the critical shortcomings of this study was the limited amount of training, only about six minutes per day for a week, at the different ankle angle. Furthermore, no information was provided on whether any of the subjects were naturally already tending toward plantarflexion or dorsiflexion in their normal pedaling. For something that we do thousands of times every ride, six minutes of training a few times a week is simply not enough time for the body to adapt. One interesting finding from this study is that although dorsiflexion seems to cost a bit more energy, no benefit seems to result from riding with a more toes-down style. The main lesson really comes from the major limitation of this study—to become proficient at anything, nothing beats repetition. If you're going to make any changes in your pedaling, body position, or new equipment, you must commit time and effort to it, not make a snap decision based on initial perceptions.

# Equipment for Optimizing Pedaling

Given the complex nature of the muscle and joint coordination required for pedaling, it may seem surprising that round chainrings and a perfectly circular pedal stroke are assumed to be optimal. Noncircular chainrings and crankarms have appeared sporadically throughout the history of the bicycle. The most systematic push occurred with Shimano's introduction of its BioPace nonround chainrings in the late 1980s. BioPace was nearly universally reviled by the cycling market for a variety of reasons, including possibly the fact that it was introduced in the lower-end 105 and Ultegra groups and not in the pro-level Dura-Ace. Scientifically, no significant differences in physiological response were found when comparing BioPace to round chainrings across a range of workloads and cadences (Cullen et al. 1992).

Other designs have been developed by small companies, often debuting with a cult following but minimal scientific research. The theory behind nonround pedaling systems is that increasing the effective crank length or chainring size during the powerful downstroke increases torque where the leg muscles are most effective. Most designs also attempt to minimize the effective crank length or chainring size during the upstroke to permit faster movement through the biomechanical dead spots. For example, Rotor chainring literature touts their 53-tooth chainring as roughly equivalent to a 56- and 51-tooth chainring during the power and dead spots of the pedal stroke, respectively (figure 8.4). This section reviews the current knowledge behind noncircular chainrings, nonconstant crankarms, and independent crankarms such as PowerCranks.

**FIGURE 8.4** The O-symetric Harmonic chainring increases the effective chainring size during the power phase.

Hunter Allen

## Noncircular Chainrings

After a few years of gaining a foothold in the pro peloton through the early 2000s, nonround chainrings have gone big time. Currently, the two major players in noncircular chainrings are O-symetric from France and Rotor from Spain. O-symetric was first popularized by Bobby Julich and achieved a big breakthrough when Bradley Wiggins used them en route to a fourth-place finish at the 2009 Tour. Rotor's first huge splash was with cyclocross, road bike, and track star Marianne Vos, who has won world championships in all disciplines with Rotor rings. Apart from the specific shape of the Rotor rings, a unique Rotor design feature is the multiple installation possibilities. Namely, the chainrings can be installed at various positions relative to the crankarms, essentially phase advancing or delaying the peak of the power stroke. Therefore, the ring position can be adjusted individually based on both personal biomechanics and the demands of the discipline. Rotor's biggest coup was Carlos Sastre's use of an unbranded chainring on otherwise traditional FSA-sponsored cranks during his 2008 Tour de France victory. With Sastre's move to the new Cervelo TestTeam (CTT) from 2009 through 2010, Rotor became the official crank and chainring sponsor for the entire team, giving the company huge credibility and pro access for testing their design. Such acceptance by professionals helped greatly with market credibility, and scientific research on the biomechanical, physiological, and performance effects of alternative pedaling systems in general has expanded. One of the first studies to compare the use of round versus Rotor chainrings at two different installation settings, done during a 10K time trial, found no difference in power output or ratings of perceived exertion (figure 8.5). But systematic scientific investigation of these two modern nonround chainrings under long-term use has yet to be performed. Therefore, it is currently impossible to assess their efficacy scientifically.

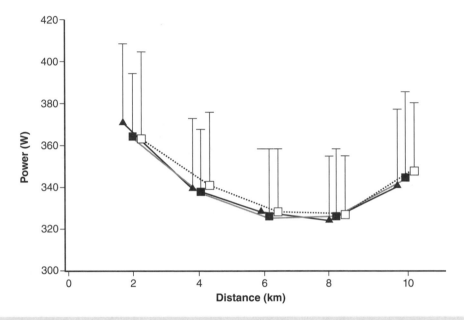

**FIGURE 8.5** Power outputs from cyclists using circular (shaded square) and Rotor chainrings set at two orientations (shaded triangle and open square) during a 10K time trial.

Adapted, by permission, from J.J. Peiffer and C.J. Abbiss, 2010, "The influence of elliptical chainrings on 10 km cycling time trial performance," *International Journal of Sports Physiology and Performance* 5(4): 459-468.

## Nonaligned Crankarms

The other approach to achieve different pedaling biomechanics is to alter the cranks rather than the chainrings. The purpose of nonconstant crankarms is similar to that of nonround chainrings, namely either to eliminate the dead spot at 0 and 180 degrees of the pedal stroke or alter the effective crank length throughout the stroke. In turn, three separate or combined designs are typical:

1. The cranks themselves change length throughout the pedal stroke.
2. The center of attachment to the bottom bracket is offset, such that round chainrings become effectively nonround.
3. The cranks are not fixed at 180 degrees apart, such that the power phase of one leg is occurring at the same time as the dead spot of the other leg.

Currently, the main commercial system is from Rotor. Before introducing the nonround Q-rings, Rotor started as a designer of a unique crank system in which the arms are not fixed at 180 degrees apart. The aim was to eliminate the dead spots at the top and bottom of the pedal stroke (Lucia et al. 2004, Rodriguez-Marroyo et al. 2009, Santalla et al. 2002). Additionally, the chainrings on the Rotor cranks are not perfectly centered on the cranks (i.e., the chainring and crank rotation axis are not the same) but can be varied. The effect is to alter the crank angle at which the effective crank arm length is maximal (i.e., where the most force can be applied). Again, the goal is to optimize and match where the human leg can biomechanically produce the most force. The Q-rings that we now commonly see are an offshoot of the whole system design in order to gain acceptance by cyclists who might balk at the different setup and higher weight.

No differences in ventilatory threshold or any other physiological parameter were reported between the standard and Rotor (position 3) cranks during the incremental test to exhaustion (Rodriguez-Marroyo et al. 2009). Similarly, no differences in any parameter were reported in the submaximal test across the five conditions (standard cranks plus Rotor in all four positions). This conclusion held true whether all five were compared or whether the normal data were compared with the Rotor position that provided optimal mechanical efficiency results for each subject. Adaptation issues aside, this finding suggests that minimal improvements can be expected with the Rotor cranks during aerobic exercise.

The primary source of difference occurred with the Wingate sprinting test, which relies strongly on massive force output and anaerobic capacity and less on aerobic efficiency. With the Wingate test, Rotor peak and mean power values were consistently higher (4 to 9 percent) than normal cranks regardless of which position was used. Statistically, significant differences were observed with position 4 (134-degree angle) and somewhat with position 3 (128 degrees). More than two-thirds (68 percent) of the subjects achieved the highest power values with position 4, and one-quarter of the subjects achieved the highest values with position 3. The proposed explanations for why the Rotor system worked best on the anaerobic test come from the biomechanical requirements that go along with high power outputs. The greater leverage (because of the longer effective crankarm length with the Rotor design), combined with the lower negative momentum during the upstroke (because of the shorter effective crankarm length in this phase), may come into play only at these high power outputs.

## Variable Crankarms

Another approach to an alternative crank system is to have the crankarms vary in length over the course of a pedal stroke, increasing it during the downstroke to maximize leverage and decreasing it during the upstroke to minimize inertial resistance. This setup achieves the same goal of altering leverage and leg speed, and such systems have received some research attention in the past decade (Belen et al. 2007a, 2007b; Hue et al. 2001, 2008; Zamparo et al. 2002). Zamparo et al. (2002) published a study comparing the biomechanics and energy requirements of this pedal system with a standard 172.5-millimeter Dura-Ace crank. Seven highly fit subjects pedaled at 60 revolutions per minute for five minutes at 50-watt increments using each of the two systems. Interestingly, no differences were observed in energy costs from 50 to 200 watts. But oxygen consumption decreased and mechanical efficiency increased slightly but significantly in the 250- to 300-watt range with the variable cranks. This finding follows the theory of increased torque on the downstroke along with decreased torque on the upstroke. Overall, the authors extrapolated this improvement to an extra kilometer over a one-hour time trial. Hue et al. (2001) also reported a faster 1-kilometer TT performance with such crankarms. But Belen et al. (2007a, 2007b) could not replicate any findings of improved performance with similar crank designs.

## PowerCranks

The final method of improving pedaling dynamics is to improve the neuromuscular process itself. Enter PowerCranks (PC), which is unlike any other crank system available. The basic idea behind PC is to make each leg independent of the other, forcing each one to pedal in a true circle and eventually to optimize its mechanics (figure 8.6). Therefore, rather than eliminating or compensating for the dead spot, PC forces you to improve your pedaling dynamics throughout the

Courtesy of PowerCranks LLC.

**FIGURE 8.6** PowerCranks feature independent crank arms, forcing each leg to apply force throughout the entire pedal stroke.

pedal cycle. This action includes forcing each leg to exert positive upward force to raise the pedal rather than rely on the downward force of the other leg to propel it upward. Theoretically, the improved upstroke may ease the force requirements of the leg performing the downstroke, resulting in a more even distribution of force throughout the various leg muscles over the pedal stroke and reduced local muscle stress and fatigue at any particular power output. Using PowerCranks theoretically also helps to minimize or eliminate pedaling asymmetry because each leg moves independently, and its motion is not affected by the other.

A huge adaptation period is required for independent crank systems, during which major stress is applied to the hip flexor, hamstrings, tibialis anterior (shins), and lower back muscles to perform the upstroke. No matter how easy you take it, these muscles will be heavily stressed, especially in the initial phase. Therefore, you must gradually build up your time and distance, and you must stretch to minimize the risk of tendinitis and other overuse injuries. Cadence drops dramatically in the initial adaptation phase, and although high cadences are possible for short periods, lower cadences are typical. Heart rate also rises by 10 to 15 beats per minute during adaptation at any particular wattage, although it gradually returns to normal levels.

The primary scientific question is whether such independent cranks are effective in altering pedaling dynamics and muscle recruitment patterns. The first systematic and controlled training study with PC was performed by Fernandez-Pena et al. (2009). Experienced cyclists with no PC experience were tested before and following 18 hours of PC training over 2 weeks and then were tested again after 18 hours of training back on normal cranks. With normal cranks, the PC training did result in greater activation of the hamstrings during the upstroke and lower activation of the quadriceps during the downstroke, and no changes were observed in the tibialis anterior. Although this finding supports the theory of improved pedaling dynamics, these changes in recruitment patterns disappeared after 2 weeks back at training on normal cranks. This result implies that constant reinforcement with PC is required to sustain the motor changes, or that more than 2 weeks may be needed to hard-wire these muscular changes. Regardless, these findings provide strong theoretical support for the potential of independent crank systems to enhance pedaling dynamics.

# Optimal Cadence

Optimal cadence means a lot of things to a lot of people depending on the context. The prevailing wisdom from older scientific studies was that the optimal cadence, in terms of efficiency (mechanical power output as a percentage of total energy turnover) was shaped like an inverted U. Peak efficiency occurred at approximately 50 to 60 revolutions per minute, far lower than the typical cadence employed by most cyclists. Certainly, multiple reasons underlie cadence selection, including matching the requirements of the event or situation, maximizing power production and efficiency, minimizing fatigue, and even maximizing comfort. Cadence may also derive from an inherent hard-wired "metronome" within the brain (Hansen and Ohnstad 2008). These reasons are all valid, and no cadence is optimal for all conditions in all cycling events. For example, the acceleration required by track sprinters leads to very high cadences of greater than 120 revolutions per minute, whereas a comfortable cadence for long endurance rides seems to be a self-selected cadence of 90 to 105 revolutions per minute on the flats for most cyclists.

## Field Studies

Often in sport science, the best way to start is by observing professionals at work. Besides being elite physical specimens who push the limits of human performance, pro cyclists generally perform near the limits of efficiency. That is, to survive and reach the pro ranks, they have voluntarily or involuntarily adopted strategies, such as choice of cadence, that are likely optimal given their individual characteristics. Lucia et al. (2001) monitored seven cyclists during Grand Tours and reported the preferred cadence during high mountains (71 plus or minus 1.4 revolutions per minute), flat individual time trials (89.3 plus or minus 1.0 revolution per minute), and flat long road stages (92.4 plus or minus 1.3 revolutions per minute) despite different heart rates and presumably power outputs.

Subsequently, 10 pro riders were tracked during the major mountain stages of the 2005 Tour de France (Vogt et al. 2008). None was among the main general classification contenders, and they typically placed 40th to 120th for most stages. SRM power meter data of 108 individual category 1 or hors catégorie (beyond categorization) climbs were analyzed, and the riders were categorized as climbers (less than 9 percent of stage-winning time) or helpers. Climbs generally involved 20 to 80 minutes at high submaximal intensities, ranging from 294 to 312 watts of average power output. The category 1 climbs, with their lower power requirements, were also accomplished at significantly higher cadences (73 plus or minus 6 revolutions per minute) compared with hors catégorie climbs (70 plus or minus 6 revolutions per minute). The climbers had a higher power output and cadences in both category 1 (321 watts, 75 revolutions per minute) and hors catégorie climbs (311 watts, 71 revolutions per minute) than the helpers did (292 watts, 71 revolutions per minute for category 1 climbs; 287 watts, 69 revolutions per minute for hors catégorie climbs). When comparing cadence as a function of power output, the data were pretty scattered at less than 250 watts. But as power output increased beyond that (250 to 750 watts), the general pattern found was a direct relationship of higher cadences with higher power outputs. This same pattern was observed when comparing distance covered with one pedal stroke versus power output. Distance covered with one stroke was the way that the authors tried to back-calculate gearing choice indirectly. Overall, it appears that no single cadence is preferred; instead, cadence varies greatly depending on the terrain and race situation.

## Optimal Cadence Testing Protocol

One simple way to find your optimal cadence is to test yourself at three different cadences across different periods. When Hunter starts coaching new athletes, he has them test their peak power output at 5 seconds, 1 minute, 5 minutes, and 20 minutes. In this initial test they pedal at their freely chosen cadence, or whatever cadence they naturally choose to ride and feels best to them. As an example, at the conclusion of the first test, the 20-minute wattage might be 265 watts, at a cadence of 87 revolutions per minute and an average heart rate of 172 (starting each test with the same initial heart rate is important). In the following week the athlete retests but now at 10 revolutions per minute below the average of the first test (in this example, at 77 revolutions per minute). In the third week the athlete tests him- or herself at 10 revolutions per minute above the average of the first test (in this example, 97 revolutions per minute). The sample athlete finds that in the lower-cadence test, the wattage average was 247 watts and the heart rate was 176 beats per minute. In the higher-cadence test, the wattage was 287 watts and the heart rate was 173 beats per minute. In this case, it's highly likely that the higher cadence is more optimal for the athlete because he or she produced 22 watts more power with an increase of only 1 heart beat per minute when at 97 revolutions per minute. Of course, you must do your best to minimize differences between the tests in variables such as weather, amount of rest, and time of day to make the test as controlled as possible. This simple test needs to be done across the multiple periods suggested because each period represents a different physiological system within the body. Although you might find that your self-selected cadence is optimal, you could find that you are more economical at a higher or lower cadence.

## Cadence Ranges for Longer Efforts

Studies by Foss and Hallen (2004, 2005) shed a few interesting ideas about the cadence mix. Specifically, they postulated that older studies found that peak efficiency occurred in cadences of 50 to 60 revolutions per minute because the tests were short (less than 10 minutes), at relatively low power outputs (about 125 watts), and were constant-load tests (ridden at the same intensity throughout) as opposed to being true time trials in which performance (highest power output achievable) was the goal.

Foss and Hallen (2004) attempted to address some of these limitations by having elite cyclists perform an incremental test to exhaustion (4 to 7 minutes) with cadences of 60, 80, 100, and 120 revolutions per minute. They found that performance was highest at 80 revolutions per minute. This finding places optimal cadence closer to the typical one employed by cyclists and brings about their interesting idea that, at a set grade, optimal cadence increases with increasing power output. Foss and Hallen (2005) attempted to address some of the problems of prior studies, namely the lack of a true performance measure and the short effort times. Again using national-level Swedish and Norwegian cyclists, the protocol involved trying to complete a set amount of work in as short a time as possible. The amount of work was individually adjusted to approximate a 30-minute time trial, and the subjects were able to self-adjust the power output. Again, cadence was fixed at 60, 80, 100, and 120 revolutions per minute. For an additional trial, subjects could freely choose cadence. The primary results of the 2005 study supported the 2004 findings (illustrated in figure 8.7) in that the optimal cadence in terms of efficiency was 80 revolutions per minute, although at 100 revolutions per minute only minor decrements were seen and indeed a slightly higher energy turnover (i.e., performance) occurred. Freely chosen cadence averaged about 90 revolutions per minute, and the results were similar to those at 80 and 100 revolutions per minute. Therefore, at realistic power outputs and with efforts typical of time trials, it appears that efficiency and performance can be achieved anywhere within the range of 80 to 100 revolutions per minute.

A similar study on cadence (Mora-Rodriguez and Aguado-Jimenez 2006) tested nine elite amateur cyclists (who had raced as elite amateurs for at least 3 years). They performed an increasing load test to exhaustion, beginning at 175 watts and increasing 25 watts every 3 minutes. This test is similar to a lactate threshold test performed in an exercise science lab. Subjects repeated this test at a constant cadence of 80, 100, and 120 revolutions per minute, along with a freely chosen

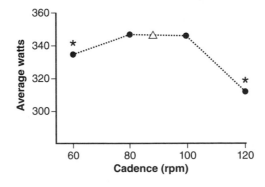

**FIGURE 8.7   Effect of cadence on average power output during a time trial.**
Circles represent set cadence, and the triangle represents freely chosen cadence (averaging 90 revolutions per minute). Cyclists worked to complete 562 watts of work.
*Different from freely chosen cadence.

cadence, which averaged 89 revolutions per minute. Although heart rate was higher with increasing cadence, gross efficiency at 275 watts was similar across the three fixed cadence conditions. In other words, the same amount of energy was required to pedal at 275 watts at 80, 100, and 120 revolutions per minute. On the other hand, impairment did occur at 120 revolutions per minute compared with 80 and 100 revolutions per minute in the peak wattage at the point of exhaustion, the wattage at ventilatory threshold (where breathing becomes labored and inefficient), and a trend toward lower wattage at lactate threshold. So although cadence didn't seem to impair performance at a high but submaximal wattage, it did seem to cause earlier fatigue at maximal sustained effort. The authors hypothesized that two factors may have caused this result:

1. Greater energy was required simply to move the legs at the higher speed, therefore causing greater fatigue (although the cyclist may be pushing against less resistance with each pedal stroke, more energy is used to move 120 times compared with 100 times, even against no resistance).

2. The higher speed of movement caused greater recruitment of fast-twitch muscle fibers, which are less efficient aerobically and produce more lactic acid.

## Effect of High Cadence on Subsequent Maximal Effort

Traditional advice is that we should save our legs during the early parts of a race by spinning as much as possible in easy gears. By doing so, our legs are fresher and have more snap to them when the going gets tough. As seen in the previous section, however, this spinning at easier wattages often comes at a higher energy cost than using a lower cadence. So is spinning indeed the best option before attacking the crunch point of the race? To investigate this question, testing riders in a time trial setting is not appropriate. Most races feature prolonged efforts at relatively low wattages, followed by a serious crunch time of maximal effort. Therefore, an interesting question arises: Does the extra energy cost of a high cadence during the easy first part of a race impair the ability to hammer at the end of a race?

Hansen et al. (2006) tested the effects in trained cyclists of prolonged submaximal riding on a subsequent 5-minute time trial. Optimal cadence was first determined by riding at 180 watts, chosen to represent a relatively easy and typical endurance effort for elite cyclists, at 35, 50, 65, 80, and 95 revolutions per minute. Calculations of the metabolically optimal cadence averaged 73 plus or minus 11 revolutions per minute as a group. Individual subjects had their optimal cadence over the entire tested range of 65 to 95 revolutions per minute. In contrast, freely chosen cadence averaged 95 plus or minus 7 revolutions per minute. The second half of the experiment involved 2.5 hours of cycling at either the optimal or freely chosen cadence, followed by a 5-minute maximal effort at a freely chosen cadence, an effort replicating the duration and intensity of the decisive parts of many races (e.g., bridging to a break, solo break, crosswind). During the 2.5 hours of cycling at 180 watts, oxygen uptake was slightly (7 percent) higher with the freely chosen cadence compared with the optimal cadence. In both cases, mean power output during the 5-minute effort was lower after 2.5 hours of cycling (8 percent in optimal, 368 watts, and 10 percent in free, 359 watts) compared with the initial baseline day (399 watts). No differences were found between optimal and free cadence except for a trend toward a higher peak oxygen uptake in the free cadence condition. Therefore, with greater subject numbers, it may be that the freely chosen cadence results in reduced metabolic efficiency during hard efforts at the end of the race. Thus, when riding in the early parts of a race, a lower cadence may leave more in the tank for the latter decisive phases of the race.

## Standing Versus Seated Pedaling

The first and most obvious weight-bearing exercise is running. A lot of energy is required not only to propel yourself forward but also to keep yourself upright and stable. Added to that is the impact force from landing on your feet with each stride. The combination of the two makes for a much higher heart rate, a greater metabolic rate, and more overall stress when running compared with cycling. Cycling is mostly a non-weight-bearing activity, and the bicycle is a highly efficient machine because it removes the impact forces and cradles your body in a position that greatly minimizes the need to support your body weight. But at times you have to stand when riding, and then you have to support a good deal of your body weight (figure 8.8). Whether it's on the flats, in the hills, or in a sprint, you are no longer supporting your weight on the saddle, and you have to rely on your muscles more to keep yourself upright.

Of course, standing typically requires more energy and makes you less economical, but it also leverages more of your body weight over the pedals and recruits additional muscles, thus making higher power output possible. For this reason, we're generally taught to keep the standing to a minimum and to stand only when we need extra power, such as when initiating an acceleration (e.g., sprint, breakaway) or when we need extra power while climbing. Wind resistance is also higher while standing because of the larger surface area exposed.

Millet et al. (2002) tested fit elite and pro cyclists riding for 6 minutes at 75 percent of $\dot{V}O_2max$ in a velodrome and while seated or standing on a 5.3 percent gradient hill. The cyclists also performed 30-second all-out sprints in the lab and while seated and standing on a gradual hill. Thanks to the improvements in technology, the researchers could take this study out into real terrain and use the subjects' own SRM-equipped bikes with portable gas analyzers, increasing

**FIGURE 8.8** Standing to execute a hard attack expends greater energy, but it does not necessarily reduce efficiency.

the applicability of the study. As expected, heart rate was about eight beats per minute higher when standing compared with seated uphill. Ventilation was also higher, although no differences were seen in oxygen consumption. Cadence was similar at just under 60 revolutions per minute in both conditions. Most important, no differences were found in either gross efficiency (about 22.5 percent) or economy (4.7 kilojoules of power per liter of oxygen). In the 30-second tests, maximum and mean power were much higher in the standing position compared with the seated position (mean power of about 820 and 650 watts, respectively), despite similar cadences and blood lactate values.

Overall, the ability to produce higher power when sprinting and standing is obvious and intuitive, as are the higher heart rates when climbing and standing. The main novelty of the study comes in the analysis of efficiency, especially the finding that no differences occur in efficiency or economy whether standing or seated. This result means that, although standing creates more stress on the aerobic and cardiovascular system, it does not necessarily cause a decrease in efficiency itself. So standing is not going to cost more energy to perform when you factor in the greater power that you are generating. One obvious caveat is that extended standing while climbing must be practiced to optimize economy. Another caveat is that all the subjects in the study were young, lean, and light, averaging 67 kilograms. For bigger riders with more weight to support, the efficiency and economy equations might be tilted in favor of sitting.

# Applying the Science

Cycling may be child's play, but pedaling a bike is not as simple as merely pushing the pedals around. Proper pedaling technique is a complex interplay of many muscles contracting and relaxing in a coordinated pattern. Therefore, small changes in the pedaling motion may have the potential to improve performance and prevent or minimize the risk of muscular injury. The physiological reasons and mechanisms behind changes in efficiency are not now fully understood but are being investigated. Trained cyclists are more economical than novice or untrained cyclists both in the muscle recruitment patterns involved in pedaling and in gross efficiency. At the highest levels of cycling, however, efficiency by itself may not predict performance. Many technological innovations that depart from the traditional round chainring and fixed crankarms have appeared on the market in recent years. Their proponents claim that these innovations enhance pedaling biomechanics, but systematic studies on their long-term effectiveness are still required. The selection of proper gearing and cadence is another important factor in optimizing both biomechanical and physiological efficiency. The ability to use power meters to perform quadrant analysis and map the relationship between force and cadence can help cyclists understand the specific neuromuscular demands of their preferred cycling discipline and provide better training specificity to what is needed to succeed in racing.

As might be expected, the optimal cadence appears to depend on the particular terrain and racing situation. Furthermore, although a higher power output appears to necessitate both a higher cadence and a higher resistance (gearing), the converse argument—that a higher cadence results in higher power output—is not necessarily true. To date, it appears that it doesn't make a huge difference whether you spend time cruising in the peloton at a high cadence or at a metabolically more efficient lower cadence. In both cases, you are going to get equally tired and you're not going to be able to hammer as hard when the "fox gets into the henhouse." Finally, we have learned in this chapter that in fit, experienced cyclists, riding position (seated or standing) does not seem to affect gross efficiency or overall economy when you factor in the higher wattages made possible by standing.

## CHAPTER 9

# Understanding Hydration and Supplements

One of the most controversial and polarizing topic in health and fitness is nutrition. New ideas, trends, and fads about what athletes should put in their bodies emerge and reemerge in other forms on a regular basis, each with adherents who swear by its benefits. New ideas about hydration, such as the potential importance of protein in rehydration fluids and the efficacy of consuming carbohydrate-based drinks during short-term, high-intensity exercise, are also emerging. The current, apparently ironclad rule is the need for drinking and ensuring adequate fluid replacement during extended periods of exercise, especially in hot environments. But until the early 1970s, when, perhaps coincidentally, the massive sports drink industry emerged, most coaches and athletes believed that drinking during a marathon was a sign of weakness and a practice to be avoided. And as difficult as it may be to believe given our current hydration-dominated mind-set, the vast majority of runners in that era completed marathons safely and without any acute or long-term health problems, despite making no effort to stay hydrated. Given this historical context, it is perhaps not surprising that the importance of high rates of fluid replacement during exercise is undergoing renewed scientific investigation.

As if the recent plethora of information on hydration were not enough to have athletes scratching their heads, a major nutritional supplement industry has arisen in recent years, offering an array of products, including compounds such as creatine and ginseng. Despite the fact that these substances are often marketed with phrases such as "scientifically proven" or "clinically tested," the lack of regulation of the industry leaves athletes to fend for themselves in terms of learning about the safety, risks, and potential side effects of taking supplements.

Athletes must be cautious in evaluating new claims and products, but they must also be open to reexamining their nutritional beliefs as new research retests and challenges commonly accepted ideas. They must also develop an understanding of the complex forces at play in the field of nutrition and the context by which claims are evaluated. Given the different opinions and conflicting interests of scientists, medical professionals, dietitians, and members of the food and diet program industries, athletes must be aware of the strengths and limitations of science (see chapter 1) and treat the latest and greatest claims with a healthy skepticism.

Specific dietary advice and detailed information on the effects of individual nutrients lie beyond the scope of this book. Many excellent books (Clark 2008, Ryan 2007) and online resources dedicated specifically to nutrition in general and sports nutrition in particular are available (see the sidebar Getting Unbiased Information on page 217 for some sample websites).

In this chapter we focus on hydration and supplements as case studies that point to the need to interpret and examine nutritional claims. The goal is to make informed decisions about how to fuel your body for training and competition.

# Physiology of Hydration

An important method of ensuring optimal performance during cycling in both normal and hot conditions is to ensure that adequate hydration is maintained. Recall from chapter 2 that roughly 80 percent of energy from metabolism results in heat rather than mechanical power to the pedals, and most of this heat must be dissipated from the body to prevent heat stress. Sweating is the dominant method of heat removal, but it results in the loss of fluid and electrolytes from the body that need to be replaced. Sweat rates exceeding 1 liter per hour are typical during moderate exercise. In an extreme case, American runner Alberto Salazar recorded a sweat rate of 3.7 liters per hour during preparation for the 1984 Olympic Marathon (Armstrong et al. 1986). The thirst response is relatively slow, and an involuntary dehydration of 2 percent or more of body weight may occur before a strong drinking response occurs. But even with an adequate fluid supply and reminders to drink, the rate of ad libitum, or at will, fluid intake rarely matches the rate at which fluid is lost through sweating. Cyclists become gradually dehydrated over the course of a prolonged ride in both comfortable and hot environments. Riders can tolerate mild dehydration during exercise to a certain extent, but too much of a deficit during exercise eventually impairs performance and makes it harder to recover adequately for subsequent training. Both the American College of Sports Medicine (ACSM, www.acsm.org) and the National Athletic Trainers' Association (NATA, www.nata.org) provide solid position stands on the major considerations in fluid replacement during exercise (Casa et al. 2000, Sawka et al. 2007).

The body is composed primarily of water, which represents 50 to 60 percent of total mass in a healthy adult. This fluid is distributed into a few major compartments (see figure 9.1), and the sweat lost during cycling comes from these compartments at various rates. Initially, a large part of sweat is taken from the approximately five liters of blood in the body, especially from the mostly liquid or plasma portion of the blood, which makes up about three liters. With this decrease in blood volume, heart rate needs to rise to maintain blood flow throughout the body. This cardiovascular drift, as this rise in heart rate is termed, can be seen even with a constant power output. As dehydration progresses, the body attempts to minimize further loss from the plasma volume by drawing fluid from the muscles and other cells. In turn, this greater level of dehydration within the cells results in changes in the muscles that impair their ability to contract and generate force.

Fluid balance during exercise is determined by a multitude of factors, including the environmental conditions, the nature and intensity of the exercise, and the characteristics of the fluid replacement. Because of the strong demand by the muscles for blood to maintain pedaling force, blood flow to other systems in

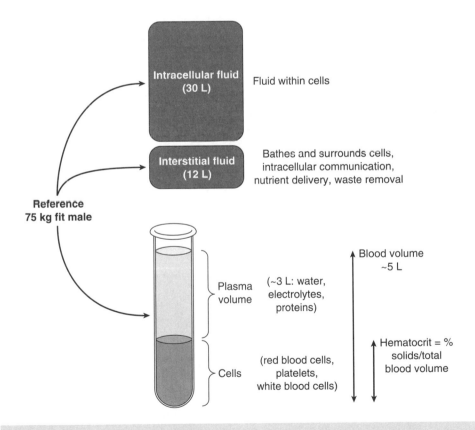

**FIGURE 9.1  Body fluid compartments.**
Adapted, by permission, from S.S. Cheung, 2010, *Advanced environmental exercise physiology* (Champaign, IL: Human Kinetics), 51.

the body may be reduced to maintain adequate blood pressure and blood flow back to the heart. Several problems can arise from this redistribution of blood:

- Resting heart rate and core temperatures progressively increase with increasing levels of dehydration (Sawka et al. 1985).

- Skin blood flow diminishes. Apart from sweating, skin blood flow is another important pathway for the body to get rid of extra heat.

- Dehydration progressively impairs the ability of the body to dispel heat through evaporation, and a higher core temperature is needed before sweating begins. Therefore, body temperature and heat exhaustion arise faster with greater rates of dehydration.

- Blood flow to the digestive system, including the stomach, intestines, and kidneys, diminishes, impairing the ability of the body to take in additional food and fluid during exercise.

- Recent research suggests that the structural integrity of the digestive system may become impaired, resulting in the leakage of materials and bacteria into the main blood stream. This condition, known as endotoxemia, has been associated with impaired muscle function (Supinski et al. 2000) and may produce an inflammatory response in the body that contributes to exercise fatigue, especially in the heat (Lambert 2004).

- Blood flow to the brain has historically been thought to be protected during exercise, but recent evidence suggests that, especially when exercise is combined with heat stress, this may not be the case. The blood–brain barrier, which protects the brain from being exposed to damaging substances in the blood, may become leakier (Watson et al. 2005). Also, reduced blood flow and heat stress may alter brain metabolism and neurochemistry, which may contribute to changes in mental arousal and fatigue (Meeusen et al. 2006).

# Performance Effects of Dehydration

Conflicting conclusions have been advanced about the influence of dehydration on anaerobic performance or sports of short duration and relatively high intensity. Using a supramaximal 30-second Wingate sprint test, some authors have reported decreases in both anaerobic power and capacity, whereas others have found no performance effects with progressive dehydration up to 5 percent of body weight (Jacobs 1980). No firm conclusion can be made about the effects of dehydration on sprinting performance because studies use a wide range of subjects, dehydration protocols, magnitude of dehydration, and exercise tests. Because exercise in the heat is often used to elicit dehydration, conclusions about the effects of fluid balance itself are sometimes confused with the effects of exercise fatigue and higher body temperatures. Overall, in reviewing the literature, Judelson et al. (2007) concluded that a sustained state of lower fluid balance can impair strength, power, and high-intensity muscular endurance by 2, 3, and 10 percent, respectively.

With aerobic exercise of lighter intensity and longer duration in the heat, during which the limit to exercise tolerance can be dominated by body temperature and heat-induced fatigue, the detrimental effect of dehydration is more distinct. Even so, significant debate remains about its true effect on competitive performance. In a hot environment, the additional stress imposed by hypohydration (a continued state of dehydration) appears to magnify the effects of heat stress and severely impairs the ability of people to tolerate exercise. In work done in Stephen's laboratory on military chemical protective clothing in the heat, researchers found a higher resting core temperature with 2 percent hypohydration, but the terminal core temperature at the point of voluntary exhaustion did not change, meaning that overall tolerance to exercise heat was less. More important, being dehydrated before exercise negated any benefits from heat acclimation or a short period of physical training, underscoring the importance of ensuring adequate hydration before exercise as a preventative countermeasure (Cheung and McLellan 1998a). Furthermore, a critical hypohydration threshold for exercise impairment does not appear to exist in the heat, where even relatively minor levels of hypohydration are sufficient to produce impairment in hot conditions.

**To optimize performance, be sure you are adequately hydrated before exercising.**

## Can Dehydration Improve the Power-to-Weight Ratio?

Athletes such as rowers, wrestlers, martial artists, and boxers often use voluntary loss of body weight and water to achieve a certain weight category before competition, but endurance athletes do not often use this practice. With the importance of the power-to-weight ratio in cycling, athletes may be tempted to consider lowering body weight as a simple strategy to improve their cycling performance. The idea is that drinking less over the course of a long race will reduce the body weight that needs to be accelerated (when sprinting) or lifted (when climbing). This strategy is obviously contingent on absolute power output not being impaired by dehydration. Would a gradual weight-cutting strategy over the course of a race be effective for a final decisive moment? Such an idea was the basis for a study at the Australian Institute of Sport (Ebert et al. 2007). Eight well-trained male cyclists consumed either 2.4 liters of a 7 percent carbohydrate drink or .4 liter of water with sufficient gels to provide equal carbohydrate consumption during a 2-hour endurance ride in a 30 °C lab temperature. The subjects then rode to exhaustion at 88 percent of maximal aerobic power. As expected, body weight was lower with the gel condition. These subjects were 1.9 kilograms lighter because of their low fluid intake, and a lower power output was sufficient for them to maintain a constant speed. But these subjects had a higher core temperature and higher heart rates at the end of the 2-hour endurance effort. On the subsequent ride to exhaustion, tolerance time was 13.9 plus or minus 5.5 minutes for the subjects with low fluid intake compared with 19.5 plus or minus 6.0 minutes for those with high fluid intake. Overall, any power-to-weight advantage from voluntary dehydration was offset by the physiological and performance impairments. These findings make it clear that fluid intake for cyclists should be based on sound hydration considerations rather than weight concerns.

# Rehydration

The degree of rehydration possible during exercise depends on a wide range of factors, such as individual drinking behavior, environmental parameters, the nature of the activity or the rules or the sport, exercise intensity, and type of fluid. Because no single guideline can be applied across all individual and situational characteristics, the best advice for athletes is to experiment with various hydration strategies and develop a plan based on individual needs. In this section, we consider some of the major factors in rehydration planning and the current recommendations for fluid composition during exercise and postexercise recovery. Table 9.1 summarizes these factors.

**TABLE 9.1.** Considerations for Developing an Individual Hydration Strategy for Exercising

| Factors | Current consensus | Developing an individual hydration strategy |
|---|---|---|
| Sweat rates and composition | A large interindividual variability exists in sweat rates and composition. Women generally have lower sweating rates than men. Increased fitness and heat acclimatization generally increases sweating rates. | Athletes should rely on individual determination of sweat rate and composition rather than general guidelines. |
| Hydration effects | Dehydration results in progressive decreases in plasma volume, which increases cardiovascular and thermal strain. Activities that rely on maximal strength, power, or anaerobic metabolism appear to be unaffected by 3 to 5 percent body weight dehydration. Aerobic capacity and submaximal exercise may become progressively impaired beyond 2 percent body weight dehydration, especially with exercise in the heat. | Athletes should strive to drink sufficient amounts to avoid dehydration beyond 2 percent of body weight over prolonged exercise. Even with minimal physical impairment, mental functioning may be impaired. |
| Rehydration fluid composition | Carbohydrate (CHO) delivery of about 60 grams per hour promotes carbohydrate availability and spares glycogen stores, enhancing submaximal exercise. CHO may have nonmetabolic benefits for high-intensity exercise shorter than one hour. CHO concentrations of 4 to 8 percent do not impair gastric emptying. Simple sugars (e.g. glucose, fructose) in combination appear to empty most rapidly, but fructose at a concentration of greater than 3 percent can decrease the GI absorption rate. Small amounts (.3 to .7 gram per liter) of sodium can increase palatability and drinking through thirst stimulation and can decrease the risk for hyponatremia. | Palatability of fluid should be a key consideration in promoting voluntary fluid consumption during exercise. Palatability varies between individuals and by conditions (e.g., less tolerance for sweetness in the heat). CHO fluids of 6 to 8 percent concentration should be consumed for prolonged exercise of longer than one hour and possibly for high-intensity exercise of less than one hour. Small amounts (.3 to .7 gram per liter) of sodium can be added to fluid. People who exercise for more than four hours should moderate their fluid intake to below sweating rates and avoid drinking only water or low-solute fluids to minimize risk of hyponatremia. |

Adapted, by permission, from S.S. Cheung, 2010, *Advanced environmental exercise physiology* (Champaign, IL: Human Kinetics), 56-57. Summary collated from Sawka et al. 2007 and Casa et al. 2000.

## Dehydration Versus Hyponatremia

Public education and policy surrounding hydration aim to strike a balance between the acceptable or safe amount of dehydration that can be tolerated and the risk of overdrinking and the development of hyponatremia, a drop in blood sodium concentration. Concern over dehydration and heat stress during exercise helped spark the promotion of awareness of the dangers of dehydration and the benefits of rehydration. This activity peaked in the mid-1990s with the American College of Sports Medicine's 1996 Position Stand on Fluid Replacement, which advocated that

> during exercise, athletes should start drinking early and at regular intervals in an attempt to consume fluids at a rate sufficient to replace all the water lost through sweating (i.e., body weight loss), or consume the maximal amount that can be tolerated. (Convertino et al. 1996)

As a result, we saw a proliferation of water bottles everywhere in gyms and shopping malls as people became paranoid about not drinking enough water.

More recent scientific research, especially from Professor Tim Noakes's group in South Africa, has questioned the need for such thorough rehydration. Noakes is particularly concerned that the prevailing emphasis on high volumes of rehydration during exercise may lead to the onset of hyponatremia, marked by a reduction in blood sodium concentrations from normal levels of 135 to 145 millimoles per liter to potentially harmful low levels below 130 millimoles per liter. This degree of dilution of the blood may produce dangerous swelling of the central nervous system and symptoms such as "confusion, disorientation, progressively worsening headache, nausea, vomiting, aphasia, impaired coordination, muscle cramps, and muscle weakness. Complications of severe hyponatremia include cerebral and pulmonary edema that can result in seizure, coma, and cardiorespiratory arrest" (Casa et al. 2005). Unfortunately, these symptoms are similar to those of severe dehydration, making the correct diagnosis and medical response by first aid and other emergency personnel critically important.

Rather than offering the message of drinking to replace sweat loss or as much as tolerable, Noakes aims for a public awareness message that encourages people to be more attuned to their sense of thirst and to use this sense as a guide to drinking during exercise (Noakes 2007). A few key observations form the primary foundation for Noakes arguments:

- Much of the research used to support the concept of drinking as much as tolerable is based on laboratory research involving minimal realistic wind speed and a set intensity of exercise. This research design may not adequately simulate real athletic situations of riding outdoors at a self-selected pace. In support, Saunders et al. (2005) demonstrated that adequate wind speed in the lab removes the differences observed in core temperatures or exercise performance between drinking as much as tolerable versus at-will drinking.

- Anecdotally, many world-class marathoners drink only small amounts of water that are well below their anticipated sweat rates. For example, Mizuki Noguchi, the winner of the women's marathon at the 2004 Athens Olympics, held with a starting temperature of 35 °C, spent only about 30 seconds drinking during the entire race (Noakes 2007). Such an apparent imbalance between fluid consumption and anticipated sweat loss calls into question whether moderate dehydration significantly impairs elite performance even in hot environments.

- Many elite runners also do not drink an enormous amount of fluids after training or throughout the day. In 14 elite Kenyan runners training with multiple daily interval and variable running workouts, fluid consumption during and after workouts did not appear to be a primary preoccupation (Fudge et al. 2008). Indeed, drinking or eating during training did not occur in this group at all, despite their losing 1.5 kilograms (2.7 percent) of body mass because of sweating. Without specific dietary counseling, daily fluid consumption generally consisted of water (.7 liter), milky tea (1.2 liters), other fluids including soft drinks and milk (.4 liter), food (1 liter), and metabolic generation of water (.5 liter), totaling 3.8 liters daily. Throughout, various hydration indices remained fairly stable and within the normal range.

Arguments such as these, along with continuing evolution of research into hydration and exercise, have led to a significant revision of the fluid replacement guidelines, specifically the ACSM's new 2007 Position Stand on Exercise and Fluid Replacement (Sawka et al. 2007). One highlighted change in the revised document is the recognition of the risks of hyponatremia from fluid consumption that exceeds the sweating rate. Specifically, the revised guideline states that the "goal of drinking during exercise is to prevent excessive (greater than 2 percent body weight loss from water deficit) dehydration and excessive changes in electrolyte balance to avert compromised performance." The guideline deliberately avoids recommending a specific volume for rehydration. Rather, the document provides information on various factors that may modify both sweating and electrolyte excretion rates, suggests methods of monitoring fluid loss, and outlines individual and situational characteristics that may affect the ability to rehydrate during exercise. Overall, the position stand suggests a range of .4 to .8 liter per hour as a starting point; large individuals who are heavy sweaters and are exercising in the heat may lean toward the higher end of this range, and small individuals who are exercising at low intensities in a cool environment may aim toward the lower rate.

## Fluid Composition

Volume considerations aside, two further points are important in the design of rehydration fluids. First, even the best drink from a scientific perspective is useless unless it is palatable and something that people want to drink in sufficient quantities to ensure adequate hydration. Therefore, scientific research has explored the effect of various drink compositions and characteristics on the rates of voluntary consumption in various populations. Second, the composition of the fluid and the nature of the exercise can have significant influence on the speed at which ingested fluids affect the body compartments because fluid must first be emptied from the stomach and absorbed from the intestines.

People have different preferences for fluid taste and temperature. Even within individuals preferences vary based on the particular situation. Anecdotal reports

©Human Kinetics

**The best sports drink in the world is worthless unless it is something that athletes find palatable and are willing to drink.**

indicate that people have less tolerance for sweet drinks in the heat. In one of the few studies that looked at voluntary drinking behavior in humans, a water temperature of 15 °C had the highest consumption rate in subjects who were allowed to choose the water temperature (Boulze et al. 1983). This cool yet not cold temperature suggests that providing ice water at events is not critical, greatly aiding the ability of event organizers to provide large volumes of fluids in the field. Flavoring of drinks, irrespective of carbohydrate content, may also aid in voluntary consumption. For example, cooling and flavoring drinks increased the consumption rate; consumption of flavored water at 15 °C was 120 percent greater than consumption of unflavored water at 40 °C (Hubbard et al. 1984). The difference in consumption rate may be explained either as an affinity for cool and flavored fluid or as a negative response to warm or unflavored fluid. Overall, the emphasis in sports nutrition should remain on individual education and the testing of various fluids in practice situations to find a range of fluids that work best.

# Consuming Carbohydrate During Short Events

Traditional nutritional advice is that solid food and carbohydrate are needed only for longer events. The rationale is that only with longer efforts do the body's glycogen stores become depleted and additional glucose becomes important. A 2004 study (Carter et al. 2004), however, suggested that carbohydrate can act as an ergogenic (performance-enhancing) aid even for short, high-intensity efforts such as a 40K time trial. These studies tested trained cyclists who completed 914 kilojoules of cycling in the lab while periodically rinsing their mouths and then spitting out either a carbohydrate solution or water. With the carbohydrate rinse, although only a miniscule amount of carbohydrate would have been absorbed by the body, completion time improved significantly, by approximately two minutes, and a higher power output was produced. In a subsequent study, however, the same research group could not find any physiological or performance differences when comparing the ingestion of an equal volume of carbohydrate drink and water during a 16K time trial (Jeukendrup et al. 2008). The van Essen and Gibala (2006) study on protein in sports drinks also provided indirect evidence that supported the performance-enhancing effects of carbohydrate in short-duration exercise. The 80K time trial was done as four 20-kilometer laps on a stationary trainer. In both the carbohydrate and carbohydrate plus protein conditions, the first 20 kilometers was done at a faster average pace than the placebo, even though glycogen stores wouldn't have become depleted yet.

The reason for improved performance from the carbohydrate mouth rinse is not clear, because too little carbohydrate would have passed through the digestive system and into the bloodstream to fuel the muscles significantly. In addition, muscle glycogen levels did not change between conditions. Also, the improvement

*(continued)*

**Consuming Carbohydrate During Short Events** *(continued)*

cannot be through the physical or psychological effects of drinking, because in both conditions subjects rinsed their mouths. One possibility is that, because the brain generally runs only on carbohydrate, some direct stimulation of carbohydrate receptors in the mouth may have altered brain activity, arousal, or the subconscious perception of effort and available energy. Namely, self-paced effort may be selected by a "smart sensor" somewhere in the brain that integrates input from throughout the body. The presence of carbohydrate may trigger sensors in the mouth to relay positive information to the brain and allow it to select a higher pace. Given such findings, even in cool temperatures in which dehydration or heat stress is not a major concern, it may be worthwhile to try a small bottle of sports drink or a gel immediately before or during short and high-intensity events of 60 to 90 minutes, including time trials, cyclocross, and many mountain biking events.

## Timing of Fluid Consumption

When developing a hydration plan for a ride or race, remember that it can take 15 to 30 minutes or more for a drink that you take to empty from the stomach and be absorbed from the intestines into the bloodstream. Gastric emptying is a dynamic function that is affected by many factors, including the rate of fluid replacement and subsequently the volume of the stomach contents. A direct relationship is observed between the amount of fluid ingested and the rate of gastric emptying. As previously noted, however, high volumes of unabsorbed fluid in the stomach may also lead to gastric discomfort. You may need to begin drinking early in a long ride because the reduced blood flow to the digestive system can inhibit the rate of gastric emptying (Rowell 1974).

Because of both the delayed thirst response and the time required for fluid absorption, athletes have traditionally been advised to drink before exercise and constantly throughout exercise rather than wait until late in the exercise to begin rehydration. The timing of fluid replacement may indeed play an important role in exercise responses, although the research into this question is somewhat equivocal. Work in Stephen's laboratory on soldiers exercising in the heat suggested that ensuring normal hydration levels before exercise is more important than drinking during exercise in maintaining performance capacity (Cheung and McLellan 1998b). Similarly, a single large intake of fluid during exercise may maintain fluid balance better than the same overall volume in smaller doses throughout exercise. In a well-controlled study, subjects who were given a set volume of carbohydrate solution in a single dose at the start of exercise had the same final heart rates and core temperatures as those who were provided the same amount in one large dose during exercise or the same amount doled out continuously throughout exercise (Montain and Coyle 1993), suggesting that the important factor is adequate early drinking rather than its timing. See table 9.2.

| TABLE 9.2 | Practical Options for Assessing Hydration Status | | |
|---|---|---|---|
| Measure | Technique | Normal hydration thresholds | Notes |
| Thirst perception | Subjective numerical ratings of thirst sensation | n/a | A visual scale used primarily for educational purposes and as a rough approximation. Regular use may serve as a stimulus to drink. |
| Body weight | Weight taken in the morning or following exercise | Less than 1 percent difference in body weight from normal baseline | Often used to estimate acute sweat loss. High practicality but potentially low reliability, even for an individual. |
| Urine color | Graded colored chart matching urine color to dehydration level | Scale ranges from 1 (very pale yellow) to 8 (brownish green). Values from 1 to 3 are considered well hydrated. | High practicality. Urine color can be influenced by diet (e.g. vitamin supplements) and also by drinking large amounts of water or hypotonic fluid. |
| Urine specific gravity | Droplet of urine measured on a handheld monitor | Less than 1.020 grams per milliliter | High practicality. Main use for chronic rather than acute hydration assessment. |
| Bioelectrical impedance | Electrical conductivity of the body used by some home and gym scales to estimate body fatness and sometimes hydration status | n/a | Not ideal for small or acute changes with fluid ingestion and sweat loss. Can be reliable and accurate for chronic changes if protocol is standardized (e.g., machine, posture, time of day). |

Adapted, by permission, from S.S. Cheung, 2010, *Advanced environmental exercise physiology* (Champaign, IL: Human Kinetics), 58-59.

## Protein Sports Drinks

Within the last five years or so, the established formula for most sports drinks, consisting of approximately 6 to 8 percent carbohydrate along with some electrolytes, changed after some research advanced the benefits of adding protein into sports drinks. The study that made the big splash was one by Saunders et al. (2004), which compared a carbohydrate-protein sports drink with another drink with the same carbohydrate content. With 75 percent and 85 percent $\dot{V}O_2$max rides to exhaustion, in which subjects were asked to ride at a set workload for as long as possible, exercise tolerance time increased dramatically to 29 percent and 45 percent longer at 75 and 85 percent of $\dot{V}O_2$max respectively. This result, in a field in which 10 percent improvement is considered astronomical, was shocking. But the study was not able to ascertain whether this huge benefit came about because of something specific about adding proteins or because the carbohydrate-protein drink had more total calories. The scientific consensus is that the ceiling for carbohydrate absorption is already reached at 6 to 8 percent concentration and that simply adding more carbohydrate does not get more into your system and may even slow things down in the digestive tract. Therefore, adding protein seemed to serve as a back-door way to cram more calories into your system.

Regardless of whether the increase in time to exhaustion in the Saunders et al. study was based on the protein content or the greater number of calories, many companies jumped on the bandwagon of adding protein and touting its inclusion in their sports drinks. A subsequent study, however, further investigated the benefits of protein in sports drinks and offered conflicting evidence. Researchers van Essen and Gibala (2006) tested two types of noncommercial drinks (6 percent carbohydrate and 6 percent carbohydrate plus 2 percent whey protein) and a placebo. One nice touch was that the drink powder for all three drinks was produced by the same source to be as identical in aesthetics (taste, color, and so on) as possible, offering subjects no clues as to their content. A further modification to the study design by van Essen and Gibala was the use of an 80K time trial protocol in which subjects were asked to complete the ride as fast as possible with no pacing or timing cues, rather than the ride-to-exhaustion protocol of Saunders et al. (2004). This procedure was done on the grounds that a time trial is more applied and realistic. Indeed, a general trend has been to move away from the ride-to-exhaustion style of testing because of its high variability, attributed to motivational factors as well as individual differences. The 80K time trial also ensured that glycogen stores would be significantly depleted and the ingested calories would really come into play. Both the carbohydrate (135 minutes plus or minus 9 minutes) and carbohydrate plus protein (135 minutes plus or minus 9 minutes) groups had faster completion times than placebo (144 minutes plus or minus 10 minutes), but no differences were found between the two carbohydrate drinks.

The rate of fluid ingestion may be one of the major reasons for the difference between the two studies. Saunders et al. (2004) had a relatively low (500 milliliters per hour) drinking rate, resulting in about 37 grams per hour of carbohydrate replacement. This quantity is much lower than the 60 grams per hour recommended to maximize carbohydrate replacement in the body. Therefore, the extra protein may play an important role only when carbohydrate replacement is less than optimal. Regardless, the jury is still out on how important protein is during cycling.

## Hyperhydration

One common misconception is that if a little of something is good, more must be better. In the case of hydration, the importance of promoting adequate hydration before exercise can lead to the notion that hyperhydration, or the attainment of a higher-than-normal body fluid balance, before exercise can prolong tolerance to exercise- and heat-related stress. Hyperhydration may be achieved by drinking large amounts of water or other fluids in the days and hours before a competition. But besides increasing the need to urinate during competition, this high level of water consumption can dilute plasma sodium and enhance the risk of dilutional hyponatremia. Another method of achieving hyperhydration is through the ingestion of a glycerol solution, which aids in the retention of fluid. The total amount of hyperhydration possible, however, is relatively small at about 1 to 2 percent above normal body weight. This state is inherently unstable, because the body will rapidly strive to increase fluid excretion to return to baseline hydration levels, such that proper timing would be essential if this practice is employed. Furthermore, no scientific study has been able to demonstrate a clear thermoregulatory or performance advantage from this practice (Latzka et al. 1997, 1998). Therefore, the best suggestion remains to focus on ensuring that you are normally hydrated before exercise in the heat.

## Recovery Hydration

Many athletic and occupational situations require consecutive bouts of exercise with only a short recovery period after each. These short rest breaks can range from 30 minutes to an hour between track cycling heats, to the 18 hours of recovery available between race stages in summer weather in events such as the Tour de France. With the known effect of proper hydration on tolerance for hot-weather exercise, planning hydration strategies is critical not just for the exercise itself but also for the recovery period. But compared with the research done on hydration during exercise, relatively minimal investigation has been performed on recovery and hydration.

A research group in Aberdeen, Scotland, performed an excellent series of studies during the mid-1990s to isolate the effects of various drink characteristics on fluid balance recovery. A summary of the primary findings from these studies are presented in table 9.3 on page 210. Note the important caveat of the general context of this series being the return of body weight to preexercise weight rather than any performance testing postrecovery. The consensus from these studies suggested that adequate recovery rehydration requires the consumption of much more fluid (about 150 percent) than that lost through sweating to compensate for fluid excretion through urination. Research has yet to be done, however, on the effect of various recovery rehydration fluids and protocols on actual aerobic and anaerobic exercise capacity. Such work would assist in planning how much rehydration recovery is possible or required between events in a stage race. It could also aid in determining when aggressive rehydration strategies, such as intravenous fluid infusion, are appropriate.

### TABLE 9.3 Summary of a Series of Studies on Rehydration

| Composition | Study | Best practice conclusions |
|---|---|---|
| Volume | Shirreffs et al. 1996 | Sodium and volume interact in rehydration. Rehydration volume must exceed sweat loss, placing great emphasis on palatability. |
| Sodium | Shirreffs and Maughan 1998 | Sodium is essential for rehydration, but balance is needed in determining sodium and may be case specific based on individual sweat composition. |
| Potassium | Maughan et al. 1994 | Potassium may be useful in low concentrations to offset urinary potassium loss from sodium ingestion. |
| Carbohydrate | Maughan et al. 1994 | Carbohydrate alone is not sufficient for optimal rehydration. It offers no additional benefit above electrolyte solution for fluid balance but is likely critical for substrate recovery. |
| Solid versus liquid | Maughan et al. 1996 | Food ingestion does not impair rehydration and may increase palatability and voluntary fluid consumption. |
| Alcohol | Shirreffs and Maughan 1997 | Alcohol at less than 2 percent concentration does not serve as a significant diuretic or impair rehydration. |

Adapted, by permission, from S.S. Cheung, 2010, *Advanced environmental exercise physiology* (Champaign, IL: Human Kinetics), 65-66.

## Q&A With Brian Roy: Drinking While Riding

| | |
|---|---|
| **Current position** | Associate professor, director of the Centre for Muscle Metabolism and Biophysics, Brock University. |
| **Professional relationship/ background with cycling** | I consult regularly with numerous teams, individual cyclists, and triathletes to help develop nutritional strategies to enhance their training and performance. |
| **Personal background with cycling** | Avid recreational cyclist. |
| **Favorite ride (either one you've done or always wanted to do)** | The Great Ocean Road, Victoria, Australia. |
| **Favorite cycling-related experience** | Being in Paris for the start of the 2003 Tour de France. |

**Brian, most of the talk about the importance of adequate hydration revolves around the cardiovascular implications of sweating and blood volume changes. One of your research areas focuses on the effects of hydration on the muscles. Can you tell us a little bit about how dehydration affects muscle and muscle function?**

Hydration can affect the function of many physiological systems within the body. In our lab we have been investigating how acute changes in muscle hydration influence muscle metabolism. We have established that acute decreases in muscle hydration can have dramatic and potentially detrimental metabolic effects. More specifically, we have shown that decreases in muscle hydration result in increased rates of glycogen depletion and turnover. For cyclists, this means that hydration is important not only for maintaining thermoregulation and cardiovascular function but also for possibly delaying the onset of fatigue related to muscle glycogen depletion.

 **There's been a fair bit of scientific and public policy debate about the need to drink during exercise versus the risk for hyponatremia. What's the perspective from the muscle function angle?**

Hyponatremia is an interesting physiological condition because it can result from two possible yet opposite causes—excessive water or fluid intake and excessive fluid loss. Both can lead to abnormally low plasma sodium concentrations. The most logical advice is to try to match fluid intake to fluid loss during exercise while avoiding excessive fluid intake.

Some people believe that consuming sports drinks with sodium prevents hyponatremia, but generally the sodium content of sports drinks is inadequate, especially for those athletes who are "salty sweaters."

As for muscle function, low plasma sodium concentrations would theoretically lead to a decline in muscle excitability and thus function. But it is difficult to assess muscle function with hyponatremia because it has wide-ranging effects on multiple body systems.

 **What are some of the main considerations when picking a drink to consume during exercise and for recovery after exercise?**

Many factors are important, but probably the main consideration is that the goals of nutritional intake during exercise are different from those postexercise. Generally, nutrition during exercise is undertaken to help delay fatigue related to factors such as fluid loss, glycogen depletion, electrolyte losses, and heat stress. Sports drinks designed to be used during exercise should contain some carbohydrate (5 to 8 percent) and electrolytes. But the three most important characteristics for a sports drink are that it tastes good to encourage drinking, that it can be absorbed rapidly from the digestive system, and that it causes little or no gastrointestinal distress.

In regard to recovery beverages, a growing trend is to include some high-quality protein sources in addition to carbohydrate and electrolytes. The

*(continued)*

theory is that the protein may enhance training adaptations by altering protein turnover. This topic needs to be investigated further, but there is growing evidence that low-fat milk-based drinks facilitate adaptations to resistance training when taken postexercise in men and women.

Besides macronutrients such as protein and carbohydrate, antioxidants are commonly used in recovery drinks. If you are healthy, you don't really need to include any antioxidants in a recovery beverage. The current research literature suggests that the reactive oxygen species that are produced during exercise may contribute to the beneficial adaptations that athletes seek from training. Reactive oxygen species are clearly a stimulus to upregulate the body's natural antioxidant systems, but they may also contribute to many of the other adaptations that occur in skeletal muscle with training. Although the use of supplemental antioxidants in extreme circumstances may offer some potential, such as in athletes who are at great risk for overtraining injuries, for most athletes they are unnecessary.

 **After exercise, athletes are told about the importance of a glycogen window for maximizing recovery. What's actually going on in the muscles itself, and what should cyclists be doing to take advantage of it?**

Consuming energy as soon as possible following the completion of training is critical, especially in the form of high glycemic index carbohydrate. This need is related to the influence that exercise and training have on the protein that is responsible for bringing carbohydrate into the muscle. During exercise a special population of these proteins moves to the surface of the muscle that is working, and they help bring carbohydrate into the working muscle. They stay on the surface of the muscle for up to four hours following the workout. When you consume carbohydrate to refuel, blood insulin rises, which then acts on the muscle to recruit a second separate population of these proteins to the surface of the muscles. So, you then have two separate populations of these proteins available to bring carbohydrate into the muscle, leading to even greater rates of muscle glycogen recovery.

 **One of the "newest" recovery drinks that's been highly touted is chocolate milk. What is so special about chocolate milk, and what is the evidence?**

There has definitely been growing interest in milk, especially chocolate milk as an endurance exercise recovery beverage. Remember that the goals of postexercise nutritional intake are to replenish fuel and fluids and to promote muscle recovery and adaptation. Low-fat chocolate milk has a number of characteristics similar to those of the traditional sports recovery beverage. First, it contains carbohydrate, specifically lactose and sucrose, in amounts similar to the amount of carbohydrate found in commercially available sports drinks. Also, milk contains casein and whey proteins in a ratio of 3 to 1, which provides for slower digestion and absorption of these proteins, resulting in sustained elevation of blood amino acid concentrations. Finally, milk has naturally high concentrations of electrolytes, which are lost through sweating during exercise and which aid in fluid recovery following exercise.

But limited scientific research has been done about the efficacy of low-fat milk and chocolate milk as sports beverages. The scientific studies that have been done suggest that milk is as effective as commercially available sports drinks at facilitating recovery for additional performance and rehydration, although no direct measures of muscle glycogen in humans have been made. More research is needed to understand how milk promotes recovery after exercise, how the physiological mechanisms operate, and how these mechanisms may influence subsequent performance. I still recommend it to the athletes whom I work with because it is a tasty alternative to the traditional sports drinks that they normally consume during longer training sessions.

## Developing a Personal Hydration Plan

Forget the hype. It is time to unveil the magic answer to just what you should be putting in your bottle! Of course, the magic answer is, "It depends." During riding, the ideal drink composition is infinitely variable depending on temperature, exercise intensity, and personal preference. Therefore, you have to try different drinks in different situations and see what works best for you rather than simply follow the pack or accept manufacturers' claims at face value. Here are some considerations and rules of thumb that have passed the test of science as opposed to being hyped by marketing:

- Besides getting water into your system, the overall goal is to get about 40 to 60 grams of carbohydrate into your body each hour during exercise. For reference, 60 grams of carbohydrate works out to about one large water bottle of most common sports drinks mixed at full strength. More is not necessarily better here because the body can't seem to absorb more than 60 grams per hour and cramming in more carbohydrate may simply cause gastric distress. Don't get too hung up on what kind of carbohydrate you use, although fructose, commonly found in apple juice, seems to take longer to absorb than other types.

- Generally, the sweet spot at which fluid enters your bloodstream fastest is with a carbohydrate concentration of 2 to 8 percent (for reference, Coke is about 10 percent, and Gatorade is about 6 percent). On a hot day, you'll generally have decreased tolerance for sweetness, so dilute your drink. Don't worry that you won't be getting enough carbohydrate because you'll likely compensate by drinking more fluid without even making a conscious effort to do so.

- Unless you're into ultraendurance events, you won't lose an abundance of electrolytes (salts and minerals) through your sweat during exercise, and what you do lose you will easily replace with a balanced diet. But electrolytes do tend to improve taste and help improve absorption of carbohydrate, so you'll generally want to include moderate amounts of electrolytes (mainly sodium) in your drink (Coke has almost none, and Gatorade has a moderate amount). Most sports drinks already have an appropriate amount.

- If you are a salty sweater, you may need to supplement your sports drink with extra electrolytes, such as a full or partial salt tablet. People vary widely in the saltiness of their sweat. Although you could take a sweat sample and have it tested to determine the precise electrolyte concentration, a simpler method of determining whether you are a salty sweater is to see how much dried salt stays on your clothing after riding. If the salt stains on your jerseys or shorts are far more extensive than those of your training partners, your sweat likely has a high electrolyte content and you may wish to consider adding salt to your sports drink.

# Supplements

Smart training, hard work, and sound nutrition will get you close to your genetic potential. But in looking for that final edge, some athletes turn to nutritional supplements. The supplements industry is a massive growth industry in both senses of the word. It is a multi-billion-dollar market, and it offers endless claims of magical results. Athletes are certainly a major segment of the supplement market because they use supplements at a much higher rate than the general population does. For example, 88.4 percent of the 583 elite Canadian juniors through national-class athletes reported using at least one dietary supplement during the previous six months (Erdman et al. 2006). The supplement-using athletes use three supplements each on average, including sports drinks (22.4 percent), sports bars (14.0 percent), multivitamins and minerals (13.5 percent), protein supplements (9.0 percent), and vitamin C (6.4 percent).

But how do you figure out what is sound science and what is simply marketing? The smart athlete should start by being extremely skeptical about the efficacy of any supplement. Being skeptical is not the same as being cynical; it simply means that you should explore the scientific data rather than just accept claims at face value. For several reasons, the caveat "Buyer beware" is particularly apt.

Unlike medicines and drugs, which are closely regulated by governmental agencies, supplements have no regulations for testing and certification. Medicines undergo extensive and scientifically rigorous testing to see whether they work as advertised, are safe, and have potential side effects. In contrast, supplements are not required to undergo testing, so you have only the promise of the companies who make them that the supplements actually work. Some supplements have potentially serious side effects that even the scientific community may not be aware of. This problem is a function of the constantly increasing number of supplements appearing on the market, coupled with the relative lack of scientific testing.

©Vincent Zuber/Custom Medical Photo Stock

**Before taking any supplement, decide whether it is truly necessary for you and research the product and company carefully.**

The history of cycling in the past decade, as with other sports, is rife with "unintentional" doping cases, in which athletes test positive and blame the result on the supplements that they were taking. Although some athletes who make such claims may have knowingly ingested banned substances, unintentional doping is entirely possible because not only is no testing done for efficacy but no screening of supplements is done by any regulatory agency to test their contents. Athletes have no guarantees about how pure the product is or even whether the ingredients shown on the label are actually included within the product! Worse yet, supplements may be contaminated with substances not listed on the label, which can lead to positive drug tests and allergic reactions. A 2001–2002 study of 634 commercially available supplements purchased in multiple countries, from both retail outlets and the Internet, found that 15 percent were contaminated with substances banned by the World Anti-Doping Association and not included in the labeling (Geyer et al. 2004). Products tested in this study included both hormonal and nonhormonal supplements such as vitamins. Contaminating substances included caffeine, which is no longer banned, as well as substances banned in or out of competition such as ephedrine and other stimulants, precursors to testosterone, and anabolic steroids. The situation has not improved since and likely will become worse with the ready availability of generic bulk substances to manufacturers and the massive increase in supplement production in countries with lax regulatory standards (Geyer et al. 2008).

Let's illustrate the difference between a pharmaceutical medicine and a supplement with some examples. Ibuprofen (Advil) is an example of a pharmaceutical that is officially recognized and regulated by national health agencies such as Health Canada and the Food and Drug Administration in the United States. This recognition means that ibuprofen was investigated for as long as a decade and underwent hundreds of scientific studies to examine its effectiveness, test the limits of its usefulness, and determine both short-term and long-term potential side effects before it appeared on the market. The sale of ibuprofen has been closely regulated, and independent testing is regularly performed on all ibuprofen medicine to ensure quality control, proper dosage, and lack of contamination.

Contrast ibuprofen to creatine, one of the most popular supplements among athletes. Creatine is atypical among supplements in that it has undergone hundreds of scientific studies examining its efficacy for improving athletic performance. Because of this, we know that it has specific benefits for athletes in certain settings, and we have a fairly good idea of proper dosages and side effects. So far, so good, although this level of scrutiny is generally not applied to most supplements.

Ginseng is another popular supplement found in many energy drinks and bars, but only about 20 studies have been conducted on its use during exercise. About half found no benefit, and half found some benefit for aerobic performance. But this lack of consensus has not stopped many manufacturers from touting ginseng as a wonder tonic and using the virtually meaningless phrase "clinically proven" in its marketing.

Why are supplements such as creatine and ginseng not under review by national health regulatory bodies? As big and lucrative as the supplement industry is, it pales in comparison to the size of the pharmaceutical business. Therefore, the regulators of the health industry are far more concerned, appropriately so, with the larger picture of medicinal effects and the prevention or cure of illnesses in the general population than they are with the ergogenic effects of supplements in the much smaller demographic of athletes who wish to improve their performance. Only in extreme cases, such as that recently seen with ephedra—a stimulant often used in weight-loss supplements—in which far too many deaths occurred in otherwise healthy people, did regulatory bodies step in and investigate a supplement. From an economic perspective, pharmaceutical companies have minimal incentive to fund research on whether ginseng, for example, improves aerobic capacity or alertness. The military actively researches the ergogenic effects of drugs and supplements on exercise, but the findings often remain classified, and studies are often performed at dosages quite different from those that might benefit civilian athletes.

Keep in mind that not every supplement is contaminated, and not every company is intentionally dishonest. But supplements are not regulated, and athletes should not assume that they are safe and effective.

# Getting Unbiased Information

Some supplements definitely work, some probably work, some have little to no effect, and some may be problematic or even harmful. The key is to become educated on the science underlying the claims of manufacturers and not simply take the marketing department's word for it. In other words, it's your body and you need to be a smart consumer! Part of evaluating the science is making sure that conflicts of interest are not present. Scientists should not have any financial stake in the outcome of their research. In the nutrition and supplements industry, just as in the pharmaceutical industry, steering clear of financial conflicts of interest can be exceedingly difficult. The field is huge, and the financial rewards can be great if a company finds something that works. As such, few scientific studies are not in some way supported by commercial interests. In addition, it's difficult to define exactly when a conflict of interest arises. If a study on sports drinks received no money from any manufacturer but the researchers did receive free product, does this contribution constitute a conflict of interest?

So if you are checking out promotional literature or, better yet, the scientific papers behind the marketing hype, look for any obvious conflicts of interest and for full disclosure of any potential ones. One simple way is to follow the money trail and determine who sponsored or funded the research. Were any of the authors paid or were they employed, currently or previously, by a company with a vested interest in the results? Answers to these questions can usually be found in the acknowledgements or at the beginning of the paper, where the authors' names and affiliations are listed.

In evaluating the scientific validity and integrity of online resources, aim for objective sites that are not a marketing arm of a commercial company, thus minimizing, although not necessarily completely eliminating, the risk of conflicts of interest. Many major nonprofit organizations derive at least partial sponsorship from commercial companies. The following home pages and websites are maintained by respected sport science organizations:

Australian Institute of Sport nutrition site: www.ausport.gov.au/ais/nutrition

Coaching Association of Canada nutrition site: www.coach.ca/sport-nutrition-tips-513426

World Anti-Doping Agency: www.wada-ama.org

American College of Sports Medicine: www.acsm.org

National Athletic Trainers' Association: www.nata.org

Canadian Society for Exercise Physiology: www.csep.ca

European College of Sport Science: www.ecss.mobi

# Applying the Science

Although sound general principles are available to ensure proper hydration and guide the use of supplements, as with training itself, no single template will work for every rider. All athletes have their own personalized hydration goals, depending on individual physiology (e.g., level and saltiness of sweat) and race demands. Riders need to experiment with various drinks and nutritional choices while exercising and see for themselves what works best for them. Weighing yourself before and after training in various weather conditions can give you a ballpark figure for your sweating rate, and you can use that to plan your on-the-bike hydration strategy. Inspecting the saltiness of your clothes after workouts can give you insight into the amount of electrolytes you tend to lose through sweat and whether you might need to enhance your electrolyte intake during or postexercise. Finally, you should experiment with various compositions of fluids to determine both what tastes best to you and what keeps your energy levels highest over the duration of your training rides or races. When considering supplements, the best approach for cyclists is self-education. Learn about what you are putting into your body by going directly to the research or to scientifically reliable resources rather than relying on second-hand information or manufacturer claims.

## CHAPTER 10

# Dealing With Environmental Stress

Cycling is a sport of freedom. For the most part, it is not confined to indoor arenas or to stadiums. Rather, the epic nature of the sport reflects the fact that it usually takes place in the great outdoors, over all sorts of terrain and in all kinds of weather. At races like the Tour of Qinqai Lakes in the high plains of China, cyclists must adapt to the decreased oxygen available at high altitudes. Early season classics take place in the cold and rain of northern Europe, while the same roads are scorching hot in the heat of summer during the Grand Tours. Bike-racing fans will likely never forget Andy Hampsten's epic ride over the Gavia pass in a blizzard during the 1988 Giro d'Italia. Every year, the Ironman triathlons that take place in Penticton, Kona, and elsewhere occur in extremely hot weather, causing some athletes to succumb to heat exhaustion. The environment, therefore, becomes a major determinant of how a ride or race plays out, and it can greatly affect performance. At the same time, by understanding the effects of environmental stress on how the body responds, cyclists can minimize the negative effects and even use challenging environmental conditions to maximize their capacity.

Our bias is that nothing replaces smart training and nutrition to maximize your genetic potential. But just as "free" speed can be found through a lighter or faster bike or wheels (free in terms of laying your watts onto the road, but not free to your wallet!), improved physiological performance can also be obtained through a range of ergogenic aids. The recovery modalities in chapter 5 can help you retain and maintain your physiological capacity day to day, and they are somewhat analogous to making sure that your bike is tuned and the tires are inflated. In contrast, a number of ergogenic aids, based on manipulating environmental stress and forcing your body to adapt, have been proposed as being able either

©Panoramic/Icon SMI

**With the right clothing and preparation, cycling in the cold can even be fun!**

to help your body make a quantum jump in physiological capacity or to allow you to overcome extreme environmental conditions. In this chapter we examine hypoxic (oxygen-reduced), or altitude, training and cooling devices, two training aids that have become common among professional cyclists and are beginning to be marketed to the larger recreational and age-group market.

# Hypoxic Training

At the 1968 Summer Olympics in Mexico City, at an elevation of 2,240 meters above sea level, Bob Beamon broke the long jump world record by a phenomenal 55 centimeters. This feat literally launched the field of altitude physiology research. At the same time, natives of Kenya and Ethiopia, both situated in the highlands of Africa, emerged as outstanding performers in middle- to long-distance running events at the Mexico City Olympics, further spurring research on the concept of altitude training and its potential benefits to exercise performance at lower altitudes. Most of the studies in the initial era of altitude research focused on athletes who adapted by both training and living at altitude. The second wave of research branched away from this, exploring such concepts as living at high altitudes while training at lower altitudes. This line of research has been aided by technological advances in the development of relatively portable and inexpensive altitude tents or rooms, permitting athletes to control oxygen levels during both training and recovery without the logistical and financial expense of protracted field-based training camps. Hypoxic systems, offered by companies such as Colorado Altitude Training and Altitude Tech, are becoming more common with professional cycling teams and individuals, and such devices are now marketed to recreational and age-group athletes. The most comprehensive and practical book specifically devoted to the use of altitude training in sports was written by Dr. Randy Wilber of the United States Olympic Committee (Wilber 2004).

The leading theoretical explanation of how altitude training can improve endurance performance is simple. According to this model, decreased oxygen availability, because of lower partial pressure of oxygen ($PO_2$) at altitude, stimulates the kidneys to increase their production and secretion of erythropoietin (EPO). In turn, EPO acts on the marrow within the long bones to increase red blood cell production (Mackenzie et al. 2008). This increase in hemoglobin or red blood cell mass should therefore contribute to an increase in blood volume and oxygen-carrying capacity, ultimately producing an increase in aerobic capacity.

Although this theory is compelling and the individual links have been clearly demonstrated in a number of studies, other mechanisms may be of equal or greater prominence (Gore et al. 2007), as outlined in figure 10.1. Especially notable are a number of studies that have demonstrated an improvement in aerobic capacity or exercise performance without any changes in blood variables (Gore et al.

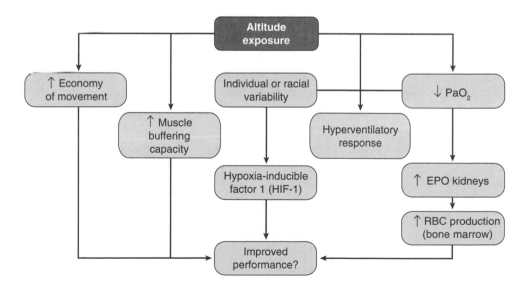

**FIGURE 10.1 Schematic of hematopoietic model of hypoxic improvement.**

Reprinted, by permission, from S.S. Cheung, 2010, *Advanced environmental exercise physiology* (Champaign, IL: Human Kinetics), 129.

2007, Hahn et al. 2001). Low oxygen levels affect many physiological systems, and changes within each of them may help to explain improved performance following hypoxic training. Possibilities include changes in submaximal oxygen requirements and lactate tolerance.

- Intriguingly, hypoxic exposure appears to elicit a marked improvement in economy of movement. Reductions in submaximal oxygen requirements of 3 to 10 percent have been reported in a number of independent research laboratories (Neya et al. 2007, Saunders et al. 2004). The exact reasons behind this change in economy are unknown, but they are likely related to adaptations within the metabolic processes in muscles.

- The ability of the body and the skeletal muscles to tolerate and buffer against lactate may improve following hypoxic training. Two to three weeks of altitude exposure above 2,000 meters results in enhanced muscle buffering in trained individuals (Gore et al. 2001).

Many questions remain about altitude training, including individual variability in response, the rate and physiological mechanisms underlying adaptation, and its optimal implementation for various sports.

## Live High, Train High

Traditionally, altitude training involved having the athlete move to a training base at altitude, live and train there for a period of weeks or more, and then return to competition at sea level. Such live high, train high (LHTH) protocols were the earliest ones employed because they were the main practical option before the advent of portable hypoxic facilities. When evaluating the LHTH literature, consider the non-altitude-related factors that may have enhanced performance. Namely, even for national-caliber athletes, such altitude camps may be a unique experience in that they have full access to coaches, masseurs, mechanics, and a peer group of training partners that they may not have at home. Many of the LHTH studies did not incorporate a control group that trained in a similar camp at sea level, making it difficult to isolate the effects of altitude. Despite its long history, the results of LHTH protocols for sea-level performance remain equivocal in both the scientific literature and actual practice.

The classic study concluding that LHTH had no effect was conducted in 1975 on trained male distance runners (Adams et al. 1975). The study featured a repeated measures crossover design in which one group underwent three weeks of sea-level training followed by three weeks of training at 2,300 meters and the other matched group of subjects had the reverse order of conditions (i.e., three weeks of altitude training followed by three weeks of sea-level training). The critical finding with aerobic capacity was that, compared with preexperimental baseline values at sea level, neither group demonstrated any increase in $\dot{V}O_2$max when tested at sea level after returning from altitude.

But some well-controlled studies have demonstrated an enhancement of aerobic performance from LHTH protocols (Daniels and Oldridge 1970). Six U.S. national team distance runners completed two 14-day LHTH blocks at 2,300 meters, during which the normal sea-level training loads were employed from the beginning of camp. These blocks were separated by a 5-day period during which the athletes competed in elite events. Competitions also occurred in the 5 days following the second 14-day LHTH block. Aerobic capacity testing following the initial and final LHTH blocks elicited a 4 percent and 5 percent increase, respectively, in $\dot{V}O_2$max compared with preexperimental values. Exercise performance also benefitted, and a significant 3 percent improvement was seen in 3-mile (5 km) race pace at the end of all LHTH blocks. From an applied perspective, the most important finding was that all but one athlete set personal records in competition over the course of the study, and each of those five subsequently reset their records. Besides the small sample size, concerns about the execution of this study have focused primarily on the lack of a control group of elite athletes training at a sea-level camp.

Long-term living at moderate altitudes is popular among endurance athletes, as evidenced by the many elite cyclists and triathletes who have chosen to live in Boulder, Colorado. Shorter-term altitude camps for athletes may be effective in improving performance, although widely disparate results have been reported across different studies using various test measures. In addition, the training-camp effect of most of these studies cannot be ignored as a reason for performance gains. Even for professional athletes, the opportunity to do a focused training block with peers and without daily distractions from family, groceries, laundry, and bike maintenance would likely result in significant fitness and performance improvement regardless of location or altitude.

## Live Low, Train High

Not all athletes have the means or desire to make a permanent move to a higher altitude or to attend a high-altitude camp. One option springing up in some elite training centers is to use hypoxic facilities during training itself but otherwise to live in a low-altitude environment, creating a situation of live low, train high, or LLTH. The bulk of the existing LLTH literature shows that this approach has minimal ergogenic benefit. In a recent survey of various altitude-training modalities, Wilber (2007) reported that only a small number of controlled LLTH studies on trained or elite athletes demonstrated significant improvements in subjects' blood parameters, aerobic capacity, or work performance.

Courtesy of Altitudetech Inc.

**Portable systems enable athletes to train in a hypoxic environment.**

One of the major limitations of LLTH is that athletes are relatively constrained to a laboratory environment or a training base at altitude during the training sessions. From a practical perspective, human athletes cannot train exclusively in an artificial laboratory environment. For example, few cyclists can maintain motivation to log large amounts of training hours on a stationary bike indoors. Therefore, the concept of replacing only part of an athlete's training with a hypoxic stimulus has been investigated. In one study, trained cyclists performed three 30-minute laboratory bouts a week of either hypoxic (oxygen reduced) or normoxic (normal oxygen) workouts at the estimated anaerobic threshold for six weeks (Ventura et al. 2003). The subjects self-determined the remainder of the training week. But no significant changes were observed in $\dot{V}O_2$max, maximal power output, or time trial performance in either the hypoxic

A hypoxic tent can enable cyclists to live high and train low.

Courtesy of Altitudetech Inc.

or normoxic training groups. In contrast, elite runners who trained twice per week in a hypoxic (14.5 percent inspired oxygen) environment experienced a significant improvement in $V'O_2$max and time to exhaustion at a high-intensity workload, and no improvements were observed in a normoxic group (Dufour et al. 2006, Ponsot et al. 2006).

## Live High, Train Low

The late 1990s saw a new paradigm emerge in altitude training. To maximize the physiological adaptation from exposure to hypoxia yet minimize the reduction in exercise capacity typically observed at altitude, Ben Levine and Jim Stray-Gundersen (1997) proposed a live high, train low (LHTL) altitude-training model. With LHTL, athletes experience passive hypoxia during rest or sleep to elicit altitude adaptation, typically 8 to 10 hours daily at altitudes ranging from 2,000 to 2,700 meters. Regular training is performed at altitudes as close to sea level as practical, typically at less than 1,000 meters.

The classic initial LHTL study investigated 13 male and female collegiate runners over a 28-day period. The subjects resided at Park City, Utah, (2,500 meters) and trained at Salt Lake City (1,250 meters) (Levine and Stray-Gundersen 1997). Thirteen additional runners were in a live high, train high (LHTH) group, and a third control group of 13 male and female runners trained and resided at the lower altitude (LLTL). Figure 10.2 presents the data for blood volume, red blood cell mass, and 5K time trial performance for each of the three groups before training, following 4 weeks of standardized sea-level training, and after the experimental training (LLTL, LLTH, LHTL). The LHTL group demonstrated a strong linkage between elevated blood response and ultimately higher $\dot{V}O_2$max and exercise performance. Specifically, red blood cell mass, hemoglobin, and treadmill $\dot{V}O_2$max all increased following the LHTL training period, whereas no significant changes in these variables were observed in the control group or in 5,000-meter run times. In the LHTL group, however, 5,000-meter run times improved by an average of 13.4 seconds 3 days postaltitude, and this improvement was maintained in continued testing at weekly intervals up to 3 weeks postaltitude. Such clean demarcation of responses in a well-controlled study generated excitement about the potential for LHTL training and helped to popularize the blood response model for hypoxic adaptations. As with other modes of altitude training, however, the scientific literature does not universally confirm the efficacy of LHTL training, and a number of studies on elite athletes have not been able to demonstrate significant blood response following a LHTL regimen (Gore et al. 2006).

Following this initial introduction of the LHTL model, much research has gone into refining the application of this research to elite athletes. One LHTL variation by the same research group involved further partitioning the training component. Base training was performed at altitude (2,500 meters) and only

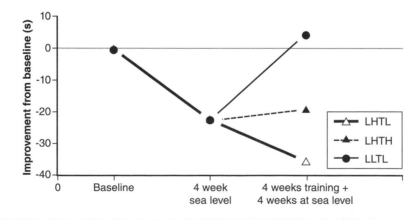

**FIGURE 10.2** Relative improvements in 5000 m run times after periods of sea level and LHTH, LLTH, and LHTL training regimens.

Data from Levine and Stray-Gundersen 1997.

the interval training sessions were done at the lower altitude (Stray-Gundersen et al. 2001). The major findings of their original LHTL study were replicated, including elevated EPO, hemoglobin, and $\dot{V}O_2max$ coupled with improved 3,000-meter run times. Notably, these improvements were found in elite rather than collegiate-level athletes, but one limitation of the study was the lack of a control group for comparison. Other variations of this model have included refining and individualizing the altitude employed for both rest and training, and attempting to determine the optimal progression of altitude throughout a block of training. By and large, of the various hypoxic manipulations, the live high, train low model has demonstrated the most evidence for ergogenic benefit for sea-level performance (Wilber 2007).

## Individual Variability in Hypoxic Response

When contemplating whether to use hypoxic training, keep in mind that, as with training itself, everyone responds differently and no general template can be applied. Thirty-two elite male and female middle- to long-distance collegiate runners performed various training protocols, including live high, train low; live high, train high; and live high, train high base, train low interval during 4 weeks of living at 2,500 meters (see table 10.1) (Chapman et al. 1998). A distinct categorization of subjects into groups of responders and nonresponders was observed, regardless of sex or training program at altitude. The responder group (n = 17), who decreased their 5,000-meter run times by 4 percent compared with prealtitude times, demonstrated a significant elevation of serum EPO concentrations within 30 hours of initial arrival at altitude, and they maintained this increase after 14 days of exposure. At the conclusion of the 4 weeks of exposure, responders exhibited

**TABLE 10.1    Individual Variability in Performance Following Variations of a 28-Day Live High, Train Low Altitude-Training Protocol**

|  | NONRESPONDERS (N = 15) | | RESPONDERS (N = 17) | |
|---|---|---|---|---|
|  | Prealtitude | Postaltitude | Prealtitude | Postaltitude |
| 5,000 m run time (min:s) | 17:24 (:91) | 17:38 (:98)* | 17:11 (:76) | 16:34 (:75)*† |
| $\dot{V}O_2max$ (ml × min$^{-1}$ × kg$^{-1}$) | 64.1 (4.4) | 64.4 (4.7) | 65.0 (5.8) | 69.2 (6.8)* † |
| Maximal steady state $\dot{V}O_2$ (ml × min$^{-1}$ × kg$^{-1}$) | 50.2 (8.5) | 52.4 (4.9) | 54.2 (5.3) | 59.0 (9.1)* † |

Means (standard deviation)
*Significantly different from prealtitude.
†Significantly different from nonresponders.

Reprinted, by permission, from S.S. Cheung, 2010, *Advanced environmental exercise physiology* (Champaign, IL: Human Kinetics), 134. Data from Chapman et al. 1998.

an increased red blood cell volume and $\dot{V}O_2$max. In sharp contrast, nonresponders (n = 15), who averaged a 1 percent slower 5,000-meter time postaltitude, demonstrated only a slight EPO increase at 30 hours into exposure. Beyond this initial elevation, no hematological or aerobic changes occurred at any further point of the altitude exposure in this group, and the EPO concentrations decreased back to near sea-level values by 14 days following altitude exposure. Furthermore, nonresponders had a significantly lower average velocity during interval training at altitude after 2 weeks compared with responders.

Clearly, the Chapman et al. (1998) study highlights that hypoxic exposure cannot be generalized as having a consistent ergogenic benefit. But note that a disproportionate percentage of the nonresponders were from the live high, train high group (82 percent of the responders were from the two variants of live high, train low), such that the nonresponse may be more a reflection of the lack of efficacy of training at high altitudes. Also, no sex-specific response pattern can be generalized; a roughly equal distribution of men and women was found in the responder and nonresponder groups. In summary, predicting who will benefit from altitude training remains extremely difficult, and customizing that training to suit individual characteristics is a further challenge.

## Respiratory Training

At the end of the day, almost all cycling disciplines ultimately revolve around endurance, which in turn relies on maximizing aerobic capacity and oxygen uptake. This connection explains the obsession with maximal oxygen uptake ($\dot{V}O_2$max) and lactate threshold measures. When you hear talk of power-to-weight ratio or sustained power, that idea also relies on aerobic capacity to generate watts. Improving aerobic capacity involves improving the metabolic efficiency of your muscles, neural recruitment patterns, and the oxygen delivery to those muscles through the respiratory system (lungs) and cardiovascular system (heart).

Because of the importance of oxygen uptake, a recurring target for ergogenic aids is the respiratory system itself. Considering that respiratory muscles can be responsible for nearly 10 percent of the total oxygen requirement during maximal exercise (Vogiatzis et al. 2009), a strong case can certainly be made for respiratory training (Romer and Polkey 2008). Why not be more efficient with oxygen use in the respiratory muscles and divert the extra oxygen to the cycling muscles? With that in mind, a number of training systems have been marketed with the promise of improving the strength of the respiratory muscles. Such respiratory systems, including the PowerLung and PowerBreathe, are touted as having the ability to train, in an adjustable fashion, both the inspiratory and expiratory muscles, and to work in a more advanced fashion than simply limiting airflow (i.e., breathing through a straw). Much of the work on respiratory limits to exercise has focused on patients with respiratory diseases such as severe asthma or chronic obstructive pulmonary disorders. Relatively less work has examined exercise limits in trained athletes. Scientific validation of these systems and of using respiratory training for athletes in general is relatively rare, and findings are somewhat inconclusive. Wide variation between training and testing protocol is one potential reason.

Overall, studies on respiratory training have been performed on a range of athletes, and many seem to suggest some benefit in both perception of effort and exercise performance. Kilding et al. (2010) found slight improvement in swimming performance in club-level swimmers at 100- to 400-meter distances after 6 weeks of inspiratory muscle training. Voliantis et al. (2001) reported improved distance during a 6-minute maximal rowing ergometer test, along with a faster 5,000-meter time trial in 14 competitive female rowers after 11 weeks of inspiratory muscle training. Five weeks of respiratory muscle training seemed to improve intermittent sprinting performance in soccer players (Nicks et al. 2009).

In cycling, the evidence is somewhat more equivocal. Many studies seem to find an improvement in respiratory muscle function that did not translate to better aerobic capacity or cycling performance. For example, Guenette et al. (2006) completed both $\dot{V}O_2max$ and time-to-exhaustion exercise tolerance tests before and after 5 weeks of training with a PowerLung. They reported that mean inspiratory pressure generated by the respiratory muscles increased by about 37 percent. No changes were found in $\dot{V}O_2max$ with respiratory training, although there was some evidence of improved exercise tolerance time in those untrained subjects. In an earlier study, subjects improved respiratory muscle endurance with 4 weeks of inspiratory training, but this improvement did not translate into either a higher $\dot{V}O_2max$ or an improved tolerance to high-intensity exercise (Fairbarn et al. 1991). One exception reported an increased diaphragm thickness and improved respiratory function, along with a 36 percent increased time to exhaustion when cycling at 75 percent of maximal power (Gething et al. 2004b). The same group also investigated whether there was a dose response in terms of intensity of respiratory training. Training for 6 weeks at both 80 percent and 100 percent maximal inspiratory pressure improved respiratory muscle performance, but only the 100-percent condition elicited a reduction in heart rate and perceived exertion during a moderate cycling test (Gething et al. 2004a).

What does this all mean in terms of whether respiratory muscle training is effective as an ergogenic aid for cyclists? Clearly, the function and endurance of the respiratory muscles themselves can be enhanced by specific respiratory muscle training. But the response in actual performance improvement seems to be highly variable, especially in self-paced time trial efforts. Overall, respiratory training definitely does not appear to be a magic bullet that can replace normal training, nor does it seem able to produce the large potential changes in performance seen with altitude training. At best, it may serve as a final ergogenic tool for those who have already optimized their training, and then only after some trial-and-error testing.

# Heat Stress

At the Olympics in Atlanta in 1996 and Athens in 2004, sport scientists, coaches, and athletes alike knew that heat, humidity, and even air pollution would be environmental factors that could seriously affect the performance of the athletes. The positive aspect was that, just as the 1968 Mexico City Games kick-started scientific and applied interest in altitude training that still hasn't abated, these recent Games spurred a lot of fundamental and applied research into ways to minimize the potentially debilitating effects of heat.

Climatic warming, along with growing participation in extreme or ultraendurance sports and other outdoor activities, has contributed to the increased incidence of serious exertional heat illnesses worldwide. Hot temperatures can severely impair exercise capacity and lead to risks of heat illnesses. A rise in body temperature can arise through a combination of exercise-induced metabolic heat production, environmental conditions (temperature, humidity), and the wearing of clothing that impairs evaporative heat transfer (figure 10.3). Hyperthermia, heat exhaustion, and heatstroke have become well recognized as major risks of exercising in hot environments. An excellent book on this topic specifically for coaches and athletes was written by Dr. Lawrence Armstrong (2007) of the University of Connecticut. Furthermore, exertional heat illness can occur even in cool weather. In one case study a well-trained male collapsed near the finish of a marathon in 6 °C ambient conditions and presented a rectal temperature of 40.7 °C approximately 30 minutes postcollapse (Roberts 2006). Dr. Armstrong led the American College of Sports Medicine Position Stand on Exertional Heat Illness (Armstrong et al. 2007), emphasizing that heat exhaustion and exertional heatstroke "occur worldwide with prolonged intense activity in almost every venue (e.g., cycling, running races, American football, soccer)." Although they occur most frequently in hot and humid conditions, such problems can occur even in cool conditions with intense or prolonged exercise such as marathons or Ironman triathlons.

## Effects of Heat Stress

Heat stress and hyperthermia can undoubtedly have a serious negative effect on exercise performance and the health and safety of athletes. Besides causing physiological effects, a higher ambient temperature may alter voluntary effort; the extra heat stress may cause the brain to reduce the willingness to work hard in order to avoid the risk of heat illness. Consider these findings:

- Stephen's lab has demonstrated that the ability of the brain to recruit muscles to contract forcefully is reduced when body temperature is high (Morrison et al. 2004, Thomas et al. 2006).

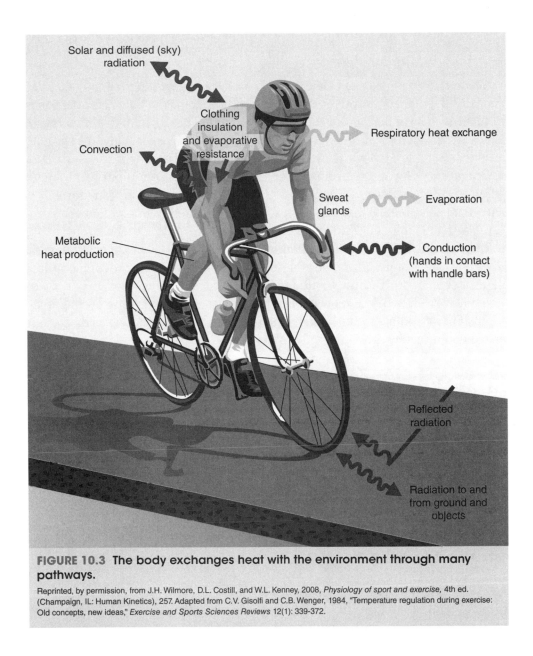

**FIGURE 10.3** The body exchanges heat with the environment through many pathways.

Reprinted, by permission, from J.H. Wilmore, D.L. Costill, and W.L. Kenney, 2008, *Physiology of sport and exercise,* 4th ed. (Champaign, IL: Human Kinetics), 257. Adapted from C.V. Gisolfi and C.B. Wenger, 1984, "Temperature regulation during exercise: Old concepts, new ideas," *Exercise and Sports Sciences Reviews* 12(1): 339-372.

- When trained cyclists rode at 70 percent of max in lab temperatures of 4, 10, 20, and 30 °C, the longest tolerance time was at 10 °C. Cyclists produced progressively lower times at 20 and 30 °C (Galloway and Maughan 1997). This result suggests that heat stress may be an issue even in temperatures that we typically think of as comfortable.

- When tasked to adjust power output to maintain a constant perceived effort similar to that needed for a 20K to 40K time trial pace, the rate of decline in voluntary power output was higher in hot (35 °C) compared with cooler (15 and 25 °C) environments (Tucker et al. 2006).

Given that hyperthermia clearly impairs physiological function and exercise capacity, the main question for athletes is just how hot is too hot. This question is difficult to answer, because a slight or even significant rise in body temperature is not always an indication of problems during exercise, especially in fit or elite athletes. In table 10.2 we see that, while 8K running times were slower in hot temperatures, the overall average running speed in both conditions were similar whether subjects were <40 °C or >40 °C in core temperature. Ultramarathoners can exercise at maximal capacity for four hours in moderate ambient temperatures with only minor elevations in core temperature, suggesting a strong ability to thermoregulate even under conditions of high metabolic heat production. At the same time, some endurance athletes can sustain elevated core temperatures of greater than 40 °C throughout a marathon or triathlon without major issues (Kenefick et al. 2007). Especially in cycling outdoors, where the cycling itself often generates a high wind speed, high temperatures may not be as dangerous as expected (see Q & A with Dr. Lars Nybo).

**TABLE 10.2 Relationship Between Temperature and Running Performance in Fit Athletes**

| Ambient temperature | 8K run times (s) | Athlete's core temperature | Average running speed (m/min) |
|---|---|---|---|
| Cool (17 °C) | 1,657 | <40 °C | 282 |
| Warm (30 °C) | 1,768 | >40 °C | 279 |

Data from Ely et al. 2009.

## Heat Adaptation

Heat acclimation generally elicits a lower resting core temperature, greater plasma volume, and an increased sweating rate (Cheung et al. 2000). Heat acclimation can be achieved by a variety of heat exposure protocols. People vary in the frequency, duration, and intensity of heat stress required to attain and maintain adaptation. In healthy adults, the primary stimulus for heat acclimation appears to be a sustained elevation in core temperature of 1 to 2 °C for 60 to 90 minutes over 4 to 10 days. Aerobic fitness decreases the required stimulus and the amount of stimulus needed to maintain or reacclimate to heat (Pandolf et al. 1977). The environment is also a significant component of a heat acclimation program. Wearing heavy sweat clothing in a cool environment may elicit the same increased sweating response as standard heat exposure does (Dawson

1994). Therefore, training indoors with a lower fan speed or wearing an extra clothing layer may be a useful method if you are training in a cold environment but travelling to a race where you expect hot conditions. Overall, the thing to focus on with heat acclimation appears to be getting your core temperature to rise to the point where your sweating response is strongly stimulated and to maintain that high temperature and sweating for about 60 to 90 minutes a session for four to eight sessions, depending on fitness. Passive heat exposure, such as sitting in a sauna, can possibly provide the same stimulus but is not really practical because staying in the sauna for long periods may be dangerous, and time spent in the sauna is time that you're not spending on training itself. Many people believe that they can stay in an air-conditioned environment much of the day and then acclimatize by riding for two or three hours each day in the heat. To acclimatize fully to the heat and humidity, however, you need to minimize the time that you spend in an air-conditioned car, home, and office because the acclimatization process occurs not just during exercise but also from living in the environment 24/7.

## Protective Effects of Aerobic Fitness

Aerobic fitness provides protective physiological responses to exercise similar to those from acclimatization to hot environments (Cheung et al. 2000). These benefits include greater evaporative heat dissipation through improved sweating response, resulting from both lower core temperature thresholds for the initiation of sweating and greater sensitivity of sweating response to increasing core temperatures. Improved aerobic capacity also leads to elevated plasma volume and cardiac output, minimizing the competition for blood distribution between skeletal muscle and skin (heat dissipation and sweating output) during exercise and heat stress (Sawka et al. 1992). Other important benefits of aerobic fitness are a lowered resting core temperature coupled with an elevated endpoint core temperature that can be tolerated before voluntary exhaustion (Cheung and McLellan 1998). This latter effect results directly from aerobic fitness rather than body composition because differences across fitness groups remained evident when highly and moderately fit subjects were normalized for differences in body fatness (Selkirk and McLellan 2001). Therefore, fitness appears to benefit heat tolerance because of both a greater capacity for and a slower rate of heat storage. These benefits, however, appear unique to long-term changes in aerobic fitness rather than transient changes brought about by short-term training interventions (Cheung and McLellan 1998).

## Q&A    With Lars Nybo: The Heat of Competition

| | |
|---|---|
| **Current position** | Associate professor at the University of Copenhagen. |
| **Professional relationship and background with cycling** | Coach for a Continental road team; supervisor for the national team. |
| **Personal background with cycling** | Elite rider at national level for eight years; three times Danish TT and road race champion for masters. |
| **Favorite ride (either one you've done or always wanted to do)** | Danish TT championship in 2009, a hard ride with high speed but still with rhythm and flow. |
| **Favorite cycling-related experience** | I actually like the daily training, and most training rides are good and enjoyable experiences for me. But riding in the mountains in the spring in Spain is always an event I look forward to. |

 **Lars, Denmark isn't exactly known for being the warmest place on the planet. How did you get into hyperthermia research, and can you tell us a little bit about your work?**

True, Denmark normally has a cold climate in winter and moderate temperatures during summertime. Nevertheless, there is a long tradition of research within the area of hyperthermia, and when I undertook my masters degree I was fortunate to work with some great researchers. They introduced me to the field, and this provided me with a good start.

Since then I have done several studies within the field of exercise in the heat, examining factors associated with hyperthermia-induced fatigue and central fatigue in general. Besides doing research, I teach at our department in basic and exercise physiology and I am involved in coaching road cyclists at the national and international level.

**So how does hyperthermia cause fatigue? Is it in the brain, the muscles, a combination of brain and muscles, or something else altogether?**

I think it is a big mistake to ascribe fatigue or exhaustion to a single factor. Our studies as well as those conducted in other labs, including yours, Stephen, have clearly demonstrated that what we call central fatigue and alterations of brain function are involved, but it also seems clear that cardiovascular stress, reduced oxygen delivery to the exercise muscles, and alterations in muscle metabolism may be important factors. Therefore, I would conclude that the cause of fatigue is not just one thing but a combination of central and peripheral factors all acting separately but also together.

**How big a danger is hyperthermia and heat exhaustion in cycling?**

For trained cyclists on a flat road maintaining a high velocity, convective and evaporative cooling will be greatly enhanced. Under these conditions, unless it is extremely hot or the cyclist fails to maintain water balance, it is unlikely that the cyclist will become hyperthermic. If the cyclist becomes dehydrated, however, the ability to dissipate heat will be markedly reduced and the risk of hyperthermia will increase.

During uphill cycling or other types of cycling with low velocities (mountain biking, early season cyclocross, and so on), a real threat for developing hyperthermia may be present. In hot environments the cooling capacity of the environment is reduced when the cyclist's speed is low because the air velocity declines, lowering both convective cooling and maximal evaporative capacity.

 **You've presented some really intriguing work recently arguing that top cycling performance isn't impaired in the heat but may actually be improved. How does that work?**

Because air resistance is a main factor during cycling on flat roads, performance is favored by an increase in the environmental temperature because the air density declines as the air temperature increases. A cyclist during a time trial under these conditions might be able to maintain a given velocity with a lower power output or ride at a higher average velocity by maintaining the same power output.

 **So let's say that you're helping a cyclist with a world hour record attempt at an indoor velodrome. What would you recommend the indoor temperature be, and what other temperature considerations might there be? For example, should precooling be used during warm-ups? Should the cyclist warm up on the trainer or by actually riding?**

The optimal temperature would be the maximal temperature at which the rider can maintain temperature balance without being forced to reduce power output. In other words, the environmental temperature should not be so high that it will cause hyperthermia and impair the rider's exercise capacity, but within that limit it should be as high as possible to favor the aerodynamic aspects. The precise number may depend on the specific rider's dimensions, heat production, aerodynamic position, and so on, but my best guess is an air temperature around 30 °C.

The warm-up should be conducted with an approach that will elevate the rider's body core temperature to about 38 °C and preferably with a muscle temperature around 39 °C. The warm-up could be done on trainers if adequate air cooling is provided by fans or some other means. I prefer riding the bike around the track, because the risk of becoming hyperthermic during the

*(continued)*

warm-up is markedly elevated when using trainers or stationary bikes. Also, riding the bike activates the specific and relevant muscles.

Of course the altitude issue—specifically the barometric pressure, which affects the air density—should also be considered.

 **What about triathlons? The running is done at a slower speed and comes after the bike. So would it be better to race triathlons in cooler or warmer temperatures? What steps can triathletes take to race a better run portion in hot temperatures?**

During triathlons in hot environments, hyperthermia is generally not an issue during the cycling leg, whereas overheating is a common problem during the running phase. The speed is much lower during running compared with cycling, and the resulting reduction in the capacity for dissipating heat to the environment becomes relevant.

When participating in Ironman competitions or long-distance triathlons in environments where hyperthermia is likely to occur during the final run, avoiding dehydration during the cycling phase is important. Furthermore, starting the running with a core temperature that is as low as possible may be advantageous. Any cooling that may be applied during the cycling stage may ultimately benefit the succeeding running performance. Cooling during the cycling leg may benefit water balance by lowering the requirement for sweat production, allowing the athlete to initiate the final run with a slightly lower core temperature. But cooling before the triathlon—before swimming—makes little sense because this effect will not last throughout the swim and cycling phases.

 **What would be your advice for practically implementing cooling strategies for cyclists? Should we really be concerned about precooling?**

No—for runners precooling may be relevant, but I think it is optimal to initiate cycling competitions with a normal exercise core temperature of about 38 °C. But on very hot days core temperature should certainly not be elevated above that point because it might be following an intense warm-up on a stationary trainer with little or no cooling.

## Cooling Strategies

The use of cooling protocols to improve performance or to counteract the risks of heat stress and hyperthermia has gained increasing popularity in cycling. Early athletic proponents include the Australian rowing teams, who used vests containing ice packs during warm-ups before competing in the 1996 Atlanta Olympics. Since then, teams such as Garmin began using various ice vests while warming up on stationary bikes for a time trial.

The consistent core temperatures at the point of voluntary fatigue with a constant workload in the heat would certainly suggest that the removal of heat before exercise could increase exercise tolerance by increasing possible heat storage beforehand. Although the rate of heat storage may remain unchanged with precooling, the lowered baseline temperature may enable both core temperature and heart rate to remain lower with prolonged exercise over time. Precooling also can decrease perceptions of heat stress and thereby possibly promote an upregulation of work intensity. This phenomenon has been reported in both elite runners (figure 10.4) and rowers with precooling of about 0.5 °C using cool water of about 20 °C or ice vests (Arngrïmsson et al. 2004, Booth et al. 1997). Less clear are the benefits of precooling for cycling events that rely more on short bursts of anaerobic power or strength. Precooling before intermittent cycling sprints did not result in any improved power (Cheung and Robinson 2004, Duffield et al. 2003), and a higher ambient temperature may actually facilitate higher pedaling cadences and power outputs during maximal cycling sprints (Ball et al. 1999).

Ice vests are popular because they cover the important torso region and are relatively nonconstricting compared with wearing cooling pants during cycling. They also permit the legs to exercise and get the usual benefits of warming up before competition while keeping the torso as cool as possible. Research has shown that precooling the legs eliminates most of the benefits of warming up (Sleivert et al. 2001). Cooling hoods are also often used because they theoretically keep the brain cool. Furthermore, the head and face play a major role in the overall perception of thermal stress and comfort (Cotter and Taylor 2005),

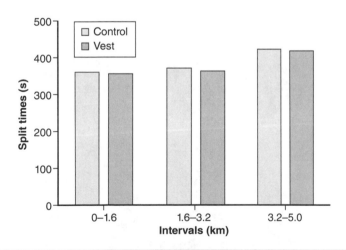

**FIGURE 10.4  Effect of precooling on runners.**
Data from Arngrïmsson et al. 2004.

and head cooling by itself can be beneficial in improving high-intensity running in the heat.

As of now, cooling suits remain impractical and expensive for all but the most well-heeled teams and athletes. Suits with water cooling require a pump and power, and the ice in the ice vests melts and needs to be replaced, thus requiring extra ice and a freezer unit.

How can you apply some of the research on cooling to your cycling performance?

- Keep as cool as possible before your event! Do everything you can to stay out of the sun and heat before the start of your event. Every bit of heat exposure is unnecessary additional stress that detracts from your training or recovery.

- Keep hydrated and drink during the days before and the morning of your event (see chapter 9). Dehydration becomes a negative spiral in that it further impairs your ability to tolerate heat stress because you have less blood volume to dissipate heat. If you have only a little bit of water left in your bottle, it is wiser to drink it rather than pour it over your head!

Cooling vests are a practical and effective option for staying cool while doing a stationary warm-up on a hot day.

Courtesy of Arctic Heat USA.

- You need to cool a good chunk of your body. You may have seen flexible gel packs shaped like tubes that you can drape around your neck and collar. It's a nice idea, but the cooling capacity of these stylish little collars is far too small to have any real effect.

- Concentrate on cooling the head and torso. Recent work from South Africa and Australia suggested that people may subconsciously select a pace based on psychological (i.e., head) perceptions of heat stress. Subjects with a hotter brain performed at a slower pace (Tucker et al. 2006, Marino et al. 2004). Avoid actively cooling your legs, which negates the benefits of your warm-up. Simple Lycra hoods with ice packs sewn inside may be an every-man's solution to precooling.

## Cold Weather

People have said that there's no such thing as bad weather, only bad clothing. Within reason, exercising outdoors even in the extreme cold is both doable and possibly even enjoyable. But there is a fine line between building toughness and getting sick. Here are some guidelines to consider when exercising in the cold.

- Research shows that inhaling very cold air during exercise causes minimal to no negative effects (Hartung et al. 1980) because the nasal passage and airways are extremely effective at warming up the air before it reaches the lungs. So in cold and dry conditions, you can safely go cycling, cross-country skiing, or snowshoeing as long as you dress appropriately and take enough to eat and drink with you.

- Warm-ups might need to be longer and possibly more intense to build up core temperature, but care must still be taken to avoid becoming too fatigued. Minimize the time between the end of the warm-up and the start of competition to ensure that your body and muscles do not cool down too much.

- Windchill is the big risk when exercising in the winter because wind greatly increases the rate of heat loss from your skin and the risk for frostnip and frostbite (Castellani et al. 2006, Noakes 2000). Consider ditching the road bike, which you generally use on exposed roads, and build up a mountain bike for ice and snow biking on tree-lined trails. Cross-training activities such as snowshoeing and cross-country skiing, which get you out on to the trails and moving at generally slower speeds, decreases the risk of windchill and heat loss from convective cooling.

- Because of the cold temperature and low humidity, you may not feel that you are sweating heavily. Your sweat rate, however, will remain near what it might be in hotter conditions because of the heat buildup from exercising. Also, the amount of heat and water that you lose from your breathing will be higher than it would be in hotter conditions. Therefore, continue to track your hydration status during winter workouts and prepare your hydration strategy appropriately.

- Be extremely careful in cold, rainy conditions. Water conducts heat 25 times as fast as air (that's why a 15 °C room is not too bad but a 15 °C pool is brutal) and greatly increasing your risk of hypothermia. On a cold and wet day, consider doing something indoors instead or make sure that you have excellent rain gear. Try to keep stops or rest breaks to a minimum because the act of exercising generates a lot of valuable heat that can keep you warm.

- Make sure that you wear quality winter underclothing that wicks sweat away from your body because trapped sweat will cool you down rapidly.

- Layering definitely works. Each layer acts as a barrier to wind, and the sum of a few layers is usually greater than one single layer of the same overall insulation. Layering also lets you customize the degree of ventilation during exercise.

- Wear a hat under your helmet. With all the superventilating helmets out on the market, you can add a layer to warm your head and still be comfortable.

# Applying the Science

Extreme conditions are an essential part of cycling and can play as much of a role in how a ride or race turns out as equipment, training, or strategy does. Riding or living at high altitude decreases the availability of oxygen to the body. Although this factor impairs exercise when you first arrive at altitude, long-term exposure to altitude can stimulate a host of adaptive changes, allowing your body to take in more oxygen or use it more effectively. Currently, the scientific evidence suggests that a live high, train low protocol of training near sea level to maximize training load and living or sleeping at a higher altitude is the best way to improve sea-level performance. But there are many potential mechanisms by which altitude training can improve performance, and the response to any altitude-training program is highly individual. Researchers have also looked at the effect of strengthening the muscles of the respiratory system. Some evidence has shown that respiratory training can provide some benefit as a means of improving performance through increasing oxygen delivery to the body.

Although some increase in body temperature during exercise is acceptable and even desirable, extreme temperatures impose extra stress on the body that diverts its focus from generating power at the muscles and delivering it to the pedals. Cooling strategies are difficult to use on the bike, and the most effective path seems to be minimizing heat increases before cycling and then staying hydrated both before and during your ride. The large amounts of heat that you generate while exercising make riding in even very cold weather safe if you take some basic precautions and wear appropriate clothing. Overall, you can view the environment as either a friend or a foe, depending on your understanding of its effects and the preparations that you make.

# References

## Chapter 1

Chapman, R.F., J. Stray-Gundersen, and B.D. Levine. 1998. Individual variation in response to altitude training. *Journal of Applied Physiology* 85:1448–1456.

Cheung, S.S., and A.M. Robinson. 2004. The influence of upper-body pre-cooling on repeated sprint performance in moderate ambient temperatures. *Journal of Sports Sciences* 22:605–612.

Conconi, F., G. Grazzi, I. Casoni, C. Guglielmini, C. Borsetto, E. Ballarin, G. Mazzoni, M. Patracchini, and F. Manfredini. 1996. The Conconi test: Methodology after 12 years of application. *International Journal of Sports Medicine* 17:509–19.

Flouris, A.D., and S.S. Cheung. 2006. Design and control optimization of microclimate liquid cooling systems underneath protective clothing. *Annals of Biomedical Engineering* 34:359–72.

Jeukendrup, A.E., and J. Martin. 2001. Improving cycling performance: How should we spend our time and money. *Sports Medicine* 31:559–69.

Levine, B.D., and J. Stray-Gundersen. 1997. "Living high–training low": Effect of moderate-altitude acclimatization with low-altitude training on performance. *Journal of Applied Physiology* 83:102–112.

Tikuisis, P., M.B. Ducharme, D. Moroz, and I. Jacobs. 1999. Physiological responses of exercised-fatigued individuals exposed to wet-cold conditions. *Journal of Applied Physiology* 86:1319–28.

## Chapter 2

Abbiss, C.R., and P.B. Laursen. 2005. Models to explain fatigue during prolonged endurance cycling. *Sports Medicine* 35:865–98.

Allen, H., and A. Coggan. 2010. *Training and racing with a power meter*. 2nd ed. Boulder, CO: VeloPress

Anish, E.J. 2005. Exercise and its effects on the central nervous system. *Current Sports Medicine Reports* 4:18–23.

Bemben, M.G., and H.S. Lamont. 2005. Creatine supplementation and exercise performance: Recent findings. *Sports Medicine* 35:107–125.

Bramble, D.M., and D.E. Lieberman. 2004. Endurance running and the evolution of Homo. *Nature* 432:345–352.

Cheung, S.S. 2010. *Advanced environmental exercise physiology*. Champaign, IL: Human Kinetics.

Coyle, E.F. 2007. Physiological regulation of marathon performance. *Sports Medicine* 37:306–311.

Enoka, R.M, and Duchateau, J. 2008. Muscle fatigue: what, why and how it influences muscle function. *Journal of Physiology* 586:11-23.

Gonzalez-Alonso, J., C. Teller, S.L. Andersen, F.B. Jensen, T. Hyldig, and B. Nielsen. 1999. Influence of body temperature on the development of fatigue during prolonged exercise in the heat. *Journal of Applied Physiology* 86:1032–1039.

Hargreaves, M. 2008. Fatigue mechanisms determining exercise performance: Integrative physiology is systems biology. *Journal of Applied Physiology* 104:1541–1542.

Joyner, M.J., and E.F. Coyle. 2008. Endurance exercise performance: The physiology of champions. *Journal of Physiology* 586:35–44.

Lambert, G.P. 2004. Role of gastrointestinal permeability in exertional heatstroke. *Exercise and Sport Sciences Reviews* 32:185–90.

Marino, F.E. 2002. Methods, advantages, and limitations of body cooling for exercise performance. *British Journal of Sports Medicine* 36:89–94.

Mauger, A.R., A.M. Jones, and C.A. Williams. 2009. Influence of feedback and prior experience on pacing during a 4-km cycle time trial. *Medicine and Science in Sports and Exercise* 41:451–458.

Meeusen, R., P. Watson, H. Hasegawa, B. Roelands, and M.F. Piacentini. 2007. Brain neurotransmitters in fatigue and overtraining. *Applied Physiology, Nutrition, and Metabolism* 32:857–864.

Nybo, L. 2008. Hyperthermia and fatigue. *Journal of Applied Physiology* 104:871–878.

Robergs, R.A., F. Ghiasvand, and D. Parker. 2004. Biochemistry of exercise-induced metabolic acidosis. *American Journal of Physiology* 287:R502–16.

Thomas, M.M., S.S. Cheung, G.C. Elder, and G.G. Sleivert. 2006. Voluntary muscle activation is impaired by core temperature rather than local muscle temperature. *Journal of Applied Physiology* 100:1361–1369.

Tucker, R., and T.D. Noakes. 2009. The physiological regulation of pacing strategy during exercise: A critical review. *British Journal of Sports Medicine* 43:e1.

# Chapter 3

Allen, H., and A. Coggan. 2010. *Training and racing with a power meter.* Boulder, CO: VeloPress.

Borg, G.A. 1982. Psychophysical bases of perceived exertion. *Medicine and Science in Sports and Exercise* 14:377-381.

Earnest, C.P., C. Foster, J. Hoyos, C.A. Muniesa, A. Santalla, and A. Lucia. 2009. Time trial exertion traits of cycling's Grand Tours. *International Journal of Sports Medicine* 30:240–244.

Friel, J. 2009. *The cyclist's training bible.* Boulder, CO: VeloPress.

Lucia, A., J. Hoyos, A. Carvajal, and J.L. Chicharro. 1999. Heart rate response to professional road cycling: The Tour de France. *International Journal of Sports Medicine* 20:167–72.

Lucia, A., J. Hoyos, A. Santalla, C. Earnest, and J.L. Chicharro. 2003. Tour de France versus Vuelta a Espana: Which is harder? *Medicine and Science in Sports and Exercise* 35:872–8.

Rodriguez-Marroyo, J.A., J. Garcia-Lopez, C.E. Juneau, and J.G. Villa. 2009. Workload demands in professional multi-stage cycling races of varying duration. *British Journal of Sports Medicine* 43:180–185.

Sawka, M.N., A.J. Young, K.B. Pandolf, R.C. Dennis, and C.R. Valeri. 1992. Erythrocyte, plasma, and blood volume of healthy young men. *Medicine and Science in Sports and Exercise* 24:47–453.

# Chapter 4

Bosquet, L., J. Montpetit, D. Arvisais, and I. Mujika. 2007. Effects of tapering on performance: A meta-analysis. *Medicine and Science in Sports and Exercise* 39:1358–1365.

Burgomaster, K.A., S.C. Hughes, G.J. Heigenhauser, S.N. Bradwell, and M.J. Gibala. 2005. Six sessions of sprint interval training increases muscle oxidative potential and cycle endurance capacity in humans. *Journal of Applied Physiology* 98:1985–1990.

Esteve-Lanao, J., C. Foster, S. Seiler, and A. Lucia. 2007. Impact of training intensity distribution on performance in endurance athletes. *Journal of Strength and Conditioning Research* 21:943–949.

Esteve-Lanao, J., A.F. San Juan, C.P. Earnest, C. Foster, and A. Lucia. 2005. How do endurance runners actually train? Relationship with competition performance. *Medicine and Science in Sports and Exercise* 37:496–504.

Faude, O., T. Meyer, J. Scharhag, F. Weins, A. Urhausen, and W. Kindermann. 2008. Volume vs. intensity in the training of competitive swimmers. *International Journal of Sports Medicine* 29:906–912.

Friel, J. 2009. *The cyclist's training bible*. 4th ed. Boulder, CO: VeloPress.

Gibala, M.J. 2007. High-intensity interval training: A time-efficient strategy for health promotion? *Current Sports Medicine Reports* 6:211–213.

Gibala, M.J., J.P. Little, M. van Essen, G.P. Wilkin, K.A. Burgomaster, A. Safdar, S. Raha, and M.A. Tarnopolsky. 2006. Short-term sprint interval versus traditional endurance training: Similar initial adaptations in human skeletal muscle and exercise performance. *Journal of Physiology* 575:901–911.

Guellich, A., S. Seiler, and E. Emrich. 2009. Training methods and intensity distribution of young world-class rowers. *International Journal of Sports Physiology and Performance* 4:448–460.

Houmard, J.A. 2009. Endurance athletes: What is the optimal training strategy? *International Journal of Sports Medicine* 30:313–314.

Mujika, I., S. Padilla, D. Pyne, and T. Busso. 2004. Physiological changes associated with the pre-event taper in athletes. *Sports Medicine* 34:891–927.

Paton, C.D., and W.G. Hopkins. 2004. Effects of high-intensity training on performance and physiology of endurance athletes. *Sportscience* 8:25–40.

Pyne, D.B., I. Mujika, and T. Reilly. 2009. Peaking for optimal performance: Research limitations and future directions. *Journal of Sports Sciences* 27:195–202.

Sassi, A., F.M. Impellizzeri, A. Morelli, P. Menaspa, and E. Rampinini. 2008. Seasonal changes in aerobic fitness indices in elite cyclists. *Applied Physiology, Nutrition, and Metabolism* 33:735–742.

Seiler, K.S., and G.O. Kjerland. 2006. Quantifying training intensity distribution in elite endurance athletes: Is there evidence for an "optimal" distribution? *Scandinavian Journal of Medicine & Science in Sports* 16:49–56.

Thomas, L., I. Mujika, and T. Busso. 2009. Computer simulations assessing the potential performance benefit of a final increase in training during pre-event taper. *Journal of Strength and Conditioning Research* 23:1729–1736.

Thomas, L., I. Mujika, and T. Busso. 2008. A model study of optimal training reduction during pre-event taper in elite swimmers. *Journal of Sports Sciences* 26:643–652.

Trinity, J.D., M.D. Pahnke, E.C. Reese, and E.F. Coyle. 2006. Maximal mechanical power during a taper in elite swimmers. *Medicine and Science in Sports and Exercise* 38:1643–1649.

Trinity, J.D., M.D. Pahnke, J.A. Sterkel, and E.F. Coyle. 2008. Maximal power and performance during a swim taper. *International Journal of Sports Medicine* 29:500–506.

## Chapter 5

Ali, A., M.P. Caine, and B.G. Snow. 2007. Graduated compression stockings: Physiological and perceptual responses during and after exercise. *Journal of Sports Sciences* 25:413–419.

Barnett, A. 2006. Using recovery modalities between training sessions in elite athletes: Does it help? *Sports Medicine* 36:781–796.

Bosquet, L., F.X. Gamelin, and S. Berthoin. 2008. Reliability of postexercise heart rate recovery. *International Journal of Sports Medicine* 29:238–243.

Bosquet, L., L. Leger, and P. Legros. 2001. Blood lactate response to overtraining in male endurance athletes. *European Journal of Applied Physiology* 84:107–114.

Bosquet, L., S. Merkari, D. Arvisais, and A.E. Aubert. 2008. Is heart rate a convenient tool to monitor over-reaching? A systematic review of the literature. *British Journal of Sports Medicine* 42:709–714.

Bringard, A., S. Perrey, and N. Belluye. 2006. Aerobic energy cost and sensation responses during submaximal running exercise—positive effects of wearing compression tights. *International Journal of Sports Medicine* 27:373–378.

Carrillo, A.E., R.J. Murphy, and S.S. Cheung. 2008. Vitamin C supplementation and salivary immune function following exercise-heat stress. *International Journal of Sports Physiology and Performance* 3:516–530.

Davies, V., K.G. Thompson, and S.M. Cooper. 2009. The effects of compression garments on recovery. *Journal of Strength and Conditioning Research* 23:1786–1794.

Duffield, R., J. Cannon, and M. King. 2010. The effects of compression garments on recovery of muscle performance following high-intensity sprint and plyometric exercise. *Journal of Science and Medicine in Sport* 13:136–140.

Fu, F.H., H.W. Cen, and R.G. Eston. 1997. The effects of cryotherapy on muscle damage in rats subjected to endurance training. *Scandinavian Journal of Medicine & Science in Sports* 7:358–362.

Gustafsson, H., H.C. Holmberg, and P. Hassmen. 2008. An elite endurance athlete's recovery from underperformance aided by a multidisciplinary sport science support team. *European Journal of Sport Science* 8:267–276.

Howatson, G., S. Goodall, and K.A. van Someren. 2009. The influence of cold water immersions on adaptation following a single bout of damaging exercise. *European Journal of Applied Physiology* 105:615–621.

Howatson, G., and K.A. van Someren. 2008. The prevention and treatment of exercise-induced muscle damage. *Sports Medicine* 38:483–503.

Kellmann, M., and K.W. Kallus. 2001. *Recovery-Stress Questionnaire for Athletes: User manual.* Champaign, IL: Human Kinetics.

Lemyre, P.N., G.C. Roberts, and J. Stray-Gundersen. 2007. Motivation, overtraining, and burnout: Can self-determined motivation predict overtraining and burnout in elite athletes? *European Journal of Sport Science* 7:115–126.

Maton, B., G. Thiney, S. Dang, S. Tra, S. Bassez, P. Wicart, and A. Ouchene. 2006a. Human muscle fatigue and elastic compressive stockings. *European Journal of Applied Physiology* 97:432–442.

Maton, B., G. Thiney, A. Ouchene, P. Flaud, and P. Barthelemy. 2006b. Intramuscular pressure and surface EMG in voluntary ankle dorsal flexion: Influence of elastic compressive stockings. *Journal of Electromyography and Kinesiology* 16:291–302.

McGinley, C., A. Shafat, and A.E. Donnelly. 2009. Does antioxidant vitamin supplementation protect against muscle damage? *Sports Medicine* 39:1011–1032.

McNicol, A.J., B.J. O'Brien, C.D. Paton, and W.L. Knez. 2009. The effects of increased absolute training intensity on adaptations to endurance exercise training. *Journal of Science and Medicine in Sport* 12:485–489.

Meeusen, R., M. Duclos, M. Gleeson, G. Rietjens, J. Steinacker, and A. Urhausen. 2006. Prevention, diagnosis and treatment of the overtraining syndrome. *European Journal of Sport Science* 6:1–14.

Meeusen, R., E. Nederhof, L. Buyse, B. Roelands, G. De Schutter, and M.F. Piacentini. 2010. Diagnosing overtraining in athletes using the two bout exercise protocol. *British Journal of Sports Medicine* 44:642-648.

Miller, E.R., 3rd, R. Pastor-Barriuso, D. Dalal, R.A. Riemersma, L.J. Appel, and E. Guallar. 2005. Meta-analysis: High-dosage vitamin E supplementation may increase all-cause mortality. *Annals of Internal Medicine* 142:37–46.

Nederhof, E., K. Lemmink, J. Zwerver, and T. Mulder. 2007. The effect of high load training on psychomotor speed. *International Journal of Sports Medicine* 28:595–601.

Nederhof, E., K.A. Lemmink, C. Visscher, R. Meeusen, and T. Mulder. 2006. Psycho-motor speed: Possibly a new marker for overtraining syndrome. *Sports Medicine* 36:817–828.

Nederhof, E., J. Zwerver, M. Brink, R. Meeusen, and K. Lemmink. 2008. Different diagnostic tools in nonfunctional overreaching. *International Journal of Sports Medicine* 29:590–597.

Peters, E.M., J.M. Goetzsche, B. Grobbelaar, and T.D. Noakes. 1993. Vitamin C supple-mentation reduces the incidence of postrace symptoms of upper-respiratory-tract infection in ultramarathon runners. *American Journal of Clinical Nutrition* 57:170–174.

Robson-Ansley, P.J., M. Gleeson, and L. Ansley. 2009. Fatigue management in the preparation of Olympic athletes. *Journal of Sports Sciences* 27:1409-1420.

Toumi, H., and T.M. Best. 2003. The inflammatory response: Friend or enemy for muscle injury? *British Journal of Sports Medicine* 37:284–286.

Vaile, J., S. Halson, N. Gill, and B. Dawson. 2008a. Effect of cold water immersion on repeat cycling performance and thermoregulation in the heat. *Journal of Sports Sciences* 26:431–440.

Vaile, J., S. Halson, N. Gill, and B. Dawson. 2008b. Effect of hydrotherapy on recovery from fatigue. *International Journal of Sports Medicine* 29:539–544.

Vaile, J., S. Halson, N. Gill, and B. Dawson. 2008c. Effect of hydrotherapy on the signs and symptoms of delayed onset muscle soreness. *European Journal of Applied Physiology* 102:447–455.

Yamane, M., H. Teruya, M. Nakano, R. Ogai, N. Ohnishi, and M. Kosaka. 2006. Post-exercise leg and forearm flexor muscle cooling in humans attenuates endurance and resistance training effects on muscle performance and on circulatory adapta-tion. *European Journal of Applied Physiology* 96:572–580.

# Chapter 6

Abbiss, C.R., and P.B. Laursen. 2008. Describing and understanding pacing strategies during athletic competition. *Sports Medicine* 38:239–252.

Abbiss, C.R., G. Levin, M.R. McGuigan, and P.B. Laursen. 2008. Reliability of power output during dynamic cycling. *International Journal of Sports Medicine* 29:574–578.

Aisbett, B., P. Le Rossignol, G.K. McConell, C.R. Abbiss, and R. Snow. 2009a. Effects of starting strategy on 5-min cycling time-trial performance. *Journal of Sports Sciences* 27:1201–1209.

Aisbett, B., P. Lerossignol, G.K. McConell, C.R. Abbiss, and R. Snow. 2009b. Influence of all-out and fast start on 5-min cycling time trial performance. *Medicine and Science in Sports and Exercise* 41:1965-1971.

Atkinson, G., and A. Brunskill. 2000. Pacing strategies during a cycling time trial with simulated headwinds and tailwinds. *Ergonomics* 43:1449–1460.

Bishop, D. 2003a. Warm up I: Potential mechanisms and the effects of passive warm up on exercise performance. *Sports Medicine* 33:439–454.

Bishop, D. 2003b. Warm up II: Performance changes following active warm up and how to structure the warm up. *Sports Medicine* 33:483–498.

Craig, A.D. 2002. How do you feel? Interoception: The sense of the physiological condition of the body. *Nature Reviews Neuroscience* 3:655–666.

Foster, C., K. Hendrickson, K. Peyer, B. Reiner, J.J. Dekoning, A. Lucia, R. Battista, F. Hettinga, J. Porcari, and G. Wright. 2009. Pattern of developing the performance template. *British Journal of Sports Medicine* 43:765-769.

Hajoglou, A., C. Foster, J.J. De Koning, A. Lucia, T.W. Kernozek, and J.P. Porcari. 2005. Effect of warm up on cycle time trial performance. *Medicine and Science in Sports and Exercise* 37:1608–1614.

Hulleman, M., J.J. De Koning, F.J. Hettinga, and C. Foster. 2007. The effect of extrinsic motivation on cycle time trial performance. *Medicine and Science in Sports and Exercise* 39:709–715.

Laursen, P.B., C.M. Shing, and D.G. Jenkins. 2003. Reproducibility of a laboratory-based 40-km cycle time-trial on a stationary wind-trainer in highly trained cyclists. *International Journal of Sports Medicine* 24:481–485.

Mandengue, S.H., I. Miladi, D. Bishop, A. Temfemo, F. Cisse, and S. Ahmaidi. 2009. Methodological approach for determining optimal active warm-up intensity: Predictive equations. *Science & Sports* 24:9–14.

Mandengue, S.H., D. Seck, D. Bishop, F. Cisse, P. Tsala-Mbala, and S. Ahmaidi. 2005. Are athletes able to self-select their optimal warm up? *Journal of Science and Medicine in Sport* 8:26–34.

Mauger, A.R., A.M. Jones, and C.A. Williams. 2009. Influence of feedback and prior experience on pacing during a 4-km cycle time trial. *Medicine and Science in Sports and Exercise* 41:451–458.

## Chapter 8

Belen, L., M. Habrard, J.P. Micallef, and D. Le Gallais. 2007a. The performance and efficiency of cycling with a carbon fiber eccentric chainring during incremental exercise. *Journal of Sports Medicine and Physical Fitness* 47:40–45.

Belen, L., M. Habrard, J.P. Micallef, S. Perrey, and D. Le Gallais. 2007b. Cycling performance and mechanical variables using a new prototype chainring. *European Journal of Applied Physiology* 101:721–726.

Bini, R.R., and F. Diefenthaeler. 2009. Mechanical work and coordinative pattern of cycling: A literature review. *Kinesiology* 41:25–39.

Cannon, D.T., F.W. Kolkhorst, and D.J. Cipriani. 2007. Effect of pedaling technique on muscle activity and cycling efficiency. *European Journal of Applied Physiology* 99:659–664.

Carpes, F.P., M. Rossato, I.E. Faria, and C. Bolli Mota. 2007. Bilateral pedaling asymmetry during a simulated 40-km cycling time-trial. *Journal of Sports Medicine and Physical Fitness* 47:51–57.

Chapman, A.R., B. Vicenzino, P. Blanch, and P.W. Hodges. 2008. Patterns of leg muscle recruitment vary between novice and highly trained cyclists. *Journal of Electromyography and Kinesiology* 18:359–371.

Chapman, A.R., B. Vicenzino, P. Blanch, J.J. Knox, and P.W. Hodges. 2006. Leg muscle recruitment in highly trained cyclists. *Journal of Sports Science* 24:115–24.

Coyle, E.F. 2005. Improved muscular efficiency displayed as Tour de France champion matures. *Journal of Applied Physiology* 98:2191–6.

Coyle, E.F., L.S. Sidossis, J.F. Horowitz, and J.D. Beltz. 1992. Cycling efficiency is related to the percentage of type I muscle fibers. *Medicine and Science in Sports and Exercise* 24:782–788.

Cullen, L.K., K. Andrew, K.R. Lair, M.J. Widger, and B.F. Timson. 1992. Efficiency of trained cyclists using circular and noncircular chainrings. *International Journal of Sports Medicine* 13:264–269.

Daly, D.J., and P.R. Cavanagh. 1976. Asymmetry in bicycle ergometer pedaling. *Medicine and Science in Sports* 8:204–208.

Fernandez-Pena, E., F. Lucertini, and M. Ditroilo. 2009. Training with independent cranks alters muscle coordination pattern in cyclists. *Journal of Strength and Conditioning* 23:1764–1772.

Foss, O., and J. Hallen. 2005. Cadence and performance in elite cyclists. *European Journal of Applied Physiology* 93:453–62.

Foss, O., and J. Hallen. 2004. The most economical cadence increases with increasing workload. *European Journal of Applied Physiology* 92:443–51.

Garry, R.C., and G.M. Wishart. 1934. The efficiency of bicycle pedaling in the trained subject. *Journal of Physiology* 82:200–206.

Hansen, E.A., K. Jensen, and P.K. Pedersen. 2006. Performance following prolonged sub-maximal cycling at optimal versus freely chosen pedal rate. *European Journal of Applied Physiology* 98:227–33.

Hansen, E.A., and A.E. Ohnstad. 2008. Evidence for freely chosen pedaling rate during submaximal cycling to be a robust innate voluntary motor rhythm. *Experimental Brain Research* 186:365–373.

Hopker, J., D. Coleman, and L. Passfield. 2009a. Changes in cycling efficiency during a competitive season. *Medicine and Science in Sports and Exercise* 41:912–919.

Hopker, J., L. Passfield, D. Coleman, S. Jobson, L. Edwards, and H. Carter. 2009b. The effects of training on gross efficiency in cycling: A review. *International Journal of Sports Medicine* 30:845-850.

Hopker, J.G., D.A. Coleman, and J.D. Wiles. 2007. Differences in efficiency between trained and recreational cyclists. *Applied Physiology, Nutrition, and Metabolism* 32:1036–1042.

Hue, O., O. Galy, C. Hertogh, J.F. Casties, and C. Prefaut. 2001. Enhancing cycling performance using an eccentric chainring. *Medicine and Science in Sports and Exercise* 33:1006–1010.

Hue, O., S. Racinais, K. Chamari, M. Damiani, C. Hertogh, and S. Blonc. 2008. Does an eccentric chainring improve conventional parameters of neuromuscular power? *Journal of Science and Medicine in Sport* 11:264–270.

Lucia, A., J. Balmer, R.C. Davison, M. Perez, A. Santalla, and P.M. Smith. 2004. Effects of the rotor pedaling system on the performance of trained cyclists during incremental and constant-load cycle-ergometer tests. *International Journal of Sports Medicine* 25:479–85.

Lucia, A., J. Hoyos, and J.L. Chicharro. 2001. Preferred pedaling cadence in professional cycling. *Medicine and Science in Sports and Exercise* 33:1361–6.

Lucia, A., J. Hoyos, M. Perez, A. Santalla, and J.L. Chicharro. 2002. Inverse relationship between V\od\O$_2$max and economy/efficiency in world-class cyclists. *Medicine and Science in Sports and Exercise* 34:2079–84.

Millet, G.P., C. Tronche, N. Fuster, and R. Candau. 2002. Level ground and uphill cycling efficiency in seated and standing positions. *Medicine and Science in Sports and Exercise* 34:1645–52.

Mora-Rodriguez, R., and R. Aguado-Jimenez. 2006. Performance at high pedaling cadences in well-trained cyclists. *Medicine and Science in Sports and Exercise* 38:953–957.

Rodriguez-Marroyo, J.A., J. Garcia-Lopez, K. Chamari, A. Cordova, O. Hue, and J.G. Villa. 2009. The rotor pedaling system improves anaerobic but not aerobic cycling performance in professional cyclists. *European Journal of Applied Physiology* 106:87–94.

Santalla, A., J.M. Manzano, M. Perez, and A. Lucia. 2002. A new pedaling design: The Rotor—effects on cycling performance. *Medicine and Science in Sports and Exercise* 34:1854–8.

Smak, W., R.R. Neptune, and M.L. Hull. 1999. The influence of pedaling rate on bilateral asymmetry in cycling. *Journal of Biomechanics* 32:899–906.

So, R.C.H., J.K.F. Ng, and G.Y.F. Ng. 2005. Muscle recruitment pattern in cycling: A review. *Physical Therapy in Sport* 6:89–96.

Vogt, S., K. Roecker, Y.O. Schumacher, T. Pottgiesser, H.H. Dickhuth, A. Schmid, and L. Heinrich. 2008. Cadence-power-relationship during decisive mountain ascents at the Tour de France. *International Journal of Sports Medicine* 29:244–250.

Zamparo, P., A. Minetti, and P. di Prampero. 2002. Mechanical efficiency of cycling with a new developed pedal-crank. *Journal of Biomechanics* 35:1387.

# Chapter 9

Armstrong, L.E., R.W. Hubbard, B.H. Jones, and J.T. Daniels. 1986. Preparing Alberto Salazar for the heat of the 1984 Olympic marathon. *Physician and Sportsmedicine* 14:73–81.

Boulze, D., P. Montastruc, and M. Cabanac. 1983. Water intake, pleasure and water temperature in humans. *Physiology and Behavior* 30:97–102.

Carter, J.M., A.E. Jeukendrup, and D.A. Jones. 2004. The effect of carbohydrate mouth rinse on 1-h cycle time trial performance. *Medicine and Science in Sports and Exercise* 36:2107–11.

Casa, D.J., L.E. Armstrong, S.K. Hillman, S.J. Montain, R.V. Reiff, B.S. Rich, W.O. Roberts, and J.A. Stone. 2000. National Athletic Trainers' Association position statement: Fluid replacement for athletes. *Journal of Athletic Training* 35:212–224.

Casa, D.J., P.M. Clarkson, and W.O. Roberts. 2005. American College of Sports Medicine roundtable on hydration and physical activity: Consensus statements. *Current Sports Medicine Report* 4:115–27.

Cheung, S.S., and T.M. McLellan. 1998a. Influence of heat acclimation, aerobic fitness, and hydration effects on tolerance during uncompensable heat stress. *Journal of Applied Physiology* 84:1731–1739.

Cheung, S.S., and T.M. McLellan. 1998b. Influence of hydration status and fluid replacement on tolerance during uncompensable heat stress. *European Journal of Applied Physiology* 77:139–148.

Clark, N. 2008. *Nancy Clark's sports nutrition guidebook.* Champaign, IL: Human Kinetics.

Convertino, V.A., L.E. Armstrong, E.F. Coyle, G.W. Mack, M.N. Sawka, L.C. Senay, and W.M. Sherman. 1996. American College of Sports Medicine position stand. Exercise and fluid replacement. *Medicine and Science in Sports and Exercise* 28:i–vii.

Ebert, T.R., D.T. Martin, N. Bullock, I. Mujika, M.J. Quod, L.A. Farthing, L.M. Burke, and R.T. Withers. 2007. Influence of hydration status on thermoregulation and cycling hill climbing. *Medicine and Science in Sports and Exercise* 39:323–329.

Erdman, K.A., T.S. Fung, and R.A. Reimer. 2006. Influence of performance level on dietary supplementation in elite Canadian athletes. *Medicine and Science in Sports and Exercise* 38:349–56.

Fudge, B.W., C. Easton, D. Kingsmore, F.K. Kiplamai, V.O. Onywera, K.R. Westerterp, B. Kayser, T.D. Noakes, and Y.P. Pitsiladis. 2008. Elite Kenyan endurance runners are hydrated day-to-day with ad libitum fluid intake. *Medicine and Science in Sports and Exercise* 40:1171–1179.

Geyer, H., M.K. Parr, U. Mareck, U. Reinhart, Y. Schrader, and W. Schanzer. 2004. Analysis of non-hormonal nutritional supplements for anabolic-androgenic steroids—results of an international study. *International Journal of Sports Medicine* 25.124–129.

Geyer, H., M.K. Parr, K. Koehler, U. Mareck, W. Schänzer, and M. Thevis. 2008. Nutritional supplements cross-contaminated and faked with doping substances. *Journal of Mass Spectrometry* 43:892–902.

Hubbard, R.W., B.L. Sandick, W.T. Matthew, R.P. Francesconi, J.B. Sampson, M.J. Durkot, O. Maller, and D.B. Engell. 1984. Voluntary dehydration and alliesthesia for water. *Journal of Applied Physiology* 57:858–875.

Jacobs, I. 1980. The effects of thermal dehydration on performance of the Wingate anaerobic test. *International Journal of Sports Medicine* 1:21–24.

Jeukendrup, A.E., S. Hopkins, L.F. Aragon-Vargas, and C. Hulston. 2008. No effect of carbohydrate feeding on 16 km cycling time trial performance. *European Journal of Applied Physiology* 104:831–837.

Judelson, D.A., C.M. Maresh, J.M. Anderson, L.E. Armstrong, D.J. Casa, W.J. Kraemer, and J.S. Volek. 2007. Hydration and muscular performance: Does fluid balance affect strength, power and high-intensity endurance? *Sports Medicine* 37:907–921.

Lambert, G.P. 2004. Role of gastrointestinal permeability in exertional heatstroke. *Exercise and Sport Sciences Reviews* 32:185–90.

Latzka, W.A., M.N. Sawka, S.J. Montain, G.S. Skrinar, R.A. Fielding, R.P. Matott, and K.B. Pandolf. 1998. Hyperhydration: Tolerance and cardiovascular effects during uncompensable exercise-heat stress. *Journal of Applied Physiology* 84:1858–64.

Latzka, W.A., M.N. Sawka, S.J. Montain, G.S. Skrinar, R.A. Fielding, R.P. Matott, and K.B. Pandolf. 1997. Hyperhydration: Thermoregulatory effects during compensable exercise-heat stress. *Journal of Applied Physiology* 83:860–866.

Maughan, R.J., J.B. Leiper, and S.M. Shirreffs. 1996. Restoration of fluid balance after exercise-induced dehydration: Effects of food and fluid intake. *European Journal of Applied Physiology* 73:317–25.

Maughan, R.J., J.H. Owen, S.M. Shirreffs, and J.B. Leiper. 1994. Post-exercise rehydration in man: Effects of electrolyte addition to ingested fluids. *European Journal of Applied Physiology* 69:209–215.

Meeusen, R., P. Watson, H. Hasegawa, B. Roelands, and M.F. Piacentini. 2006. Central fatigue: The serotonin hypothesis and beyond. *Sports Medicine* 36:881–909.

Montain, S.J., and E.F. Coyle. 1993. Influence of the timing of fluid ingestion on temperature regulation during exercise. *Journal of Applied Physiology* 75:688–695.

Noakes, T.D. 2007. Drinking guidelines for exercise: What evidence is there that athletes should drink "as much as tolerable," "to replace the weight lost during exercise" or "ad libitum"? *Journal of Sports Sciences* 25:781–796.

Rowell, L.B. 1974. Human cardiovascular adjustments to exercise and thermal stress. *Physiological Reviews* 54:75–159.

Ryan, M. 2007. *Sports nutrition for endurance athletes*. Boulder, CO: VeloPress.

Saunders, A.G., J.P. Dugas, R. Tucker, M.I. Lambert, and T.D. Noakes. 2005. The effects of different air velocities on heat storage and body temperature in humans cycling in a hot, humid environment. *Acta Physiologica Scandinavica* 183:241–55.

Saunders, M.J., M.D. Kane, and M.K. Todd. 2004. Effects of a carbohydrate-protein beverage on cycling endurance and muscle damage. *Medicine and Science in Sports and Exercise* 36:1233–8.

Sawka, M.N., L.M. Burke, E.R. Eichner, R.J. Maughan, S.J. Montain, and N.S. Stachenfeld. 2007. American College of Sports Medicine position stand. Exercise and fluid replacement. *Medicine and Science in Sports and Exercise* 39:377–90.

Sawka, M.N., A.J. Young, R.P. Francesconi, S.R. Muza, and K.B. Pandolf. 1985. Thermoregulatory and blood responses during exercise at graded hypohydration levels. *Journal of Applied Physiology* 59:1394–1401.

Shirreffs, S.M., and R.J. Maughan. 1998. Volume repletion after exercise-induced volume depletion in humans: Replacement of water and sodium losses. *American Journal of Physiology* 274:F868–75.

Shirreffs, S.M., and R.J. Maughan. 1997. Restoration of fluid balance after exercise-induced dehydration: Effects of alcohol consumption. *Journal of Applied Physiology* 83:1152–8.

Shirreffs, S.M., A.J. Taylor, J.B. Leiper, and R.J. Maughan. 1996. Post-exercise rehydration in man: Effects of volume consumed and drink sodium content. *Medicine and Science in Sports and Exercise* 28:1260–1271.

Supinski, G., D. Nethery, T.M. Nosek, L.A. Callahan, D. Stofan, and A. DiMarco. 2000. Endotoxin administration alters the force vs. pCa relationship of skeletal muscle fibers. *American Journal of Physiology* 278:R891–6.

van Essen, M., and M.J. Gibala. 2006. Failure of protein to improve time trial performance when added to a sports drink. *Medicine and Science in Sports and Exercise* 38:1476–1483.

Watson, P., S.M. Shirreffs, and R.J. Maughan. 2005. Blood-brain barrier integrity may be threatened by exercise in a warm environment. *American Journal of Physiology* 288:R1689–94.

## Chapter 10

Adams, W.C., E.M. Bernauer, D.B. Dill, and B.J. B. Jr. 1975. Effects of equivalent sea-level and altitude training on V\od\O$_2$max and running performance. *Journal of Applied Physiology* 39:262–6.

Armstrong, L.E. 2007. *Exertional heat illness.* Champaign, IL: Human Kinetics.

Armstrong, L.E., D.J. Casa, M. Millard-Stafford, D.S. Moran, S.W. Pyne, and W.O. Roberts. 2007. American College of Sports Medicine position stand. Exertional heat illness during training and competition. *Medicine and Science in Sports and Exercise* 39:556–72.

Arngrímsson, S.Á., D.S. Petitt, M.G. Stueck, D.K. Jorgensen, and K.J. Cureton. 2004. Cooling vest worn during active warm-up improves 5-km run performance in the heat. *Journal of Applied Physiology* 96:1867–74.

Ball, D., C. Burrows, and A.J. Sargeant. 1999. Human power output during repeated sprint cycle exercise: The influence of thermal stress. *European Journal of Applied Physiology* 79:360–366.

Booth, J., F. Marino, and J.J. Ward. 1997. Improved running performance in hot humid conditions following whole body precooling. *Medicine and Science in Sports and Exercise* 29:943–949.

Castellani, J.W., A.J. Young, M.B. Ducharme, G.G. Giesbrecht, E. Glickman, and R.E. Sallis. 2006. American College of Sports Medicine position stand: Prevention of cold injuries during exercise. *Medicine and Science in Sports and Exercise* 38:2012–29.

Chapman, R.F., J. Stray-Gundersen, and B.D. Levine. 1998. Individual variation in response to altitude training. *Journal of Applied Physiology* 85:1448–1456.

Cheung, S.S., and T.M. McLellan. 1998. Influence of heat acclimation, aerobic fitness, and hydration effects on tolerance during uncompensable heat stress. *Journal of Applied Physiology* 84:1731–1739.

Cheung, S.S., T.M. McLellan, and S. Tenaglia. 2000. The thermophysiology of uncompensable heat stress. Physiological manipulations and individual characteristics. *Sports Medicine* 29:329–59.

Cheung, S.S., and A.M. Robinson. 2004. The influence of upper-body pre-cooling on repeated sprint performance in moderate ambient temperatures. *Journal of Sports Sciences* 22:605–612.

Cotter, J.D., and N.A.S. Taylor. 2005. The distribution of cutaneous sudomotor and alliesthesial thermosensitivity in mildly heat-stressed humans: An open-loop approach. *Journal of Physiology* 565:335–45.

Daniels, J., and N. Oldridge. 1970. The effects of alternate exposure to altitude and sea level on world class middle-distance runners. *Medicine and Science in Sports* 2:107–112.

Dawson, B.T. 1994. Exercise training in sweat clothing in cool conditions to improve heat tolerance. *Sports Medicine* 17:233–244.

Duffield, R., B. Dawson, D. Bishop, M. Fitzsimons, and S. Lawrence. 2003. Effect of wearing an ice cooling jacket on repeat sprint performance in warm/humid conditions. *British Journal of Sports Medicine* 37:164–9.

Dufour, S.P., E. Ponsot, J. Zoll, S. Doutreleau, E. Lonsdorfer-Wolf, B. Geny, E. Lampert, M. Fluck, H. Hoppeler, V. Billat, B. Mettauer, R. Richard, and J. Lonsdorfer. 2006. Exercise training in normobaric hypoxia in endurance runners. I. Improvement in aerobic performance capacity. *Journal of Applied Physiology* 100:1238–1248.

Ely, B.R., Ely, M.R., Cheuvront, S.N., Kenefick, R.W., DeGroot, D.W., Montain, S.J. Evidence against a 40° C core temperature threshold for fatigue in humans. *Journal of Applied Physiology* 107:1519-1525, 2009.

Fairbarn, M.S., K.C. Coutts, R.L. Pardy, and D.C. McKenzie. 1991. Improved respiratory muscle endurance of highly trained cyclists and the effects on maximal exercise performance. *International Journal of Sports Medicine* 12:66–70.

Galloway, S.D., and R.J. Maughan. 1997. Effects of ambient temperature on the capacity to perform prolonged cycle exercise in man. *Medicine and Science in Sports and Exercise* 29:1240–9.

Gething, A.D., L. Passfield, and B. Davies. 2004a. The effects of different inspiratory muscle training intensities on exercising heart rate and perceived exertion. *European Journal of Applied Physiology* 92:50–55.

Gething, A.D., M. Williams, and B. Davies. 2004b. Inspiratory resistive loading improves cycling capacity: A placebo controlled trial. *British Journal of Sports Medicine* 38:730–736.

Gore, C.J., S.A. Clark, and P.U. Saunders. 2007. Nonhematological mechanisms of improved sea-level performance after hypoxic exposure. *Medicine and Science in Sports and Exercise* 39:1600–1609.

Gore, C.J., A.G. Hahn, R.J. Aughey, D.T. Martin, M.J. Ashenden, S.A. Clark, A.P. Garnham, A.D. Roberts, G.J. Slater, and M.J. McKenna. 2001. Live high:train low increases muscle buffer capacity and submaximal cycling efficiency. *Acta Physiologica Scandinavica* 173:275–286.

Gore, C.J., F.A. Rodriguez, M.J. Truijens, N.E. Townsend, J. Stray-Gundersen, and B.D. Levine. 2006. Increased serum erythropoietin but not red cell production after 4 wk of intermittent hypobaric hypoxia (4,000–5,500 m). *Journal of Applied Physiology* 101:1386–1393.

Guenette, J.A., A.M. Martens, A.L. Lee, G.D. Tyler, J.C. Richards, G.E. Foster, D.E. Warburton, and A.W. Sheel. 2006. Variable effects of respiratory muscle training on cycle exercise performance in men and women. *Applied Physiology, Nutrition, and Metabolism* 31:159–166.

Hahn, A.G., C.J. Gore, D.T. Martin, M.J. Ashenden, A.D. Roberts, and P.A. Logan. 2001. An evaluation of the concept of living at moderate altitude and training at sea level. *Comparative Biochemistry and Physiology A: Molecular and Integrative Physiology* 128:777–89.

Hartung, G.H., L.G. Myhre, and S.A. Nunneley. 1980. Physiological effects of cold air inhalation during exercise. *Aviation, Space and Environmental Medicine* 51:591–594.

Kenefick, R.W., S.N. Cheuvront, and M.N. Sawka. 2007. Thermoregulatory function during the marathon. *Sports Medicine* 37:312–315.

Kilding, A.E., S. Brown, and A.K. McConnell. 2010. Inspiratory muscle training improves 100 and 200 m swimming performance. *European Journal of Applied Physiology* 108:505–511.

Levine, B.D., and J. Stray-Gundersen. 1997. "Living high-training low": Effect of moderate-altitude acclimatization with low-altitude training on performance. *Journal of Applied Physiology* 83:102–112.

Mackenzie, R.W., P.W. Watt, and N.S. Maxwell. 2008. Acute normobaric hypoxia stimulates erythropoietin release. *High Altitude Medicine & Biology* 9:28–37.

Marino, F.E., M.I. Lambert, T.D. Noakes. Superior performance of African runners in warm humid but not in cool environmental conditions. *Journal of Applied Physiology* 96:124-130.

Morrison, S., G.G. Sleivert, and S.S. Cheung. 2004. Passive hyperthermia reduces voluntary activation and isometric force production. *European Journal of Applied Physiology* 91:729–36.

Neya, M., T. Enoki, Y. Kumai, T. Sugoh, and T. Kawahara. 2007. The effects of nightly normobaric hypoxia and high intensity training under intermittent normobaric hypoxia on running economy and hemoglobin mass. *Journal of Applied Physiology* 103:828–834.

Nicks, C.R., D.W. Morgan, D.K. Fuller, and J.L. Caputo. 2009. The influence of respiratory muscle training upon intermittent exercise performance. *International Journal of Sports Medicine* 30:16–21.

Noakes, T.D. 2000. Exercise and the cold. *Ergonomics* 43:1461–79.

Pandolf, K.B., R.L. Burse, and R.F. Goldman. 1977. Role of physical fitness in heat acclimatization, decay and reinduction. *Ergonomics* 20:399–408.

Ponsot, E., S.P. Dufour, J. Zoll, S. Doutrelau, B. N'Guessan, B. Geny, H. Hoppeler, E. Lampert, B. Mettauer, R. Ventura-Clapier, and R. Richard. 2006. Exercise training in normobaric hypoxia in endurance runners. II. Improvement of mitochondrial properties in skeletal muscle. *Journal of Applied Physiology* 100:1249–1257.

Roberts, W.O. 2006. Exertional heat stroke during a cool weather marathon: A case study. *Medicine and Science in Sports and Exercise* 38:1197–203.

Romer, L.M., and M.I. Polkey. 2008. Exercise-induced respiratory muscle fatigue: Implications for performance. *Journal of Applied Physiology* 104:879–888.

Saunders, P.U., R.D. Telford, D.B. Pyne, R.B. Cunningham, C.J. Gore, A.G. Hahn, and J.A. Hawley. 2004. Improved running economy in elite runners after 20 days of simulated moderate-altitude exposure. *Journal of Applied Physiology* 96:931–937.

Sawka, M.N., A.J. Young, K.B. Pandolf, R.C. Dennis, and C.R. Valeri. 1992. Erythrocyte, plasma, and blood volume of healthy young men. *Medicine and Science in Sports and Exercise* 24:447–453.

Selkirk, G.A., and T.M. McLellan. 2001. Influence of aerobic fitness and body fatness on tolerance to uncompensable heat stress. *Journal of Applied Physiology* 91:2055–63.

Sleivert, G.G., J.D. Cotter, W.S. Roberts, and M.A. Febbraio. The influence of whole-body vs. torso pre-cooling on physiological strain and performance of high-intensity exercise in the heat. *Comparative Biochemistry and Physiology A: Molecular and Integrative Physiology* 128:657-666.

Stray-Gundersen, J., R.F. Chapman, and B.D. Levine. 2001. "Living high-training low" altitude training improves sea level performance in male and female elite runners. *Journal of Applied Physiology* 91:1113–1120.

Thomas, M.M., S.S. Cheung, G.C. Elder, and G.G. Sleivert. 2006. Voluntary muscle activation is impaired by core temperature rather than local muscle temperature. *Journal of Applied Physiology* 100:1361–1369.Tucker, R., T. Marle, E.V. Lambert, and T.D. Noakes. 2006. The rate of heat storage mediates an anticipatory reduction in exercise intensity during cycling at a fixed rating of perceived exertion. *Journal of Physiology* 574:905–15.

Ventura, N., H. Hoppeler, R. Seiler, A. Binggeli, P. Mullis, and M. Vogt. 2003. The response of trained athletes to six weeks of endurance training in hypoxia or normoxia. *International Journal of Sports Medicine* 24:166–172.

Vogiatzis, I., D. Athanasopoulos, H. Habazettl, W.M. Kuebler, H. Wagner, C. Roussos, P.D. Wagner, and S. Zakynthinos. 2009. Intercostal muscle blood flow limitation in athletes during maximal exercise. *Journal of Physiology* 587:3665–3677.

Volianitis, S., A.K. McConnell, Y. Koutedakis, L. McNaughton, K. Backx, and D.A. Jones. 2001. Inspiratory muscle training improves rowing performance. *Medicine and Science in Sports and Exercise* 33:803–9.

Wilber, R.L. 2007. Application of altitude/hypoxic training by elite athletes. *Medicine and Science in Sports and Exercise* 39:1610–1624.

Wilber, R.L. 2004. *Altitude training and athletic performance*. Champaign, IL: Human Kinetics.

# INDEX

*Note:* The italicized *f* and *t* following page numbers refer to figures and tables, respectively.

## A

Abbiss, Chris  26-28
ACSM. *See* American College of Sports Medicine
active recovery rides  78-79
adaptation
  cardiovascular  42
    heat acclimation  232-233
    muscular  115-116
    physical limits to  97
    PowerCranks and  187
    as scientific limitation  12-13
    in training  28-29
adenosine triphosphate (ATP)  16
aerobic metabolism  19-20, 126
aerobic (endurance) training
  heat tolerance and  233
  vs. high-intensity training  71-72, 72*f*, 80-81
  low-intensity training  77-80
  sweet-spot training  75-77, 75*f*
aerodynamics  3, 3*t*, 173
all-out start  136, 136*f*
altitude tents  5, 221
altitude training. *See* hypoxic training
American College of Sports Medicine (ACSM)
  Position Stand on Exertional Heat Illness  230
  Position Stand on Fluid Replacement  196, 202, 203
anaerobic glycolysis  18-19
anaerobic threshold  32
ankling technique  181-182, 181*f*
Anquetil, Jacques  181
antioxidants  116-117, 212
Armstrong, Lance  171, 175, 181
asymmetry, in pedaling  179-180
ATP-PC system  16-17

## B

balance point, in bike fit  151
banned substances  215

## bike fit

bike fit
  benefits of proper fit  150-151
  BikeFit  165-168
  changes in  169
  goals and  169
  individuality in  149, 168
  injury risk and  149, 153
  Retül system  154-160
  Serotta Personal Fit System  160-165
  systems overview  151
  Wobble-Naught system  151-154
bike fitters  161-162
BikeFit  165-168
BioPace nonround chainrings  182
block training  85-86
blood-brain barrier  198
body cooling (cryotherapy)  117-120, 118*f*
body fluid compartments  197, 197*f*
body mass calculators  46
body temperature
  dehydration and  198
  fatigue and  34-36
  as performance monitor  66
  warm-ups and  126, 127
body weight
  as hydration monitor  207*t*
  power-to-weight ratio  55, 200
Borg scale  40-41
Botero, Santiago  181
brain function
  dehydration and  198
  glycogen stores and  20
  heat stress and  35, 230
  psychological training  37, 95
  role in fatigue  27-28, 33, 36-37
  warm-ups and  126
burnout  114-115

## C

cadence
  high  171, 191-192
  optimal  187-188

# About the Authors

**Hunter Allen** is a former professional cyclist, renowned coach, and expert in using power meters to train endurance athletes. As a professional racer for 17 years, he earned more than 40 career victories in competitions around the world. He was considered a great all-arounder who had the race tactics and skills essential for success at a professional level. Upon retiring from racing, Allen became a USAC elite-level cycling coach and certified nutrition consultant. He has coached more than 400 athletes, including Olympic cyclists, champions of the European road racing circuit, and champion mountain bikers. Allen is a frequent presenter at USA Cycling's coaching certification courses and was a technical consultant to the 2008 USA Cycling BMX Olympic team.

Allen writes for *Road* magazine (www.roadmagazine.net) and UK-based *Cycling Weekly,* and he coauthored *Training and Racing With a Power Meter.* Allen is the founder of Peaks Coaching Group (www.PeaksCoachingGroup. com), which specializes in training cyclists and other endurance athletes. He is a codeveloper of TrainingPeaks WKO software, a leading program for analyzing data from power meters. His passion is applying science and technology toward improving athletic performance.

Allen lives in Bedford, Virginia, with his wife and three children.

As the science and training editor for *PezCyclingNews.com*, **Stephen Cheung, PhD,** focuses on translating cutting-edge scientific research into practical guidance for both cyclists and coaches. Cheung has authored more than 100 articles that cover respiratory training, altitude training, precooling and fatigue in the heat, hydration, optimal cadence, pacing strategies, jet lag, supplements, hypoxic stress, and the reliability of exercise testing protocols.

Cheung holds a Canada research chair in environmental ergonomics at Brock University, where his research focuses on the effects of thermal stress on human physiology and performance. He is also the author of *Advanced Environmental Exercise Physiology* (Human Kinetics, 2009). Cheung helped to establish the sport science support network for the Canadian Sport Centre in Atlantic Canada and has consulted with the Canadian national rowing and snowboard teams on specific sport performance projects. Cheung has also served as a cycling official and as a board member of the Canadian Cycling Association.

Cheung is a passionate cyclist who has been commuting and competing on the road for more than 25 years. The highlight of his cycling experiences was meeting his wife, Debbie, during a cross-Canada ride in 1996.